S0-BCP-285

Where were you when?

Where were

you when?

180 Unforgettable Moments in Living History

Ian Harrison

Reader's Digest

The Reader's Digest Association, Inc.
Pleasantville/New York • Montreal • Australia

A READER'S DIGEST BOOK

This edition published by The Reader's Digest Association, Inc.,
by arrangement with Collins & Brown, an imprint of Anova Books Ltd.

Text copyright © 2006 Anova Books Ltd.

All rights reserved. Unauthorized reproduction, in any manner, is prohibited.

Reader's Digest is a registered trademark of The Reader's Digest Association, Inc.

FOR COLLINS & BROWN
Project Editor: Victoria Alers-Hankey
Copy Editor: Barbara Dixon
Designer: Thomas Keenes and Ben Cracknell

FOR READER'S DIGEST
U.S. Project Editor: Marilyn Knowlton
U.S. Consulting Editor: Nancy Shuker
U.S. Copy Editor: Barbara Booth
Canadian Project Editor: Robert Ronald
Australian Project Editor: Annette Carter
Associate Art Director: George McKeon
Executive Editor, Trade Publishing: Dolores York
Vice President and Publisher: Harold Clarke

ISBN 10: 0-7621-0838-X (paperback)

Address any comments about *Where Were You When?* to:
        The Reader's Digest Association, Inc.
        Adult Trade Publishing
        Reader's Digest Road
        Pleasantville, NY 10570-7000

For more Reader's Digest products and information, visit our website:
        www.rd.com (in the United States)
        www.readersdigest.ca (in Canada)
        www.readersdigest.com.au (in Australia)
        www.readersdigest.com.nz (in New Zealand)
        www.rdasia.com (in Asia)

Repro by Classicscan, Singapore
Printed and bound by Craftprint, Singapore

1 3 5 7 9 10 8 6 4 2 (paperback)

"History with its flickering lamp stumbles along the trail of the past, trying to reconstruct its scenes, to revive its echoes, and kindle with pale gleams the passion of former days."

—WINSTON CHURCHILL

Contents

Foreword by Buzz Aldrin 8

1980–1989

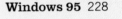

1990–2005

Foreword

By the last decade of the 20th century, media hyperbole had cheapened phrases such as "epoch-making," "historic moment" and "the eyes of the world," so for me to be part of a *genuinely* epoch-making historic moment on July 20, 1969, watched by one-fifth of the world's population, was both an honor and a privilege. When Neil Armstrong and I walked on the Moon, we were doing something that human beings had dreamed of for centuries. As a race, humankind had truly taken a "giant leap," and as individuals, that moment inspired people the world over to remember where they were when it happened. I certainly remember where I was!

Many people think of "history" as a dry, academic study, but in fact, it's the opposite—truly memorable historic moments are about excitement and exhilaration or, all too often, death and destruction; but rarely boredom and academia. The moments about which people ask, "Where were you when…?" are part of our heritage. They belong to all of us, whether we were participants or observers—and sometimes watching events unfold makes them seem more real than actually taking part in them. When we returned from the Moon and saw the reaction of the people, I said to Neil Armstrong and Mike Collins, "We missed the whole thing," because we didn't share the moment of exhilaration here on Earth. We were out of town doing something else.

My interest in space began early, but I never dreamed that one day I would be an astronaut. As a youngster, I read of Buck Rogers and Flash Gordon; as a student, I immersed myself in the genre of science fiction; then as a fighter pilot, I observed the selection of America's first Mercury astronauts. All this was fascinating, but I really didn't think I would ever be a part of it. When Neil and I finally stood on the Moon, we were aware that the eyes of the world were upon us. We were farther away from the rest of humanity than anyone had ever ventured, and yet we felt closer to humanity than any two humans had ever been as the largest audience in history witnessed what we were doing. When we touched down, I looked at Neil and he looked at me. I patted him on the shoulder, and he said, "Houston, Tranquility Base. The Eagle has landed." And that lifted a lot of apprehension and pressure from people all over the world. We were onstage, but it was a very unusual stage.

Looking back at the Earth from the Moon was an unforgettable experience—a brilliant jewel in the black velvet sky, four times the size of a full Moon seen from Earth. And the Moon itself was described by my words on first landing, "magnificent desolation"; *magnificent* for the achievement of being there, and *desolate* for the eons of lifelessness. Walking on the Moon was really a lot easier than we had been led to believe. The horizon clearly curved away, and the sky was black as could be—crystal clear visibility with no air.

Since the completion of the Apollo program in the early 1970s, we have not been back to the Moon. And yet, the most important legacy of Apollo is that it should mark the beginning, not the end, of manned space exploration and travel. Without a question, Mars is the objective that should dominate this century's space exploration efforts. Mars is there, waiting to be reached. We need to evolve the potential for journeying beyond the Moon, perhaps visiting the asteroids on the way to the moons of Mars, then supporting landings on Mars itself. All of this should be viewed with the objective of permanent occupancy on Mars. To do that, we have to reduce the cost of getting into space, increase public involvement and build the next generation space shuttle that can carry an adequate number of people; something that will take some significant engineering feats as well as a better understanding of physics. I think humans will reach Mars, and I would like to see it happen in my lifetime. I would dearly love to be around when people start asking one another, "Where were you when humans first walked on Mars?"

Good luck, best wishes and *ad astra* (to the stars)!

Buzz Aldrin

Buzz Aldrin

1939–1949

1939

TIMELINE

Outbreak of World War II

World War II began with Adolf Hitler's invasion of Poland on September 1, 1939, prompting Britain and France to declare war on Germany.

World War I was supposedly "the war to end all wars," but the resulting uneasy peace was dependent on a precarious balance of power in Europe. That balance was upset by Führer Adolf Hitler's remilitarization of Germany, his alliance with Italian dictator Mussolini, and his expansion of Germany's borders by the annexation of Austria and parts of Czechoslovakia. In March 1939, hoping to discourage further German expansion, Britain, France, and Poland agreed to a military alliance. Crucially, Britain and the Soviet Union (USSR) could not reach an agreement, and the USSR instead signed a nonaggression treaty with Hitler, making war inevitable.

Practically speaking, World War II began just before dawn on September 1, 1939, when some 1.25 million German troops swept across their country's border into Poland. Dispensing with the formality of officially declaring war, Hitler had set in motion Operation *Fall Weiss* (White Plan) as the army crossed the border, the Luftwaffe (German air force) began bombing Polish cities—including Warsaw, Lodz and Krakow—and the German navy started shelling the Polish port of Danzig. Polish defenses soon succumbed when Poland became the first country to experience the German blitzkreig, or "lightning war."

"SO NOW WHAT?"

Officially the war did not begin until two days later, at 11:00 A.M. on September 3, at the expiry of a British ultimatum for German withdrawal from Poland. British prime minister Neville Chamberlain announced to the British people, "This country is now at war with Germany" and at midday the French delivered an ultimatum to Germany to withdraw by September 4, but accepting that this was not going to happen, preempted their own deadline by declaring war at 5:00 that same afternoon.

Hitler reportedly believed that European powers would react passively, as they had done over Austria and Czechoslovakia, and when informed of the declarations of war he asked, "So now what?" The answer was a second world war.

Where were you when?

Our cavalry regiment, accompanied by anti tank guns, was sent to the front line, where we managed to destroy eight German tanks before our ammunition ran out. The German Panzers then pushed us back toward the Vistula, and we were subjected to artillery fire. Though we fought like lions, there was no escape, and we had no alternative but to swim the river with our horses... Many of our soldiers could not swim. As they fought to stay above the water, they were dispatched at will by the Luftwaffe. The Vistula was full of the bloodied bodies of men and horses.

—Michael Krupa, Polish cavalry officer, in his book *Shallow Graves in Siberia*

HITLER'S RISE TO POWER

Adolf Hitler came to power by exploiting popular resentment at the depressed economic and social conditions that had arisen as a result of severe reparations imposed on Germany after World War I, and which were exacerbated by worldwide depression. People wanted someone to blame for their misery, and Hitler channeled their resentment toward non-Aryan minorities, the weak federal government, and a lack of *lebensraum* ("living space"). As leader of the National Socialist Party (the Nazis), Hitler won important election victories in 1930 and 1932; he became chancellor in 1933, and in 1934 he proclaimed the Third Reich, of which he became Führer, assuming absolute power by suspending the constitution and using violence and murder to silence all opposition.

Above The reality of occupation: After the conquest of Poland, German troops parade through Warsaw in front of Adolf Hitler (October 5, 1939).

Opposite Residents of the Polish capital, Warsaw, read Hitler's ultimatum—capitulation or invasion. The following day the Luftwaffe launched its first air raid on the city, marking the outbreak of World War II (August 31, 1939).

1939

THE WIZARD OF OZ

Along with Clark Gable's missing out on an Oscar, the other disappointment for *Gone With the Wind* was that Max Steiner didn't win one for his memorable score. That Oscar went to Herbert Stothart for the score of another MGM film, *The Wizard of Oz*—probably the most famous and best-loved children's classic outside Disney. *The Wizard of Oz* had its premiere in New York on August 18, 1939, and made an immediate star of 17-year-old Judy Garland, who played Dorothy. The *Wizard*'s other Oscar, of course, was for best song—awarded to Harold Arlen and E. Y. (Yip) Harburg for "Over the Rainbow." ⌐

Release of *Gone With the Wind*

After two years' prepublicity and a year in production, *Gone With the Wind* was released on December 15, 1939, in Atlanta, Georgia.

Soon after she married in 1925, budding U.S. novelist Margaret Mitchell began writing what would be her only book: *Ba! Ba! Black Sheep*. Ten years later her Civil War epic was complete, and after publication in 1936 under its new title, *Gone With the Wind*, it won the Pulitzer Prize and eventually sold more than 25 million copies worldwide. It also caught the attention of the film industry, although Irving Thalberg of MGM reputedly advised Louis B. Mayer not to bid for the film rights, telling him, "Forget it, Louis. No Civil War picture ever made a nickel." In fact, if receipts are adjusted for inflation, it went on to become financially the most successful film ever released.

TALENT CONTESTS

MGM did buy the rights to the book and immediately went into overdrive with a massive pre-publicity campaign/casting recruitment drive, with talent contests and screen tests held across the United States, giving people the impression that the central role of Scarlett O'Hara was open to any woman in America. Realistically, the part was expected to go to an A-list Hollywood star, but in the end, it went to the relatively unknown English actress Vivien Leigh, whose performance made her the first Briton to win the Oscar for Best Actress.

The prepublicity and the separate premieres in Atlanta, New York and Los Angeles on December 15, 19 and 28, 1939, ensured that the 3-hour-and-40-minute film was an immediate hit, breaking all box-office records in America and earning a then world record $18,000 in advance sales for the British premiere on April 17, 1940. The film was nominated for 13 Oscars and won eight of them, plus a special award for achievement in the use of color—the big surprise was that Clark Gable missed out on an Oscar for his portrayal of Rhett Butler. His response to the Academy on hearing the winner announced might well have been, "Frankly, my dear, I don't give a damn."

Where were you when?

The lights darkened, and the studio trademark appeared on the screen…When the main title came on, the house went mad… The film took over and the hours sped by. The applause was enormous, and when the lights came on, everyone stood up, but most of them didn't move. It was as though something wonderful or terrible had happened. Half an hour later there were still people standing around.

—Irene Selznick, wife of producer David Selznick, describing in her memoirs a sneak preview that took place in October 1939

Above Judy Garland wearing the famous ruby slippers in a still from *The Wizard of Oz* (1939).

Opposite Clark Gable and Vivien Leigh as Rhett Butler and Scarlet O'Hara (1939).

1940

Dunkirk

The need to evacuate troops from mainland Europe to England via Dunkirk was a tactical blow, but the operation itself was a huge success.

The speed and power of the German invasion of the Low Countries in May 1940, eight months into World War II, split the Allied defenses and forced the evacuation of more than 300,000 troops from Dunkirk in France. Code-named Operation Dynamo, the evacuation began on May 27, assisted by massive aerial bombardment by the RAF, heavy shelling of the coastal area by the Royal Navy and brave rear-guard action from British, French and Belgian ground troops—some Belgians continued fighting even after their king surrendered to Hitler.

At first, Operation Dynamo seemed a hopeless exercise. The British government expected to evacuate no more than 45,000 troops, but Admiral Sir Bertram Home Ramsey, the naval officer in charge, mobilized a massive armada of hundreds of vessels, including fishing boats, river cruisers and private yachts, transforming the operation into a triumph in retreat. Only 7,669 men were evacuated on the first day, but the numbers rose daily until by May 30 more than 50,000 per day were leaving Dunkirk and neighboring beaches. Embarkation was disciplined despite heavy attacks from the German army, navy and air force, and one soldier said of the lines of men wading to the ships and boats, "[There was] no bunching, no pushing—much more orderly even than a waiting theater queue."

"WE SHALL NEVER SURRENDER"

At 3:40 A.M. on June 4 the destroyer *Shikari* left Dunkirk, the last ship to depart, and at dawn the Germans reached the beaches. Some 200 Allied ships had been sunk and 177 aircraft shot down during Operation Dynamo. Furthermore, some 60,000 vehicles, 2,000 field guns and nearly 700,000 tons of ammunition, fuel and supplies had been left on the beaches, along with some 2,000 wounded who could not be transported. But in nine days 338,226 men had been saved, providing a huge morale booster and giving credence to British prime minister Winston Churchill's parliamentary speech later on June 4: "We shall fight on the beaches, we shall fight on the landing grounds, we shall fight in the fields and in the streets, we shall fight in the hills; we shall never surrender."

THE BUILD-UP TO OPERATION DYNAMO

After the sudden fall of Poland to Germany in 1939 (see p. 12), there was a six-month period of "phoney war," when little fighting took place, before World War II began in earnest with the German invasion of Norway and Denmark in April 1940. Then, on May 10, the Germans invaded the Low Countries and France. British and French forces moved north to join the Belgian army, but disastrously for the Allies, the Germans attacked farther south than was thought possible, splitting the Allied forces. As a result, the British Expeditionary Force (BEF) eventually retreated to the French coast, and on May 26 the British government ordered the evacuation of the BEF from mainland Europe.

TIMELINE

05/10/40 Germany invades Belgium, Luxembourg and the Netherlands, subsequently driving the Allies back to the French coast.

05/15/40 The Dutch army surrenders to the Germans.

05/20/40 German forces reach the French coast, splitting Allied defenses.

05/25/40 The BEF retreats to the French coast at Dunkirk.

05/26/40 The British government orders the evacuation of the BEF.

05/27/40 Operation Dynamo begins, and 7,669 men are evacuated to England.

05/28/40 Operation Dynamo continues and 17,804 men are evacuated. King Leopold of Belgium surrenders his country to the Germans.

05/29/40 47,310 men are evacuated.

05/30/40 52,823 men are evacuated.

05/31/40 68,104 men are evacuated.

06/01/40 64,229 men are evacuated.

04/02/06 80,287 men are evacuated.

06/04/40 The last ship leaves Dunkirk after the successful evacuation of some 224,000 British and some 114,000 French and Belgian troops.

Where were you when?

The man in the stretcher above me had been bleeding badly, and I kept having to wipe his blood from my face. When the ambulance reached the beach, the door opened and I saw a gray lifeboat at the water's edge, a man in a dark blue naval overcoat standing by it. He came over. "Can you get off your stretcher?" I shook my head. "Well, I'm very sorry, we can't take you. Your stretcher would take up the places of four men. Orders are only those who can stand or sit." I said nothing. I was too tired to argue.

—Jimmy Langley, Platoon Commander, Coldstream Guards

Above Crew members of the French destroyer *Bourrasque*, sunk by a mine at Dunkirk, are hauled aboard a British vessel from their sinking life raft.

Opposite Even with the evacuation ships as close as possible to the beach, soldiers have to stand chest-high in the sea awaiting their turn to embark.

1940

TIMELINE

07/02/40 Hitler begins planning the invasion of Britain, code-named Operation Sealion.

07/40– 08/40 The Luftwaffe begins intensively bombing ships, forcing the RAF to divert resources into attacking fighter escorts.

07/13/40 Hitler issues Directive No. 15, detailing how the army, navy and air force will be deployed in the invasion of Britain.

08/13/40 Code-named Adlertag ("Eagle Day") by the Germans. The Luftwaffe begins attacking British airfields and aircraft factories.

09/07/40 The Luftwaffe begins the Blitz on London (see p. 20).

09/15/40 The Luftwaffe suffers heavy losses attacking London, forcing Hitler, on September 17, to postpone his planned invasion.

10/12/40 Hitler abandons his plans to invade Britain.

A crowd gathers to watch a film about the RAF, which had recently defeated the Luftwaffe in the Battle of Britain. Films shown on mobile screens such as this were used to boost morale and raise money for the war effort (October 1940).

The Battle of Britain

No words sum up this battle better than Winston Churchill's, "Never in the field of human conflict was so much owed by so many to so few."

After the conquest of France, Adolf Hitler began planning Operation Sealion—the invasion of Britain. In order to land an invasion force against Britain's superior navy, Germany would require complete supremacy in the air, and so it was that the Battle of Britain was fought entirely in the skies. The battle began in earnest on August 13, 1940—code-named Eagle Day by the Germans—when the Luftwaffe (German air force), under the command of Herman Goëring, began the large-scale bombing of British airfields and aircraft factories in an effort to destroy the RAF. But the Germans had not counted on the skill, determination and stamina of British pilots, the maneuverability of the British Spitfire and Hurricane aircraft, or the advantage provided by Britain's secret chain of south-coast radar stations, the first in the world. At first the Germans consistently lost more aircraft than the British, but in late August Goëring changed tactics, concentrating greater firepower on a smaller number of targets, and the RAF began to lose planes and pilots faster than it could replace them. Then Goëring made a decision that would cost him the battle: On September 7 he began bombing London.

TACTICAL ERROR

Historians disagree as to whether Goëring made this decision in order to achieve a breakthrough, not realizing how close the RAF was to capitulation or whether it was a misguided retaliation for RAF raids on Berlin. Whatever the reason, it was the break the RAF needed. The bombing of London marked the start of the Blitz (see p. 20), which was disastrous for London, but by taking Luftwaffe resources away from bombing Britain's airfields, it allowed the RAF to regroup. On September 15 came the decisive raid on London—the Luftwaffe lost nearly three times as many aircraft as the RAF, and the Germans had to accept that far from being defeated, the RAF was gaining strength. Two days later Hitler postponed Operation Sealion "until further orders," abandoning it altogether on October 12. The Battle of Britain had been won and lost, and September 15 is celebrated annually as Battle of Britain Day in memory of the pilots of the RAF—"the Few" to whom so much is owed by so many.

Where were you when?

I was the typical little snotty-nosed schoolboy with a cloth cap and short pants and a gas-mask box over my shoulder— to keep my sweet ration in! Little boys like me didn't realize people were killing each other. Life was one huge excitement going to school in North London and diving out of the bus to hear the rattle of machine-gun fire and watch the Spitfires and Hurricanes and Messerschmidts covering the sky.

—David Shepherd, Sussex, England

Hurricane and Spitfire aircraft in flight

THEIR FINEST HOUR

British prime minister Winston Churchill knew that the Battle of Britain would be long and tough, and on June 18, after the evacuation from Dunkirk (see p. 16) and with the fall of France inevitable, he announced that Britain would fight on alone, saying, "The Battle of France is over; I expect that the Battle of Britain is about to begin." He went on to exhort the people, "Let us brace ourselves to our duties and so bear ourselves that if the British Empire and its Commonwealth last for a thousand years, men will still say, "This was their finest hour. "

1940

TIMELINE

A statue on City Hall Tower in Dresden overlooks the ruins of the city after air raids by the RAF and USAF.

The Blitz

To the Germans, blitzkrieg meant "lightning war," but for Britain the "Blitz" meant eight long, slow months of devastating air raids.

The first country to experience blitzkrieg was Poland (see p. 12), when the German navy and air force began bombarding that country's major cities and ports and the swift, mobile armored units of the German army swept across the border. Compared with the trenches of World War I, "lightning war" was an apt term for this new form of warfare. In Britain the RAF prevented the process of blitzkrieg from progressing beyond the stage of aerial bombardment, and "lightning war" turned into a slow war of attrition as the Luftwaffe attempted to bomb the country into submission.

THE BLITZ ON LONDON

Air raids on London began on "Black Saturday," September 7, 1940, and continued every night for more than two months with the exception of November 2, when bad weather grounded the Luftwaffe. However, the Blitz on London did not have the desired effect. It was a tactical error in that it allowed the RAF to regroup and ultimately win the Battle of Britain (see p. 18), and it was a psychological error in that it did not break the morale of Londoners, but instead made them more defiant and more supportive of Prime Minister Winston Churchill's dogged determination to fight on at all costs.

THE BLITZ ON BRITAIN

The Blitz was soon extended to most of Britain. When it became clear that the capital would not be bombed into submission, the Luftwaffe began systematically bombing other industrial cities important to the war effort, as well as continuing intermittent raids on London. After the almost total destruction of Coventry on November 14, 1940, the Germans coined a new verb: *Coventrisieren*, "to annihilate or raze to the ground." Over the coming months many other cities would be Coventrized, including Belfast, Birmingham, Bristol, Glasgow, Hull, Liverpool, Manchester, Plymouth, Portsmouth, Sheffield and Southampton. Some 42,000 people were killed and countless homes and historic buildings destroyed in the eight months of the Blitz, but Britain did not buckle, and reprieve eventually came with Hitler's decision to turn instead on his former ally, the USSR.

AIR RAIDS ON GERMANY

Britain was not the only country to suffer sustained aerial bombardment. Most occupied European countries were bombed by the RAF (and, later, USAF) at some stage, with German cities suffering the most devastating attacks. Cologne, Düsseldorf, Dortmund and Hamburg all suffered in the same way as British provincial cities, and Berlin, like London, was subject to a three-month campaign to bomb the city "until the heart of Nazi Germany ceases to beat." The most devastating and controversial Allied air raids of the entire war were three raids in close succession on the militarily insignificant, but culturally priceless, city of Dresden, which reduced the "Florence of the Elbe" to rubble and killed thousands of people.

Where were you when?

I was in the air-raid shelter, and suddenly from far off in the sky I heard the start of a shrieking roar, then another and another, more and more, all getting louder and nearer. I remember thinking, "Here we are with not a scratch on us, perfectly well, and in a few seconds we shall be blown to pieces and there is nothing we can do about it." Then there was a series of huge thumps. The bombs had landed very near, but not on us.

—Barbara Hayes, Surrey, England

British prime minister Winston Churchill, accompanied by his wife, Clementine, inspecting bomb damage in the City of London (1940).

1941

TIMELINE

1933 The League of Nations condemns Japan for its 1931 invasion and continuing occupation of Manchuria, China. Japan leaves the League of Nations.

1937 The U.S. applies economic sanctions against Japan in response to Japan's occupation of Peking.

1938 The U.S. provides economic aid to China in the face of further Japanese attacks on China.

1940 The U.S. bans the export of certain goods to Japan. Japan declares it will establish "a new order in greater East Asia," but states its intention to avoid conflict with the U.S.

1941 Japan takes control of Indochina. The U.S. responds by freezing Japanese deposits in the U.S. and banning the sale of aviation fuel to Japan.

10/11/41 Japanese government approval is given for the attack on Pearl Harbor.

11/26/41 The Japanese fleet leaves harbor in preparation for the attack.

12/07/41 Japan attacks the U.S. fleet at anchor in Pearl Harbor.

"Tora! Tora! Tora!"

THE DAY OF SHAME

The Japanese attack on Pearl Harbor took place with no declaration of war, leading Americans to call it the Day of Shame. In fact, just as shamefully, the Japanese had intended to declare war at the exact moment the attack began in order to comply with the articles (but not the spirit) of the 1907 Hague Convention on war without losing the treacherous and deadly element of surprise. The Japanese government sent the declaration to its diplomats in Washington, D.C., but the transcription of the message was delayed and war was not declared until after the attack had begun. However, even if this technicality had been met, the result would have been the same—the United States was now inextricably involved in World War II.

Above Warships on fire in the U.S. naval base at Pearl Harbor, Hawaii, after the surprise attack by the Japanese that brought the United States into World War II.

Opposite Firefighters in action after the Japanese attack on Pearl Harbor.

Pearl Harbor

The surprise raid by Japan on the U.S. naval base at Pearl Harbor killed 2,403 people and precipitated the entry of America into World War II.

Throughout the 1930s Japanese expansionist policy in East Asia strained that nation's diplomatic relations with the rest of the world. As late as July 1940, Japan professed the intention to avoid a conflict with the United States, but on October 11, 1941, Admiral Isoroku Yamamoto was given approval for his plan to attack the U.S. Pacific Fleet at anchor in Pearl Harbor, Hawaii. Japan continued ostensibly negotiating with the United States until November 29, but by then the Japanese fleet had already left harbor under radio silence to take up position for the attack.

"TORA! TORA! TORA!"

On December 2 the Japanese attack fleet was put on action stations with the order *Niitaka Yama Ni Nabore* ("Climb Mount Niitaka"), and by dawn on December 7 the ships were in position 250 miles north of Hawaii. At 6:00 A.M. the first wave of 183 bombers, torpedo planes and fighter escorts took off from Japanese aircraft carriers. At 7:48 A.M. the commander of the first wave signaled *To, To, To* ("Fight, Fight, Fight") and then the infamous *Tora! Tora! Tora!* ("Tiger! Tiger! Tiger!") to indicate that they had caught the Americans unawares. Meanwhile, a second wave of 134 Japanese bombers and 36 fighter escorts had taken off from the carriers, arriving at Pearl Harbor at 8:40 A.M. to continue the destruction.

THE UNITED STATES ENTERS WORLD WAR II

At 9:45 A.M. the last of the Japanese planes returned to the carriers after a two-hour raid that had killed 2,403 American servicemen and civilians, and damaged or destroyed 19 ships and some 200 planes, at a cost of just 29 Japanese planes and 64 dead or missing servicemen. The previous day, U.S. president Franklin Roosevelt had appealed directly to Japan's emperor Hirohito to avoid war with the United States—the following day Roosevelt asked Congress for authorization to go to war against Japan. With the official declaration by Congress the war already raging in Europe, Africa, and Asia expanded to become a second world war in fact as well as in name.

Where were you when?

Between the time I left for sunday school and when I returned home two hours later, the chatty, lighthearted atmosphere of my safe haven had taken a drastic turn. Tense feelings and serious uncertainty had invaded during my short absence.

—Jacqueline Morgan, Wyoming

1942

TIMELINE

05/27/42 A Japanese invasion fleet leaves its home ports to begin Operation M1: the capture of Midway Island.

05/28/42 U.S. Task Force 16 sails to intercept the Japanese fleet.

05/30/42 U.S. Task Force 17 sails from Pearl Harbor to join Task Force 16.

06/02/42 The U.S. task forces rendezvous 350 miles/560km northeast of Midway.

06/03/42 The Japanese launch a diversionary attack on U.S. bases in the Aleutian Islands but fail to draw the U.S. task forces off station.

06/04/42 Japanese aircraft attack Midway at 6:30 A.M. Between 7:00 and 9:30 U.S. bombers attack the Japanese fleet with little success. A U.S. dive-bomb attack beginning at 10:20 destroys three of the four Japanese aircraft carriers. At 2:45 P.M. the U.S. aircraft carrier *Yorktown* is hit and soon afterward U.S. planes hit the remaining Japanese carrier.

06/05/42 Japanese Admiral Yamamoto orders a withdrawal.

06/06/42 A Japanese destroyer is sunk by U.S. aircraft, and a Japanese submarine sinks a U.S. destroyer.

06/07/42 A Japanese submarine hits and sinks the damaged U.S. aircraft carrier *Yorktown*.

Pilots of a U.S. Navy torpedo bomber squadron prior to the Battle of Midway. All but one of these pilots was killed in the battle.

The Battle of Midway

The Battle of Midway was not only U.S. revenge for Pearl Harbor but also a turning point in the Pacific theater of World War II.

Often described as one of the most important naval engagements in history, the Battle of Midway gave America the upper hand in the battle for the Pacific. Hoping to surprise the United States as they had done at Pearl Harbor, a Japanese invasion fleet left Japan on May 27, 1942, with the aim of capturing the U.S. base on Midway Island and using it as a staging post for an invasion of Hawaii. But this time, having cracked the Japanese radio codes, the Americans were prepared for the attack, and on May 28 and 30 two U.S. task forces set sail to intercept the Japanese.

THE ENGAGEMENT

After a diversionary Japanese attack on the Aleutian Islands (in the Bering Sea, forming the southwest tip of Alaska), the battle proper began at 6:30 A.M. on June 4, when Japanese bombers attacked Midway. They inflicted considerable damage, but American planes prevented them from destroying the U.S. base on the island, and shortly afterward American aircraft twice attacked the Japanese fleet. Both attacks were repelled by Japanese antiaircraft fire before a third sortie succeeded in destroying three of the four Japanese aircraft carriers.

JAPANESE WITHDRAWAL

The Japanese struck back, damaging the U.S. carrier *Yorktown* with aircraft from their surviving carrier, *Hiryu*, but within two hours U.S. aircraft had damaged *Hiryu* so badly that it was later scuttled by the Japanese. In the early hours of June 5 Japanese admiral Isoroku Yamamoto ordered a withdrawal, after which the Americans succeeded in sinking one more cruiser, on June 6, before losing contact with the invasion fleet. The Battle of Midway was won and lost, putting an end to Japan's ability to mount strategic attacks in the Pacific and giving the United States superiority in this vital theater of war.

Where were you when?

The newspapers are all howling over "our great victory at Midway." Seems as though the Japs got a good pasting. That's the first fight I've been in with them that my side won.

—James Clair Nolan, U.S. Navy pilot, diary entry for June 6, 1942

The Battle of Midway was won and lost, putting an end to Japan's ability to mount strategic attacks in the Pacific.

Prior to the Battle of Midway, a squadron of U.S. Douglas Dauntless dive bombers patrols above the coral reefs off Midway Island in search of the Japanese.

OPERATION JUBILEE: THE RAID ON DIEPPE

While the U.S. was gaining the upper hand in the Pacific at Midway, the Allies in Europe were planning to open a second front to prevent German expansion in the east. Lacking the logistics for a full-scale invasion, the Allies planned a series of raids along a front extending from France to Norway, the first major raid taking place at Dieppe, France, on August 19 1942. The 2nd Canadian Division, with British, U.S. and French troops, endured a disastrous nine-hour battle with German defenses, eventually withdrawing with close to 4,000 casualties from a landing force of approximately 6,000. The debacle was officially justified as providing experience necessary for eventual success on D-Day, but many critics agreed with the German assessment that the raid "defied all military reason."

1944

TIMELINE

05/08/44 Eisenhower fixes the date of the D-Day landings as June 5, 6 or 7. Forces and equipment made ready for the invasion begin to move toward their embarkation points.

06/01/44 The BBC transmits a coded alert to the French Resistance, warning of the impending invasion. The message is the first verse of Paul Verlaine's poem *Chanson d'Automne*.

06/02/44 Eisenhower issues orders for the invasion to begin on June 5.

06/04/44 Eisenhower orders a 24-hour delay due to adverse weather conditions.

06/05/44 Paratroopers and glider-borne infantry leave Britain at about 10.00 P.M. and, following an Allied aerial bombardment, deploy over Normandy at about midnight to prepare the way for the ground forces. A fleet of nearly 3,000 landing ships and support vessels leaves Britain for France.

06/06/44 The first landing craft go ashore at 6:35 A.M., landing U.S. forces on Utah beach; German forces think that it is a diversion from the real invasion. The first landing craft carrying British forces go ashore at 7:25 A.M. Approximately 150,000 troops are landed on five beaches with the loss of approximately 10,000 lives.

The D-Day landings

The D-Day landings, involving 150,000 troops from the United States, Britain and Canada, constituted the greatest amphibious military operation in history.

There is no mystique to the code-name D-Day—like H-Hour, it is simply military terminology for the time at which a plan will go into action. The plan in this case was Operation Overlord, the Allied invasion of German-occupied Europe, which had such a decisive effect on the outcome of the Second World War that the humble term D-Day was elevated from military jargon to the commemorative title for the greatest amphibious invasion in the history of warfare.

For more than two years Allied commanders had been secretly planning Operation Overlord, and finally, by May 1944, everything was in place. British prime minister Winston Churchill announced, "The hour of our greatest effort and action is approaching," and German commander Erwin Rommel, predicting the inevitable, told his aide, "The first 24 hours of the invasion will be decisive. For the Allies, as well as for Germany, it will be the longest day." On June 5 Allied supreme commander "Ike" Eisenhower (see below) studied the weather report and made his decision, "OK, let's go". Airborne troops landed behind enemy lines that night, and at 6:35 A.M. on June 6 the first Allied landing craft went ashore on the beaches of Normandy.

THE LONGEST DAY

Supported by three airborne divisions and a massive seaborne bombardment, more than 150,000 British, American and Canadian troops landed at five beaches code-named Utah, Omaha, Gold, Juno and Sword. German führer Hitler thought that unless the Allies captured a major port, they would be unable to land sufficient troops and equipment to mount a full-scale invasion, but he had not counted on the invention of Mulberry Ports—huge concrete blocks, providing 15 miles/24 km of floating piers and breakwaters, that were towed across the English Channel, enabling the Allies to land more than 300,000 men, 54,000 vehicles and 100,000 tons of supplies and equipment in the six days after D-Day. Casualties were heavy, but the D-Day landings enabled the Allies to liberate France and Belgium by the end of 1944 and, the following year, to win World War II.

EISENHOWER

The Supreme Commander of Allied forces on D-Day was American General "Ike" Eisenhower, who later became President of the United States. As Allied Commander-in-Chief from 1942 to 1943, Eisenhower led the successful invasions of North Africa, Sicily and Italy, gaining a reputation as an excellent military strategist and, equally important, as a tactful coordinator of his international Allied staff. In December 1943 he was appointed Supreme Allied Commander and charged with the most ambitious and crucial operation of the war: the invasion of Europe. He bravely decided to press ahead with Operation Overlord despite changeable weather, telling the troops, "The eyes of the world are upon you. The hopes and prayers of liberty-loving people everywhere march with you."

Where were you when?

The talking stopped. Men took up their rifles and machine carbines; there was a clack of bolts being drawn and rammed home. There was smoke across the beach ahead, and the black plumes of explosions, each with a cherry-red flicker at its heart. The landing craft nosed ashore through a mass of floating rubbish."

—Alexander Baron, novelist and British government observer, Normandy

Opposite En route to Normandy, American crew members of LST 317 listen tensely to their captain as his D-Day landing instructions are piped belowdecks (June 5, 1944).

Above U.S. troops disembark from their landing craft during the D-Day invasion. On the beach ahead of them, their comrades are already under heavy machine-gun fire from the Germans (June 6, 1944).

Right French soldiers parade the flags of the Allied nations during a ceremony to mark the 60th anniversary of the D-Day landings (June 6, 2004).

1945

"THAT" PHOTOGRAPH

American photographer Joe Rosenthal's image of U.S. marines raising the Stars and Stripes on Mount Suribachi is one of the world's most iconic images of war. Its evocation of team effort and invisible faces make these unknown soldiers representative of all soldiers who have performed patriotic acts in all wars. This was the second American flag to be raised on Mount Suribachi because the first, raised 90 minutes earlier, was considered too small. Rosenthal was on hand the second time to create an image that won him a Pulitzer prize, has appeared on stamps and posters worldwide, inspired a statue in the Arlington Cemetery (above) and was consciously re-created as a sign of American defiance after the attack on the World Trade Center.

The taking of Iwo Jima

As well as providing a strategic base for raids on Japan, the conquest of Iwo Jima produced one of the world's most iconic war images.

The strategic importance of Iwo Jima may have been forgotten, but a single photograph of four U.S. marines raising the Stars and Stripes on the island's highest mountain has ensured that the conquest of the island has remained in the public consciousness for more than half a century. Iwo Jima is the largest of the Volcano Islands, which lie in the western Pacific some 750 miles/1200 km south of Tokyo. Possession of the island and its two airfields was vital to the U.S. war effort because, if captured, Iwo Jima would provide a base for fighter planes escorting B-29 bombing raids on Japan.

THE BATTLE

The battle for Iwo Jima began at 9:00 A.M. on February 19, 1945, when the United States landed some 30,000 men of the 4th and 5th Marine divisions on the southeast coast of the heavily defended island. The Americans established a beachhead but suffered such heavy losses that on the third day the 3rd Marine Division, thus far held in reserve, was sent into the fray. Eventually, members of the 5th Division surrounded Mount Suribachi, and on February 23 they raised the Stars and Stripes at the summit. This symbolic victory was followed by weeks of bitter fighting before the island was finally declared safe on March 18, after which Iwo Jima was used to support bombing raids on 66 Japanese cities in an attempt to force Japan to surrender—something that was ultimately achieved only after the dropping of atomic bombs on Hiroshima and Nagasaki (see p. 36). The island was returned to Japan in 1968.

Opposite The cover of the April 9, 1945, edition of *Life* magazine shows U.S. Marines on Iwo Jima taking cover while blowing up a cave linked to a Japanese blockhouse.

Where were you when?

We went up the mountain almost in the middle, so consequently, we sent patrols around to the right and left to take care of any Japs that might come out. When we got there, I was with the group that swung to the left, and immediately the lieutenant sent a man around to look for a piece of staff that we could put the American flag on. And we used this Jap pip, and we attached the American flag on there, and we put it up. And Joe Rosenthal happened to be there and took the picture that is now famous.

—John H. Bradley, 5th Marine Division

LIFE

APRIL 9, 1945 **10** CENTS

YEARLY SUBSCRIPTION $4.50

1945

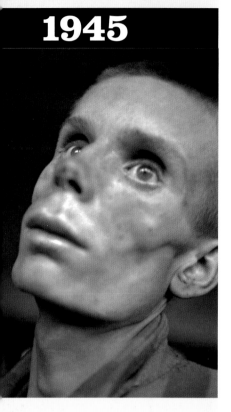

Above An emaciated unidentified 18-year-old Russian Jew on the day he was liberated from Dachau concentration camp near Munich (April 18, 1945).

Opposite American soldiers contemplate a row of cremation ovens at Buchenwald concentration camp. U.S. general George Patton ordered German civilians to view the ovens and the workings of the camp as evidence of the atrocities committed there (April 28, 1945).

Allies discover the Nazi death camps

Of all the horrors of World War II, the Nazi death camps, discovered when Allied troops liberated Europe, were by far the worst.

The Allies had known of the existence of Nazi concentration camps for much of the war, but the full abomination of their true purpose—not the concentrated internment of prisoners, but the extermination of an entire race of people—was not revealed until the first of the camps was liberated in 1945. On January 27 that year, Soviet troops entered Auschwitz, where more than 6,000 people a day had been gassed in purpose-built chambers. Three months later the Western Allies discovered, to their horror, that Auschwitz was not the only such camp: In April, British troops entered Belsen, where they discovered 40,000 emaciated prisoners dying at a rate of more than 600 a day, and that same month the Americans liberated Buchenwald, where the situation was equally bad, with 900 boys under the age of 14 among the survivors.

THE FINAL SOLUTION

In themselves, concentration camps were nothing new. Warring nations used them to intern prisoners of war, political prisoners and "enemies of the state," but in Nazi Germany the camps were used for a far more sinister purpose. Operated with no regard for international law or the conventions of war, the camps were used to imprison anyone classified by the Nazi leadership as *untermenschen* (subhuman), including Polish political prisoners, racial and religious minorities, Gypsies, homosexuals, the mentally ill and Soviet prisoners of war.

The Jewish race was the main target of Führer Adolf Hitler's hatred, and at the Wannsee Conference in January 1942 he proposed a "final solution" to the "problem" of Jews and other minorities: to systematically exterminate them. To this end, concentration camps were adapted or purpose-built as death camps, with rail links, gas chambers and ovens to transport, exterminate and dispose of, as quickly and efficiently as possible, those prisoners who were not required for medical experiments or as slave labor.

(continued on next page)

Where were you when?

I saw the faces of the people we liberated—they went through hell.

—Anatoly Shapiro, commander of the Soviet troops who liberated Auschwitz

I could not believe what I was seeing—the horror that was there. You had to pick your way through the camp because of the people who had died, some hanging from the barbed wire.

—Major Dick Williams, now 84, one of the first Allied soldiers to enter Belsen

[Belsen] is the most horrible, frightful place I have ever seen. I am told that 30,000 prisoners died in the last few months. I can well believe the figure.

—Senior British army medical officer, Belsen

1945 (Death camps cont.)

Horrified citizens of Ludwigslust, Germany, are forced to witness evidence of the atrocities committed at the nearby concentration camp, where the bodies of the victims were dumped in pits in the yard.

Three weeks after the liberation of Belsen, the camp was razed to the ground, but this did not eradicate the wrong that had been done. Perhaps more appropriately, in an attempt to ensure that the world never forgets the atrocities perpetrated there, parts of other camps have been preserved as museums commemorating the dead.

THE 60TH ANNIVERSARY

On January 27, 2005, concentration camp survivors and world leaders traveled to the southern Polish town of Oswiecim, better known by its German name of Auschwitz, to commemorate all the victims of the Holocaust on the 60th anniversary of the liberation of Auschwitz. *The Guardian* newspaper reported, "Several hundred survivors and the few living liberators of the death camp converged on the geometric expanse of barracks, furnaces, watchtowers and barbed wire that started to give up its awful secrets to an exhausted Europe 60 years ago … for the largest and last such commemoration of the wickedness that humans can inflict on one another."

Several hours of speeches, readings and ceremonies opened with the sound of an approaching train, as if arriving along the tracks that had brought more than 1 million people to their deaths at Auschwitz; the commemoration ended with the playing of a

shofar (Jewish horn) and, as the dark winter sky was lit up by a corridor of fire along the former railway, a reading of the Kaddish (the Jewish prayer for the dead).

The speeches included the testimonies of camp survivors, which, as the official Holocaust Memorial Day program points out, present a paradox: "The stories must be set down and preserved for the future, yet the reality is often beyond the capacity of language to communicate"—an observation made 60 years earlier by distinguished journalist Edward Murrow, who said in 1945, "I have reported what I saw and heard, but only part of it...for most of I have no words."

Twenty-four hours before the Memorial Day, Israeli foreign minister Silvan Shalom told U.N. delegates that as the number of survivors grows fewer, "We are on the brink of that moment when this terrible event will change—from memory to history." His point was made more poignantly by Trudy Spira, who was deported from Slovakia to Auschwitz when she was 11 and told reporters at the memorial, "It's very important. You are the last generation that can talk to the survivors; we are every day less. We can give living testimony...to let the world know, to try to get them to learn, even though they don't, so that it doesn't happen again."

> "I have reported what I saw and heard, but only part of it...for most of it I have no words."

Symbols of the lives shattered by the Nazis: Just some of the thousands of wedding rings discovered by troops of the US 1st Army in a cave adjoining Buchenwald Concentration Camp near Weimar. The rings and other valuables were stolen from prisoners before they were executed or worked to death.

1945

TIMELINE

04/29/45 German forces in Italy surrender, effective beginning May 2.

05/04/45 German forces in the Netherlands, Denmark and northwest Germany surrender.

05/06/45 German forces in Norway surrender.

05/07/45 Germany surrenders unconditionally, effective beginning May 9.

05/08/45 German surrender is ratified and celebrated in Europe as V-E Day.

05/09/45 German surrender takes effect, celebrated in the United States and USSR as V-E Day.

V-E Day

Although the war with Japan lasted until August 1945, victory in Europe was celebrated as V-E Day earlier that summer, on May 8 and 9.

After six years of war in Europe, German capitulation began with the surrender of German forces in Italy on April 29, 1945. Less than a week later, on May 4, total capitulation became inevitable with the surrender of German forces in the Netherlands, Denmark and northwest Germany to British field-marshal Montgomery at Luneburg Heath, near Hamburg. And three days after that, on May 7, German emissary General Alfred Jodl surrendered totally and unconditionally to Allied Supreme Commander General Eisenhower in Rheims, saying, "With this signature, the German people and the German armed forces are, for better or worse, delivered into the victors' hands."

V-E DAY

This acceptance of total defeat was ratified by Field Marshal Keitel in Berlin the following day, making May 8 officially the last day of war in Europe, although some fighting continued after that date. Since then, May 8 has been celebrated throughout Europe as V-E Day, while U.S. president Harry S Truman announced that Americans would celebrate on May 9, commemorating the first day of peace rather than the last day of war. Across Europe people took to the streets to celebrate victory, joyful in the midst of the death, destruction and devastation, that the war was finally over, and thankful that the Nazi grip on Europe had at last been broken.

"The German armed forces are, for better or worse, delivered into the victors' hands."

Left Civilians and soldiers dancing in Piccadilly Circus, London, to celebrate victory in Europe (May 1945).

Below Crowds on the Champs-Elysees, Paris, celebrate the end of hostilities in Europe (May 1945).

Opposite V for victory: Children sit at a V-shaped table for a victory party hosted by residents of Kentwell Close, Brockley, south London.

THE POTSDAM CONFERENCE

In July 1945 the leaders of the victorious powers met at Potsdam, Germany, to discuss the future of the continent. Effectively the conference marked the start of the cold war, as U.S. president Harry S Truman, Soviet dictator Joseph Stalin and British prime minister Winston Churchill (who, after losing a general election, was replaced during the conference by new PM Clement Attlee) failed to agree on key issues, such as free elections in Eastern European countries and where the new frontiers of Germany should be drawn. One thing the leaders did agree on was to demand the unconditional surrender of Japan, to which end, Truman informed Stalin, the United States was developing "a new weapon of unusual destructive force": the atomic bomb (see p. 36).

Where were you when?

My mother, my older sister and myself decided to go up to London for the day to experience the outburst of joy, not to mention hysteria. We found a city crammed with people singing, dancing, climbing trees, even jumping in the fountains. Toward the evening, feeling rather tired, we took refuge in a phone booth and, to prevent disturbance, wrote "Out of Order" on an envelope and pinned it to the door. We managed a few catnaps before getting the train home. I suppose it was all rather pointless, really, but it fulfilled some need to take positive action after the rules and restrictions of civilian life.

—John Allen, West Drayton, England

1945

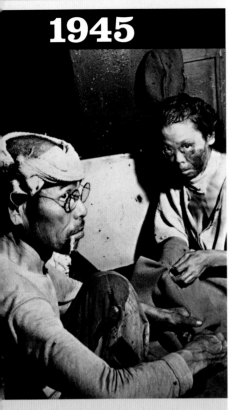

TIMELINE

07/16/45 The world's first atomic bomb is tested at Alamogordo air base, New Mexico.

08/04/45 The U.S. drops leaflets over Hiroshima, warning the inhabitants that their city will be obliterated.

08/06/45 The U.S. drops an atomic bomb on Hiroshima, Japan.

08/09/45 The U.S. drops an atomic bomb on Nagasaki, Japan.

08/10/45 Emperor Hirohito announces that Japan is prepared to make a conditional surrender.

08/14/45 Emperor Hirohito announces the unconditional surrender of Japan, celebrated in Europe as V-J Day (see p. 39).

09/02/45 Emperor Hirohito ratifies the Japanese surrender, marking the last day of World War II, celebrated in the United States as V-J Day (see p. 39).

Above Survivors of the Hiroshima bomb sit in a makeshift hospital in a bombed-out bank near the city center.

Hiroshima and Nagasaki

The dropping of atomic bombs on Hiroshima and Nagasaki brought an end to World War II, but at a terrible price to humanity.

On July 29, 1945, Japan rejected an ultimatum issued by the Allies to surrender unconditionally or suffer "complete destruction." This left two options: Invade Japan or use the awesome power of what U.S. president Harry S Truman described understatedly as "a new weapon of unusual destructive force"—the atomic bomb. U.S. military advisers considered that an invasion would incur some 1 million Allied casualties and untold civilian deaths, so Truman opted for what he considered the lesser of two evils, authorizing the immediate use of four atomic bombs. He also reiterated the call for surrender, warning the Japanese of "a rain of ruin from the air, the like of which has never been seen on this earth."

LITTLE BOY AND FAT MAN

On August 6 Operation Centerboard began. A B-29 bomber named *Enola Gay*, after the mother of the pilot, Colonel Paul W. Tibbets, took off from the Mariana Islands, in the Pacific Ocean, for the city of Hiroshima, where bombardier Major Thomas Ferebee released an atomic bomb code-named Little Boy. The tail gunner, who witnessed the explosion from 10 miles away as *Enola Gay* returned to base, voiced a thought that would be echoed around the globe: "My God. What have we done?" The city was vaporized, nearly 100,000 people were killed instantly, and up to 250,000 died of burns and radiation sickness, some of them years later.

Still the Japanese would not surrender, and on August 9 a second atomic bomb, code-named Fat Man, was dropped on the port of Nagasaki, wreaking similar destruction but with fewer casualties. The following day, Emperor Hirohito announced that Japan would surrender conditionally (see p. 39), thereby preventing the United States from dropping the remaining two atomic bombs, which had been scheduled for August 13 and 16.

THE MANHATTAN PROJECT

Manhattan Project was the codename for the most secret operation of World War II: the development of the atomic bomb. In 1939 physicist Albert Einstein advised U.S. president Franklin Roosevelt that the Germans may be developing such a bomb, and in 1942 Roosevelt authorized the launch of the $2 billion Manhattan Project, with scientific director J. Robert Oppenheimer coordinating scientists from around the world, including many from Nazi-occupied Europe. After witnessing the mushroom cloud that accompanied the test detonation of the world's first nuclear bomb on July 16, 1945, an awestruck Oppenheimer quoted from a Hindu scripture, saying, "I am become death, destroyer of worlds."

Where were you when?

"There she goes!" someone said. *Out of the belly of the bomber what looked like a black object came downward. All of us became aware of a giant flash that broke through the dark barrier of our ARC welder's lenses and flooded our cabin with an intense light. A tremendous blast-wave struck our ship and made it tremble from nose to tail. This was followed by four more blasts in rapid succession. Then, just when it appeared as though the thing had settled down into a state of permanence, there came a giant mushroom that reached a height of 45,000 feet.*

—William L. Laurence, U.S. War Department Bureau of Public Relations

One of the only buildings left standing in Hiroshima, directly beneath the epicenter of the blast.

"I am become death, destroyer of worlds."

1945

THE SURRENDER

The formal surrender on board U.S.S. *Missouri* was signed by the Japanese foreign minister Mamoru Shigemitsu and Chief of Staff Yoshijiro Umezo, and on behalf of the Allies by General Douglas MacArthur, Supreme Allied Commander in the Pacific. It was countersigned by representatives of Australia, Britain, Canada, China, France, New Zealand, the Netherlands, the United States and the USSR. The ceremony was also attended, at MacArthur's invitation, by U.S. general Jonathan Wainwright and British general Percival, who had both recently been released from Japanese prisoner-of-war camps.

Right "It's Over." Thousands of Americans celebrate V-J Day on State Street, New York.

Below Watched by U.S. general Douglas MacArthur, Japanese chief of staff General Yoshijiro Umezo signs the official surrender document on board U.S.S. *Missouri* (September 2, 1945).

V-J Day

V-J Day marked not only Victory in Japan but the end of World War II, six years and a day after the German invasion of Poland.

The day after America's second atomic bomb was dropped (see p. 36), Emperor Hirohito announced that Japan was prepared to surrender to the Allies. Military operations were immediately scaled down, and four days later Hirohito prepared to make a radio announcement of Japan's total and unconditional surrender. However, Japanese military leaders refused to accept defeat, and shortly before the announcement some 1,000 soldiers stormed the Imperial Palace hoping to prevent the announcement from being made. The Palace Guard repelled the soldiers, and that afternoon, August 14, 1945, Hirohito formally announced Japan's surrender, to the jubilation of the Allies.

"THE DAY WE HAVE BEEN WAITING FOR"

U.S. president Truman declared, "This is the day we have been waiting for since Pearl Harbor," while Britain's new prime minister, Clement Attlee, announced, "Japan has today surrendered. The last of our enemies is laid low." The war was effectively over, and August 14 was celebrated throughout Europe as V-J Day. However, there were certain formalities to be concluded, including organizing the details of the U.S. military occupation of Japan and the surrender of Japanese garrisons in Singapore and various other parts of the Pacific.

After these arrangements had been made, the surrender document was formally signed on board U.S.S. *Missouri*, at anchor in Tokyo Bay, on September 2 (see "The Surrender," opposite), a day celebrated throughout the United States as V-J Day. After the ceremony U.S. general Douglas MacArthur announced, "It is my earnest hope, and indeed the hope of all mankind, that from this solemn occasion a better world shall emerge out of the blood and carnage of the past." Japan's formal surrender marked the definitive end of World War II after 2,194 days and the loss of an estimated 55 million lives.

> "This is the day we have been waiting for since Pearl Harbor."

Where were you when?

I was on holiday in a village called Winsham on the Somerset/Dorset border where I had been evacuated for a second time in 1940/41. The Japanese surrender was announced late in the evening. Virtually the whole village turned out and was dancing and singing in the streets. Local farmers brought milk buckets full of rough cider (better than scrumpy!), and I think that this was my first introduction to alcoholic drink, at the age of 13—I have never looked back!

—Trevor Smale, Carshalton, England

THE BABY BOOM

The effects of World War II were not confined to its military outcome and the political aftermath. The war also had far-reaching effects on society, including the weakening of social hierarchies and huge demographic changes across the developed world. In Britain and some other European countries, where a large proportion of the male population had been wiped out and economies were struggling to recover from the war, the birth rate slowed down and did not pick up until the 1950s; in other countries, such as France and Italy, it increased—in France, from 600,000 births per year in 1946 to a peak rate of 850,000 per year in 1950. By comparison, America was relatively unscathed in terms of human casualties and destruction of the infrastructure, so the increase in birth rate was even greater than in France or Italy. Affluence and renewed confidence led to an unprecedented population surge beginning in the 1940s that became known as the baby boom—a surge that saw the birth of a generation of children who throughout their lives have been known as "baby boomers" or simply "boomers."

THE AMERICAN BABY BOOM

Sociologists have noted that birth rates often increase after wars and after periods of economic hardship, and for America the 1940s marked the end of both: In the early part of the decade, the nation began to recover from the worldwide economic depression of the 1930s, and 1945 marked the end of the war—the American baby boom peaked the following year. Between 1929 and 1945—16 years of depression and then war—many Americans delayed or avoided having children, either because they could not afford to or because they were on active service, but after the war millions of Americans decided to start families or enlarge them. As a result, in the 18 years between 1946 and 1964, some 76 million children were born in the United States compared with about 50 million in the previous 18 years and about 66 million in the 18 years that followed. Looked at another way, the statistics show that more American children were born in the 10 years after World War II than in the 50 years before it. This huge change in the country's demographic had major effects on the economy, the education system, the culture, and the employment market.

As World War II ended, the standard model conditions for a baby boom were exaggerated in America by the fact that the

U.S. Office of Price Management had kept prices low during the war despite the fact that wages were rising and perpetuated by the fact that as World War II gave way to the cold war, increased government spending on national defense helped to sustain full employment across the nation. As a result, between 1947 and 1960 the average disposable income in America rose by 17%, making the 1950s and early 1960s one of the most prosperous periods in U.S. history. Furthermore, the Servicemen's Readjustment Act, passed by Congress in 1944 and popularly known as the "GI Bill of Rights", guaranteed returning servicemen loans for further education or vocational training. Thus, many more couples than before had the finances, job security and aspirations to feel able to start a family. And at the same time, car ownership increased, which made the possession of suburban family homes more feasible and in turn became part of a virtuous circle that was both a result and a cause of the continuing boom.

THE EFFECTS OF THE BOOM

One of the immediate effects of this emphasis on children and suburban family life was that American women came under enormous social pressure to become "homemakers"—unlike many of their European counterparts, who now had more opportunity to break away from their traditional roles, having proved themselves the equals of men during the war in many fields previously closed to them.

The longer-term effects of the American boom relate to the sheer numbers of people at certain ages overwhelming the national infrastructure: First, schools became overcrowded, with some running two teaching shifts a day and others having to add temporary buildings; a few years later the higher-education system had to expand; after that, unemployment increased as baby boomers had to compete for jobs. As a result, the economy gradually slowed down and baby boomers tended to marry later and have smaller families, completing the circle that had begun in the 1940s. Now and for years to come, as the boomers reach retirement age, their needs will have a dramatic effect on the Social Security pension and health-care systems.

Opposite Montage portrait of dozens of baby boomers (c.1946).

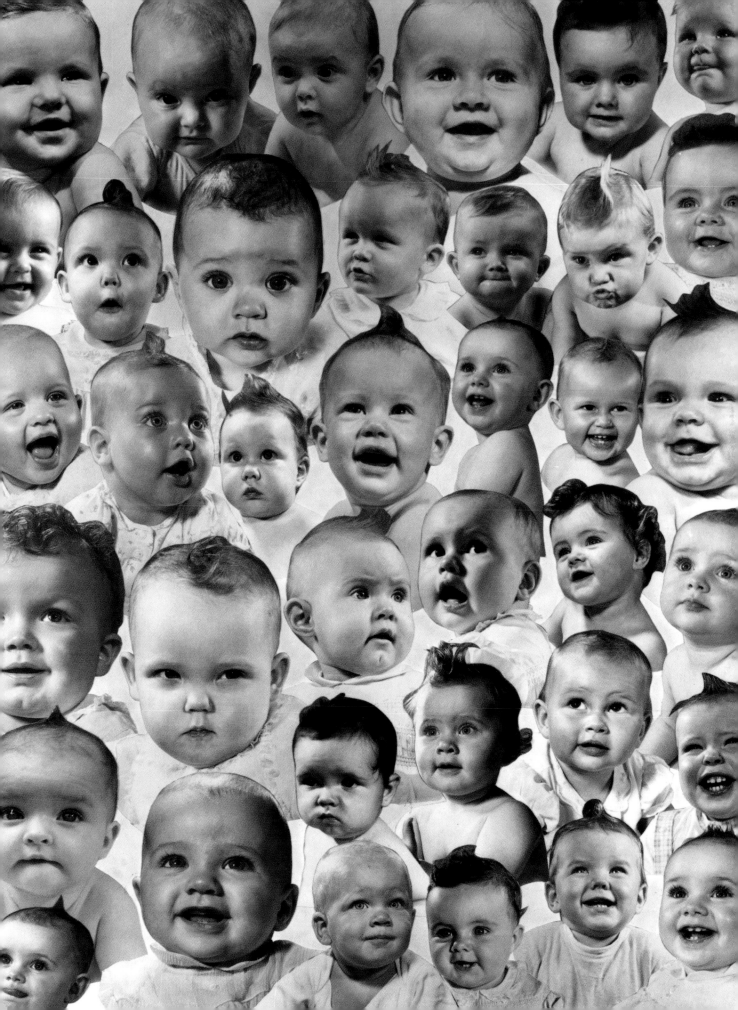

1947

TIMELINE

1885 The Indian National Congress (INC) is established to champion the cause for independence.

1919 The 1919 Government of India Act allows India some degree of power-sharing in provincial government.

1919 INC leader Mahatma Gandhi begins a campaign of civil disobedience to highlight the cause for independence.

02/11/35 The 1935 Government of India Act is passed by British parliament, allowing India greater internal self-government. Britain retains control of external affairs and national defense.

08/14/47 British rule ends at midnight, when India is partitioned into two independent dominions of the British Commonwealth: India and Pakistan. Hundreds of thousands are killed in border clashes as Muslims try to reach Pakistan and Hindus try to reach India before and after the partition deadline.

Above The signatories to partition: (l-r) Jawaharlal Nehru; Lord Ismay (adviser to Lord Mountbatten); Lord Louis Mountbatten, last viceroy of India; and Muhammad Ali Jinnah, president of the All-India Muslim League.

End of the Raj

Indian independence from Britain brought with it division and hardship for millions caught on the wrong side of the partition.

British rule in India, known as the British Raj, lasted in various forms for some 200 years. A nationalist movement—the Indian National Congress (INC)—was established in 1885 and gained strength during the 1920s through a campaign of non-violent civil disobedience led by INC leader Mahatma Gandhi (properly Mohandâs Gandhi). Gandhi succeeded in forcing various political concessions and then, after World War II, full independence—something that also entailed the partition of the subcontinent into the predominantly Hindu country of India and the predominantly Muslim Pakistan.

HANDOVER OF POWER

The handover of power was scheduled for June 1948 but was brought forward by 10 months because of fears that civil war would break out before the original deadline. Legislation was rushed through British parliament, and at midnight on August 14, 1947, power was transferred to Jawaharlal Nehru, the new prime minister of India, and Muhammad Ali Jinnah, the new governor-general of Pakistan.

TRYST WITH DESTINY

Gandhi described the granting of independence as "the noblest act of the British nation," while Nehru announced, "Long years ago we made a tryst with destiny, and now the time comes when we shall redeem our pledge, not wholly or in full measure, but substantially. At the stroke of the midnight hour, when the world sleeps, India will awake to life and freedom." By "not wholly or in full measure," Nehru was referring to the partition, something that marred the celebrations and led to the largest human migration in history, as millions of Hindus and Muslims attempted to cross to safety on the appropriate side of the divide.

> Gandhi's dream of independence had been realized, but not in the way that he had hoped.

Where were you when?

In the late spring of 1947, President Truman asked me to become the first American ambassador to India... was delighted to accept...I had acquired a genuine interest in the Indian people and the subcontinent...I sailed for India from San Francisco on May 4, 1947, and arrived at New Delhi in the latter part of June with the thermometer registering 118 degrees. When I left San Francisco, there was no serious talk of a partition of India. But by the time I arrived, one of the first things I had to do was to ask the State Department to arrange for the appointment of an ambassador to Pakistan.

—Henry Grady, U.S. Ambassador

"THE LARGEST MIGRATION IN HISTORY"

During the 1930s and 1940s Muslims in British-ruled India began campaigning for an independent Muslim state to be called Pakistan, the Urdu word for "Pure Nation." With independence came partition, intended to reflect the Muslim–Hindu divide, but inevitably millions found themselves on the "wrong" side of the partition, leading to mass migrations in both directions across the new border. In all, some 6 million Muslims crossed into Pakistan and some 4.5 million Hindus and Sikhs into India. More than half a million refugees were killed during the migration, most of them through sectarian violence rather than the other attendant dangers of disease, hunger, thirst and exposure. Gandhi's dream of independence had been realized, but not in the way that he had hoped.

Refugees in heavy-wheeled bullock carts make their way from Pakistan to India. Millions of refugees also made their way in the opposite direction.

1947

THE FIRST SUPERSONIC CAR

Scotsman Richard Noble is a man with a quest for speed, and after breaking the land speed record in 1983, he spent the 1990s in pursuit of his goal to be the first to break the sound barrier on land. With aerodynamicist Ron Ayers, he developed a jet-powered car named *Thrust SSC* (_s_uper_s_onic _c_ar) that produced nearly four times as much thrust as Chuck Yeager's Bell X-1. Noble employed ex-RAF pilot Andy Green to drive it, and on October 15, 1997, 50 years and a day after Yeager's landmark flight, Green piloted *Thrust SSC* across the sands of the Black Rock Desert, Nevada, at 763.035 mph—even without the official readout, the sonic boom was enough to confirm that it had broken the sound barrier.

Below Andy Green drives *Thrust SSC* across the Nevada desert on his way to breaking the land speed record and becoming the first human to travel at supersonic speed on the ground (October 15, 1997).

Chuck Yeager breaks the sound barrier

On October 14, 1947, American test pilot Chuck Yeager became the first human being to travel faster than the speed of sound.

In February 1945 the U.S. government began funding the development of a supersonic aircraft for scientific research. The result was the Bell X-1 rocket plane, which, because such a small rocket did not have the endurance for takeoff and ascent, had to be released airborne from a "mother plane." The Bell X-1 made an unpowered test flight on January 19, 1946, proving that the aerodynamics, including the "Thin Wing" that had been developed to reduce turbulence at high speed, were reliable. The X-1 made its first powered flight in December that year, and test flights continued throughout 1947, edging ever closer to the goal of supersonic flight.

GLAMOROUS GLENNIS

On October 14, 1947, Captain Charles "Chuck" Yeager was the pilot who made history, breaking the sound barrier by taking an X-1 named *Glamorous Glennis* to a speed of Mach 1.015, or 670 mph, at an altitude of 42,000 ft/12,800 m. The sound "barrier" is so-called because of the increased drag that an aircraft experiences from the pressure wave ahead of it as it approaches the speed of sound; at the speed of sound, the pressure wave is broken, creating the characteristic "sonic boom."

The Mach number, named after Austrian physicist Ernst Mach, is the ratio of the speed of an object to the speed of sound and is used because the speed of sound varies with temperature and altitude—in breaking the sound barrier on the ground (see "The First Supersonic Car," opposite), ex-RAF pilot Andy Green had to travel nearly 100 mph faster than Yeager had done in the air.

Looking vaguely reminiscent of James Dean, Captain Charles E. "Chuck" Yeager stands beside the plane in which he became the first human being to travel faster than the speed of sound.

Where were you when?

With the stabilizer setting at 2 degrees, the speed was allowed to increase to approximately .95 to .96. The airplane was allowed to continue to accelerate until an indication of .965 on the cockpit Machmeter was obtained. At this indication, the meter momentarily stopped and then jumped up to 1.06, and the hesitation was assumed to be caused by the effect of shock waves on the static source.

—Chuck Yeager, official flight report, October 14, 1947

Two days after Gandhi's fast in January 1948, Hindu refugee Madan Lal threw a homemade bomb at the Mahatma, but he was not injured. Meanwhile, Nathuram Godse, the 35-year-old editor and publisher of a Hindu weekly paper, traveled from Bombay to New Delhi with the specific intention of assassinating Gandhi. Godse told the court at his trial, "I sat brooding intensely on the atrocities perpetuated [*sic*] on Hinduism and on its dark and deadly future if left to face Islam outside and Gandhi inside." But Godse did not act alone. He was part of a small extremist Hindu group, eight of whom were hanged with him for conspiracy—something else that Gandhi, who decried all forms of killing, would have opposed.

Below Gandhi's niece places petals on his brow as he lies in state at Birla House in New Delhi after his assassination (January 1948).

Opposite Intrepid mourners climb a telegraph pole to get a better view of Gandhi's funeral procession (January 1948).

Assassination of Gandhi

"The Father of Indian Independence" was loved by most Indians but hated by others, one of whom shot him on January 30, 1948.

A potent mix of politician, social reformer and religious teacher, Mohandâs Karamchand Gandhi, popularly known as the Mahatma, meaning "Great Soul," spent his entire adult life campaigning for rights for Indians. After studying law in England, he moved in 1893 to South Africa, where he spent some 20 years fighting legislation that discriminated against Indians living there. Returning to India in 1914, he joined the movement for home rule and became leader of the Indian National Congress, whose cause he strengthened through his own "fasts unto death" (hunger strikes) and by organizing campaigns of public civil disobedience. Frequently imprisoned for his civil disobedience, it was at the negotiating table that he achieved his ultimate goal of independence for India (see p. 42).

THE ASSASSINATION

Gandhi's feelings on the eve of independence were mixed because he disagreed with the partition of India and foresaw the bloodshed it would bring. He advocated peace between Muslims and Hindus, and starting on January 13, 1948, he fasted for six days to reinforce his message of communal and religious tolerance. On the third day of his fast, he declared that the government of Hindu India should pay 550 million rupees to Muslim Pakistan to pay for Pakistan's share of India's prepartition assets. But it was his very tolerance, coupled with the suggestion of such a large compensation payment, that was to lead to his death at the hands of a Hindu fanatic who felt that Gandhi should not sympathize with Muslims.

On January 30, 1948, while Gandhi was on his way to a prayer meeting, Nathuram Godse (see sidebar left) stepped out of the crowd and shot him three times at point-blank range. He died 25 minutes later, and the following day more than 2 million Indians gathered for his ritual cremation. Sadly, despite the messages of peace that Gandhi had preached throughout his life, his death led to further violence, riots, arson and even greater tension between Muslims and Hindus in the newly partitioned nation.

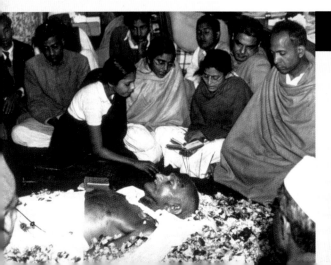

Where were you when?

At the first shot, the foot that was in motion, when he was hit, came down. He still stood on his legs when the second shot rang out, and then collapsed. The last words he uttered were, "Rama Rama."

—Pyarelal, Gandhi's secretary, writing a few days after the assassination

A ghostly hush enveloped the street we lived in. Disbelief had gripped the people, and it was too profound a grief to be articulated. Those who tried to speak about it could not do so without their eyes getting misty.

—Sivamurthy, Delhi, India

1948

The birth of Israel

The founding of the State of Israel was a long-held dream for the Jewish race but an anathema to the Arab population of Palestine.

The concept of a Jewish homeland dates back to biblical times, but the idea became a modern political reality in the late 19th century, when Hungarian Theodor Herzl established the World Zionist Organization (WZO). The stated aim of the WZO was to create a national Jewish homeland in Palestine, which was at that time a province of the Ottoman Empire with a mainly Arab population. In 1917–18, during World War I, Britain expelled the Turks from Palestine and at first declared support for the Zionist cause but later restricted Jewish immigration to Palestine after Arab violence in protest at the doubling of the Jewish population there in 10 years. The Jews in turn rioted in protest at the restrictions, resulting in a British government inquiry that recommended the partition of Palestine between Jews and Arabs.

THE PROCLAMATION OF THE STATE OF ISRAEL

At 4:00 on the afternoon of May 14, 1948, David Ben-Gurion read out Israel's Proclamation of Independence, which included the words, "On November 29, 1947, the United Nations adopted a resolution providing for an independent Jewish state in Palestine, and invited the inhabitants of the country to take the necessary steps to put this plan into effect. In the light of the natural law and the history of the Jewish people, as well as in accordance with the resolution of the United Nations, we proclaim the foundation of the Jewish state in the Holy Land, which will henceforth bear the name the State of Israel."

BIRTH OF A NATION

When World War II broke out, any action on partition was postponed. Then, in the face of continued violence from both sides, in 1947 Britain announced that it would withdraw from Palestine the following May and referred the dispute to the United Nations. The United Nations voted for partition, but not surprisingly, the Arabs did not accept the principle of partition and began guerrilla action. On May 14, 1948, the day of the British withdrawal, David Ben-Gurion proclaimed the State of Israel, with himself as prime minister, and declared that the new state would be "open for the immigration of Jews from every country in which they have been dispersed."

The new state was immediately recognized by both the United States and the USSR but not by the Arab population of Palestine, whose guerrilla action escalated into the first Arab–Israeli war. This ended in victory for Israel, and when a cease-fire was called in January 1949, Israel had extended its territory beyond that allocated by the United Nations and confirmed its existence in fact as well as in principle. Sadly for Arabs and Jews alike, the principle of partition is a dispute that has caused misery and bloodshed for more than 70 years and may never be settled.

Above Jewish refugees swim to shore from the SS *United Nations* (formerly the *Archimedes*), which deliberately ran aground at Nahariya, near Haifa, carrying 700 Central European Jewish refugees. It sailed from Bari, Italy, evading vessels of the British blockade on the way.

Opposite New prime minister David Ben-Gurion, flanked by members of his provisional government, reads Israel's proclamation of nationhood. Above him hangs a portrait of Zionist founder Theodor Herzl.

Below Just two among the many thousands who lost their homes as a consequence of the birth of Israel, an Arab mother and her child suffer quietly in Port Said, having been displaced from Haifa.

Where were you when?

While cruising through a now calm Mediterranean, we got the news on the ship's radio that the State of Israel had been declared. Somehow the Arab passengers on the Marine Carp *disappeared, maybe they moved away from where we were. Us Jews gathered in the dining hall and roared out our joy and pride. We sang "Hatikvah" and a thousand other anthems and songs, danced the hora until we dropped, cried, laughed, and carried on. The fears and doubts were kept inside, for that evening.*

—Elihu King, writing in 1993

1948

TIMELINE

03/48 Soviet representatives withdraw from the Allied Control Council (governing occupied Germany) in protest against U.S.–Anglo–French plans to unify their zones of occupation in western Germany.

04/48 The USSR begins checking and restricting road and rail traffic into Berlin.

06/21/48– The USSR begins the Berlin Blockade
06/24/48 by closing all land routes to Berlin through eastern Germany. The Allies respond by beginning the Berlin Airlift to supply the blockaded city.

09/48 An average of nearly 900 aircraft per day are supplying Berlin.

11/16/48 U.S. president Harry S Truman refuses four-way talks on Berlin unless the USSR first lifts the blockade.

05/05/49 The USSR announces that it will lift the blockade on May 12.

05/23/49 The western sector of occupied Germany becomes the Federal Republic of Germany, with Bonn as the capital. The eastern sector subsequently becomes the German Democratic Republic.

The Berlin Airlift

When the USSR blockaded Berlin in protest at U.S.–Anglo–French plans to unify western Germany, the Allies sent in vital supplies by air.

At the end of World War II, Germany was divided into four zones occupied by the United States, Britain, France and the USSR, with Berlin, like a microcosm of the country as a whole, subdivided into a four-power city, although situated deep inside the Soviet-occupied eastern sector. Tension between the Western powers and the USSR was already being labeled the "Cold War," and this tension worsened over two key issues: U.S.–Anglo–French plans to unify their zones of occupation into a single state and the U.S.-sponsored Marshall Plan for postwar economic recovery in Europe (see opposite), both of which the USSR saw as undermining its influence in eastern Germany.

THE BERLIN BLOCKADE

In April 1948 the Cold War escalated when the USSR began restricting road and rail traffic across its territory in eastern Germany into Berlin. Then, on June 24, the Soviets imposed a total blockade on the city, apparently intending to create a crisis out of which Communism could gain the ascendancy in Europe. That goal failed because of the determination of the Allies to supply the 2 million inhabitants of western Berlin by air—a mammoth exercise code-named Operation Carter Paterson but popularly known in Germany as the *Luftbrücke Berlin*: literally the "Berlin airbridge," though usually translated as the Berlin airlift.

At its height the airlift involved 895 flights per day from western Germany delivering food, fuel and other necessities during what stretched into an 11-month battle of wills between the Western powers and the USSR. Finally, the Soviets agreed to lift the blockade on May 12, 1949, and the airlift ended after some 272,000 sorties at a cost to the Western Allies of some $200 million—a dual success in that not only was a Western presence sustained in Berlin but also the matter had been settled diplomatically and not by force.

Left The border between East and West Berlin is painted across Potsdamer Strasse on the order of the British authorities.

Opposite Berliners standing in ruins at the edge of Tempelhof Airfield, looking up at a U.S. C-47 cargo plane that is bringing them food during the Berlin Airlift.

Opposite below As the food shortage becomes more desperate, a woman tends an allotment in Berliner Strasse, Western Berlin.

Where were you when?

Careful study of results to date, together with calculations of Berlin supply requirements and maximum air-transport capabilities, indicates that minimum requirements can be met by air transport.

—Sidney W. Souers, confidential report to U.S. president Harry S. Truman, Berlin, July 1948

Now and then the Russians would shoot down one of our aircraft that they claimed had intruded into their airspace... Then we would get orders to put every aircraft possible into the air—hundreds of them of all shapes and sizes. And we would fly up and down, back and forth, like some great airborne armada. Daring them to come up and fight. Of course, they never did.

—Eric Jones, then a navigator in the RAF, Gloucestershire, England

THE MARSHALL PLAN

The Marshall Plan was an aid package proposed in 1947 by U.S. secretary of state George C. Marshall as a means firstly of averting "hunger, desperation, poverty and chaos" in Europe in the aftermath of World War II, and second of creating working economies in order to maintain "political and social conditions in which free institutions can exist." The second goal was a diplomatic way of saying "to prevent an economic depression in which Communism will thrive," and was the prime reason why the Soviets objected to the plan. U.S. Congress approved $13 billion of aid to be administered through the European Recovery Program, which was established on April 2, 1948, and almost immediately afterward the USSR began restricting traffic into Berlin.

1950–1959

1950

TIMELINE

05/26/38 The House of Representatives establishes the Dies Committee, named after its chairman, Martin Dies, to investigate "un-American activities" by U.S. Nazis and Communists.

01/03/45 The House votes to give the Dies Committee permanent status as the House Un-American Activities Committee (HUAC).

02/09/50 Senator Joseph McCarthy alleges that he knows the names of 205 Communists working in the State Department.

1953 McCarthy is appointed Chairman of the Permanent Investigations Subcommittee of the Government Operations Committee and launches the McCarthy Hearings.

02/25/54 McCarthy is censured by President Dwight Eisenhower for his bullying tactics.

12/02/54 The Senate votes to condemn McCarthy for conduct unbecoming of a senator and for abuse of select committee privileges.

05/02/57 McCarthy dies of liver disease.

The McCarthy witch hunts

Joseph McCarthy's claim that Communists were working in the U.S. State Department sparked off the witch hunts known as McCarthyism.

Cold War America was a hotbed of fear and suspicion of possible Communist infiltrators and spies known as "the enemy within," and the resulting atmosphere of hysteria enabled the unscrupulous activities of one rogue senator to blight the lives of hundreds of innocent people and limit the foreign policy of two presidents. Joseph McCarthy had been a relatively low-profile Republican senator for four years when he shot to national prominence on February 9, 1950, by alleging, "I have here in my hand a list of two hundred and five members of the Communist Party still working and shaping the policy of the State Department." Setting the pattern for the so-called McCarthy Hearings that followed, the senator offered no evidence or proof of his allegations and refused to reveal the names of those he was accusing.

THE McCARTHY HEARINGS

As with medieval witch hunts, McCarthy's accusations created further hysteria that only more denunciations could allay, and over the next four years he denounced civil servants, academics and politicians with equal vigor, shaping U.S. domestic and foreign policy through the atmosphere of fear he created. In 1953 McCarthy was appointed chairman of the Senate Permanent Investigations Subcommittee, which conducted what became known as the McCarthy Hearings, legitimizing his "sensationalism, cruelty and reckless disregard for due process." The hearings also widened the scope of McCarthy's investigations and thereby the damage they caused. At the same time, the House Un-American Activities Committee (HUAC, established in 1945) was using McCarthyite tactics in its investigations of the entertainment industry.

McCarthy's misguided zeal became his own undoing when he turned his allegations and bullying tactics on the U.S. Army, earning censure from President Eisenhower, turning public opinion against himself and, finally, losing the support of the Senate, which in December 1954 voted to condemn him for "conduct unbecoming of a senator."

Where were you when?

Everywhere teachers were being fired for their associations or ideas, real or alleged, as were scientists, diplomats, postmen, actors, directors, writers—as though the "real" America was rising up against all that was not simple to understand, all that was or seemed foreign, all that implied something less reassuring than that America stood innocent and pure in a vile and sinister world beyond the borders. And from this there was no appeal.

—Arthur Miller, U.S. playwright, in his autobiography *Timebends*

THE CRUCIBLE

The most famous, eloquent and lasting rebuttal of HUAC and McCarthyism came from U.S. playwright Arthur Miller, who was sentenced to jail for refusing to cooperate with HUAC's demands to condemn Communism and denounce his friends. His rebuttal came in the form of his greatest play, *The Crucible*, which presented the infamous 17th-century witch hunts in Salem, Massachusetts, as an implicit parallel to the McCarthy Hearings. Miller later wrote, "A living connection between myself and Salem, and Salem and Washington, was made in my mind. I saw that the hearings in Washington were profoundly and even avowedly ritualistic. After all, in almost every case the Committee knew in advance [the information] they wanted the witness to give them."

Above All lenses are trained on a jovial Joseph McCarthy during a press conference.

Opposite A McCarthy-era all-American girl demonstrates anti-Communist "Red Menace" bubble gum, as marketed by the Children's Crusade Against Communism (1951).

1950

TIMELINE

06/25/50 The Communist People's Republic of North Korea invades the Republic of South Korea.

06/26/50 U.S. president Truman dispatches U.S. forces to support South Korea.

06/27/50 The United Nations (UN) votes to support the U.S. action.

09/15/50 UN forces gain the upper hand with an amphibious assault at Inchon.

10/01/50 UN forces cross the 38th parallel into North Korea.

10/19/50 UN forces capture the North Korean capital, Pyongyang.

11/24/50 UN forces launch an offensive in the Yalu valley, provoking China to reinforce the North Koreans, who together drive UN forces southward.

01/25/51 The UN halts the Communist advance and counterattacks.

06/15/51 After repelling strong Communist offensives in April and May, the front line is stabilized just north of the 38th parallel.

07/10/51 A cease-fire is called and truce talks begin.

07/27/53 An armistice is signed, ending the Korean War.

The Korean War

When Communist North Korea invaded South Korea, the United Nations intervened and, after three years of war, restored the status quo.

The Korean War provided history with two firsts, being the first major armed conflict of the Cold War and the first war to be fought under the aegis of an international body dedicated to the collective security of its members: the United Nations. It also brought the world to the brink of a third world war, just five years after the second.

At the end of World War II, the ancient kingdom of Korea was partitioned along the 38th parallel of latitude, the Communist-controlled north later becoming the People's Republic of North Korea and the anti-Communist south the Republic of South Korea. Both republics had pledged to reunify Korea by force, and on June 25, 1950, with the consent of the USSR and China, North Korean forces invaded South Korea.

THE WAR BEGINS

The U.S. ambassador in Japan cabled the White House in the United States, "To sit back now while Korea is overrun by unprovoked armed attack would probably start a disastrous chain of events leading most probably to world war." President Harry S Truman responded quickly by making what he later called "the toughest decision I had to make as U.S. president": to commit U.S. forces to support South Korea. The next day the UN Security Council voted to support the U.S. action and recommended that all member nations should "furnish such assistance as may be necessary to South Korea to repel the armed attack."

By the time the U.S.-led 15-nation task force arrived, the South Koreans had been driven back to a beachhead around Pusan in the southeast. The North Koreans won several early engagements with UN forces before an amphibious landing at Inchon, on the northwest coast, gave the UN the initiative, enabling them to drive the North Koreans back across the 38th parallel.

The Chinese then intervened, warning that they would not accept a UN occupation of North Korea. A further UN offensive in the Yalu valley, close to the Chinese border, provoked the Chinese into supporting and reinforcing the North Koreans, and a joint counterattack pushed UN forces back 75 miles south of the border.

Where were you when?

Almost at the very moment that the news of General MacArthur's relief was coming over the radio, a terrific wind blew across the camp, leveling the tents. One soldier exclaimed, "Gee, do you suppose he really is God, after all?"

—E. J. Kahn, *The Oxford Book of Military Anecdotes*

It seems strangely difficult for some to realize that here in Asia is where the Communist conspirators have elected to make their play for global conquest. As you have pointed out, we must win. There is no substitute for victory.

—General Douglas MacArthur, in an open letter to a Republican congressman

STALEMATE

On January 25, 1951, UN forces succeeded in halting the Communist advance, and several months of attacks and counterattacks eventually resulted in the front line being stabilized just north of the 38th parallel, a military stalemate that was to persist for two years. Then a simmering power struggle between the Democratic president Truman and UN commander-in-chief General MacArthur (see below), who had growing Republican support to destroy Chinese Communism, erupted into the threat of nuclear war. When Truman expressed his intention to discuss a cease-fire, MacArthur demanded that the U.S. begin an aerial bombardment of China. Truman's response was to relieve MacArthur of his command, telling the American people, "We are trying to prevent a world war, not to start one."

Peace talks began on July 10, 1951, and continued intermittently for two more years before an armistice was signed on July 27, 1953, to take effect that day. The Korean War had ended—after three years and the reported loss of 1 million lives on each side—with the restoration of the status quo, the partition being maintained close to the 38th parallel.

Above The Korean sky is filled with parachutes, men and equipment as UN airborne forces deploy for war.

Opposite U.S. artillery in action during the Korean War (1951).

Below U.S. general Douglas MacArthur roars orders from the bridge of the flagship U.S.S. *Mount McKinley* as the U.S. 1st Marine Division makes an assault landing on the Inchon beachheads.

"There is no substitute for victory."

GENERAL MACARTHUR

Douglas MacArthur was decorated 13 times for bravery in World War I and fought a brilliant campaign as Supreme Commander of Allied forces in the Pacific during World War II. He was the natural choice as UN commander-in-chief in Korea but came into conflict with President Truman over his enthusiasm for an escalation of the war rather than achieving peace, arguing "There is no substitute for victory." Having provoked Chinese intervention against Truman's instructions, MacArthur then sought support in Congress for a war against China, leaving Truman no choice but to sack him as C-in-C. In his last speech to Congress, after a brilliant career that had ended ignominiously, MacArthur famously said, "Old soldiers never die, they just fade away."

1950

TIMELINE

01/01/50 Radio Beijing announces that Tibet will be "liberated."

10/07/50 Thirty thousand Chinese troops enter Tibet with little opposition.

10/17/50 The Chinese take Chamdo, opening the route to Central Tibet.

11/50 The Republic of El Salvador raises Tibet's case with the UN, but it is dismissed as an "internal Chinese affair."

12/50 The Dalai Lama flees Tibet for the first time. He returns the following year and serves as Tibet's nominal leader until he is forced into permanent exile.

05/23/51 China issues Tibet an ultimatum to choose between "peaceful liberation" or military annihilation. Under this duress Tibet signs the 17-Point Agreement.

09/09/51 Chinese troops occupy the Tibetan capital, Lhasa.

10/26/51 According to Chinese news agency Xinhua, on this day "the Tibetan people were liberated from imperialist aggression and returned to the great family of the People's Republic of China."

China invades Tibet

In October 1950 China invaded Tibet, but Western governments dismissed it as an internal matter and did nothing to help the Tibetans.

As early as 1931, the 13th Dalai Lama prophetically warned the people of Tibet, "We must be ready to defend ourselves. Otherwise our spiritual and cultural traditions will be completely eradicated…The birthrights and property of the people will be stolen. We will become like slaves to our conquerors." China had often claimed sovereignty over the ancient kingdom of Tibet, and the Dalai Lama could see that Tibet would not survive as an independent kingdom if it continued its policy of isolating itself from the events of the outside world. On October 1, 1949, those events included the proclamation of the People's Republic of China by Chairman Mao Tse-tung, who made no secret of the fact that he considered Tibet to be a part of China.

THE INVASION

From January 1950, Chinese radio stations broadcast messages promising to "liberate" Tibet from "foreign imperialists" (referring to trade deals with Britain), and on October 7 that year the Tibetans' worst fears were realized: 30,000 highly trained, well-equipped troops of the Chinese army invaded their country. With the Tibetan army of fewer than 4,000 trained soldiers able to offer little resistance, Tibet was soon overrun, and in May 1951 the 15-year-old 14th Dalai Lama was forced to acknowledge Chinese sovereignty.

The United Nations appeared to accept Mao's position that Tibet was an integral part of China and took no action on the basis that it was an internal matter. It was not until 1959, with the loss of thousands of lives in the Tibetan Uprising against Chinese rule, that the UN condemned China's actions, but to this day the destruction continues of a people and its culture, language, religion and sacred buildings. More than 50 years after the invasion, the 13th Dalai Lama's prediction remains true: "Everyone will be forced to live in misery, and the days and nights will pass slowly, and with great suffering and terror."

Left Tibetan Youth Congress activists during a hunger strike in Bangalore, in protest at the death sentence issued by Chinese authorities to senior Tibetan religious leader Tulku Tenzin Delek Rinpoche (November 15, 2004).

Opposite A Tibetan refugee, taking with her only what she can carry on her back, walks to freedom in India (February 24, 1951).

GENOCIDE

Western governments and media often ignore the ongoing occupation of Tibet, but journalist and author Bernard Levin made his feelings clear in a 1990 article in *The Times*, "The word 'genocide' must be used with care. Our world and our century have seen countless abominable massacres, and it is easy to slip into the use of the word to denote such atrocities. We should, however, restrict it to those crimes before high heaven which are truly designated by it." Levin then listed four genocides of the preceding 60 years, "the Jewish Holocaust, the Stalin Terror, the bloodthirst of Pol Pot and the Khmer Rouge, and what was done to the people and culture of Tibet by the mad Mao Tse-tung under the name of The Cultural Revolution."

Where were you when?

Ngabo [Ngabo Ngawang Jigme, provincial governor and later first governor of Tibet under Chinese rule] *told me not to worry, there would soon be peace, just as there always had been after China had attacked Tibetan territory. I believe Ngabo had already made up his mind to sue for peace, for even as the first reports of the Chinese invasion came in, he wrote to me again, telling me not to worry, since peace would come shortly.*

—Sonam Chophel Chada, District Officer of Chamdo, one of the first places to fall to the Chinese

"The days and nights will pass slowly, and with great suffering and terror."

1952

TIMELINE

1944 British manufacturer de Havilland begins developing what will be the world's first jet airliner.

07/27/49 The de Havilland Comet makes its maiden flight.

01/22/52 The de Havilland Comet gains the world's first certificate of airworthiness to be awarded to a jet airliner and goes into freight service later the same month.

05/02/52 The de Havilland Comet goes into service as the world's first passenger jet.

08/52 In America, Boeing begins developing what will become a rival passenger jet, the 707.

1954 The Comet is grounded after three crashes in two years.

07/15/54 The Boeing 367-80, later developed as the 707, makes its maiden flight.

1955 The Boeing 707 goes into passenger service.

10/04/58 The improved de Havilland Comet 4 inaugurates the world's first transatlantic jet passenger service.

10/26/58 The Boeing 707 goes into transatlantic service.

The first jet airliner

The world's first jet airliner was the de Havilland Comet, which heralded the arrival of a new social phenomenon—the "jet set."

During the 1950s jet air travel became the ultimate luxury for those who could afford it. Many flight times were halved compared with those made by conventional aircraft, but journeys were still slow by modern standards—in May 1952 the world's first jet passenger service, a British Overseas Airways Corporation (BOAC) flight from London to Johannesburg, made five stops on the 18½-hour journey to South Africa.

This BOAC service was launched using the aircraft with which Britain hoped to gain world leadership in passenger transport design: the de Havilland Comet. Developed since 1944 as a closely guarded industrial secret, the Comet made its maiden flight in July 1949 and went into freight service in January 1952 before taking its place as the world's first jet airliner with the flight to Johannesburg on May 2 that year.

THE FIGHT FOR SUPREMACY

The Comet may have been the first jet airliner into service, but it was not the world leader for long. Three months after de Havilland's pride and joy flew to South Africa, U.S. manufacturer Boeing began developing a military and civil transport aircraft, which in 1955 went into passenger service as the Boeing 707. Meanwhile, technical problems had led to the Comet's being grounded and redesigned, but even the much improved Comet 4 could not compete with the more technologically advanced 707, which outperformed it in range, cruising speed and passenger capacity. Furthermore, with its four engines slung in pods beneath the wings, the Boeing also stole the British dream of setting the pattern for modern passenger aircraft design. But the Comet scored one more first before finally being left behind by the 707: On October 4, 1958, it was used to inaugurate the world's first transatlantic jet passenger service, 22 days ahead of the Boeing.

Left Passengers relaxing on the sleeper seats in the new Comet 4 during a demonstration flight at Hatfield (August 28, 1958).

Opposite The de Havilland Comet taxis onto the runway at London Airport in preparation for takeoff as the world's first jet passenger service (May 2, 1952).

Opposite below An early Boeing 707 takes off on a test flight.

Where were you when?

The Comet came as a revelation. I was used to flying on big, four-engine bombers, but they were powered by propeller engines. You would slowly gather speed as you trundled down the runway, then lift off at a shallow angle and climb gently into the sky. The Comet accelerated so fast it was like somebody had punched you in the back, and then you climbed up like going up stairs. It was terrifying the first time but thrilling after that.

—Eric Jones, navigator

THE JET ENGINE

The jet engine was invented in two different countries at almost the same time. In 1929 Englishman Frank Whittle conceived the idea of using a gas turbine to power a jet engine, and in 1930 he filed a patent (granted in 1931) for his "turbojet" engine, now commonly known simply as a jet engine. Whittle demonstrated the world's first jet engine on the ground in 1937, but his was not the first to be used in the air. In 1933 in Germany, Hans von Ohain had independently invented a turbojet engine, which was tested beneath a conventional aircraft in 1938 and used to propel the world's first jet-powered aircraft in August 1939.

TELEVISION COMES OF AGE

Often dismissed as purely trivial or even detrimental to culture, television is, for better or worse, the world's most powerful, influential and immediate medium of mass communication. Television enables people across the globe to witness, as they happen, events such as the moon landing, the wedding of Charles and Diana or the attacks on the World Trade Center—a globalization of shared experience that began in 1953 with the coronation of Britain's Queen Elizabeth II which was broadcast live in Britain, France, the Netherlands, and West Germany, and later the same day in Canada and the United States.

The possibilities of television took a quantum leap in the 1950s compared with the limited service and quality that had been available before World War II. In common with many other technical and social developments, the evolution of television was interrupted by the war and pursued with renewed vigor afterward. In most countries, broadcasts were suspended for the duration—the notable exception being Germany, where broadcasts continued until the Allies destroyed the national transmitter in 1943. After the war, development was resumed in Europe and America, but the speed of progress was very different on each side of the

Atlantic, and despite the excitement over the televising of the British coronation, Europe did not catch up with America until the 1960s.

THE ARRIVAL OF COLOR

In affluent postwar America the number of television sets increased from 1 million in 1949 to 10 million just two years later, and to between 50 and 60 million by the end of the 1950s. CBS (Columbia Broadcasting System) inaugurated the world's first regular color broadcast service on June 25, 1951, with a one-off afternoon variety performance featuring Ed Sullivan, Arthur Godfrey and Faye Emerson, and the next day began broadcasting the world's first color television series, *The World Is Yours*, a nature program presented by zoologist Ivan T. Sanderson. Most Europeans had to wait another 13 years for their first regular color broadcasts, with services beginning in Britain, France and Germany in 1967: Britain's color service began on BBC2 on July 1 that year with a seven-hour broadcast of the Wimbledon tennis championships.

UNDUE INFLUENCE

Meanwhile, the power of television to shape public opinion had been established, again in America, with Richard Nixon's Checkers speech during the presidential election of 1952. Nixon (the running mate of Republican candidate Dwight David Eisenhower) appeared on national television to make an emotional refutation of charges that he had received secret campaign contributions, saying that as a poor man, he had simply accepted a dog named Checkers on behalf of his children. Public reaction was so positive that Eisenhower kept Nixon as his running mate and, ultimately, vice president. It also lulled Nixon into a false sense that he understood television—something that was disproved during the presidential election of 1960, when he lost ground to John F. Kennedy after the first-ever televised election debates,

Richard Nixon making his infamous Checkers speech on television during the controversy over election campaign funding (1952).

A cooking program aired on CBS during the first week of regular color television broadcasting (June 1951).

largely due to his appearance—those listening on the radio considered that Nixon had won the debate, but television viewers favored Kennedy.

And if the political influence of television was controversial, entertainment was no less so, as evinced by the scandal over the rigging of American game shows *Twenty-One* and *The $64,000 Question* in 1958. The rigging of these shows was even more insidious than the overt manipulation of viewers by politicians, and it was investigated by the U.S. House of Representatives in 1959—a level of seriousness explained by historian Peter Thompson's description of game-rigging as "cultural engineering by rewarding contestants from deserving cultural backgrounds and defeating or excluding contestants from [other] sectors of American society."

Half a century later the debate over the power and influence of television is just as strong as it was during the 1950s. In every country that has television, there are accusations that the entertainment is vapid and caters to the lowest common denominator, that news coverage is biased, and that the political influence of both statesmen and pressure groups is related to their televised image and the amount of airtime they can afford to buy. But it can also be a force for good, disseminating knowledge and information, and enabling people the world over to share in mankind's celebrations, triumphs and tragedies.

1953

TENZING NORGAY

At the turn of the millennium, Tenzing (or Tensing) Norgay, better known as Sherpa Tensing, was named as one of *Time* magazine's "100 Heroes of the [20th] Century." As the world's most famous mountain guide, Norgay is a prime candidate for so-called "celebrity-snatching" and has been variously claimed as Indian, Nepali and Tibetan. Whatever his origins, he was a veteran Everest climber by the time of the 1953 expedition, having been a member of the British Everest Expeditions of 1935 and 1938, and having climbed to within 1,000 ft./300 m of the summit with a Swiss expedition in 1952. He was awarded the George Cross for his part in the conquest of Everest and was subsequently appointed head of the Institute of Mountaineering and president of the Sherpa Association.

The conquest of Everest

A century after it was shown to be the earth's highest point, Everest was finally conquered, by Edmund Hillary and Tenzing Norgay.

A survey carried out in 1852 showed Mount Everest to be the highest point on the surface of the earth, and over the next 101 years expeditions from several countries tried unsuccessfully to climb this mighty peak, leading many to conclude that Everest was unconquerable.

In 1924 George Mallory and Andrew Irvine climbed above 28,000 ft/8,534 m and then disappeared, raising the possibility that they may have reached the summit and died on the descent, but still noone knew whether Everest could be climbed. Then, at 11:30 A.M. on May 29, 1953, Edmund Hillary and Tenzing Norgay conquered "the unconquerable" and became the first humans known to have stood on "the roof of the world."

ON TOP OF THE WORLD

Expedition leader colonel John Hunt had decided to launch two assaults on the summit. The first pair of climbers was driven back by lack of oxygen, and then Hillary and Norgay were given their chance of making history, carrying heavier, but longer-lasting, breathing equipment. Hours after leaving their highest camp, they reached what Hillary described as "a symmetrical, beautiful snow-cone summit," where they planted flags, Norgay buried offerings to the gods of the mountain, and Hillary left a crucifix given to him by Hunt. The news reached Britain on the eve of Queen Elizabeth II's coronation (see p. 67), and *The Evening News* reported, "Today, while millions of flags deck Britain, the loneliest Union Jack in the world flies from its highest peak."

Left A portrait of Tenzing Norgay taken soon after the conquest of Everest (1953).

Opposite Edmund Hillary and Tenzing Norgay prepare to leave South Col in order to establish Camp IX, below the South Summit, before making their final historic ascent (May 1953).

Where were you when?

I looked at Tenzing and in spite of the balaclava, goggles and oxygen mask all encrusted with long icicles that concealed his face, there was no disguising his infectious grin of pure delight as he looked all round him. We shook hands, and then Tenzing threw his arms around my shoulders and we thumped each other on the back until we were almost breathless.

—Edmund Hillary

How wonderful to think of our Edward [sic] up there. Edward is up the top.

—Mrs. P. A. Hillary, Edmund's mother, when told the news by British newspaper *The Evening News*

Naturally I am extremely proud that a New Zealand member of this team has been the first Britisher to conquer the hitherto unconquerable Everest.

—Mr. S. G. Holland, then Prime Minister of New Zealand, reacting to the news

"The loneliest Union Jack in the world flies from its highest peak."

1953

HOW THE QUEEN REMEMBERED IT

On the evening of her coronation, the new Queen made a broadcast to her people, saying, "Many thousands of you came to London from all parts of the Commonwealth and Empire to join in the ceremony, but I have been conscious, too, of the millions of others who have shared in it by means of wireless or television in their homes. ... It is hard for me to find the words in which to tell you of the strength which this knowledge has given me. ... As this day draws to its close, I know that my abiding memory of it will be not only the solemnity and beauty of the ceremony but the inspiration of your loyalty and affection. I thank you all from a full heart. God bless you all."

Where were you when?

From nine this morning to six this evening, we haven't turned off the broadcast of the coronation of Queen Elizabeth. The radio seemed to come out of the night of time. It must have been an incredible spectacle to see—but it was fabulous to hear. It was related to those great bards, those troubadours who recount and embellish. The difference, in our day and age, is that in each house, the troubadour-reporter doesn't invent and doesn't try to embellish. He observes and holds his microphone toward the music, the bells, the tides of the crowd.

—Jean Cocteau, French poet, playwright and film director, diary entry for June 2, 1953

The coronation of Elizabeth II

The coronation was watched by millions of people around the world, many of whom bought their first television for the occasion.

The coronation of Queen Elizabeth II of Great Britain and Northern Ireland on June 2, 1953, was not just the dawn of what newspapers called "the new Elizabethan age," but also the coming of age of television. One newspaper announced, "This is Television's Greatest Day. That alone would make this coronation different from all others. For the first time TV is here, part of the nation's life"—and not just the British nation's life but also that of the entire developed world. For as well as 7,500 dignitaries who watched the coronation ceremony in Westminster Abbey, and some 2 million people who lined the processional route through London, more than 125 million watched on television and some 300 million listened on the radio, adding up to a total of almost one-fifth of the world's population watching or listening to this single event.

THE NOVELTY OF TELEVISION

Television was such a new phenomenon that reporters were moved to describe the process as well as the event itself: "[television made] us feel as if we were actually within the Abbey"; "Through the magic glass of the cathode tube we saw clearly the well-known faces of [the] famous"; "All these millions from Hamburg to Hollywood will see her coach jingle through rejoicing London this very day."

Viewers in Europe were able to watch the ceremony and the celebrations live, while those in North America saw them later the same day. As reported in *News Chronicle,* marveling at the wonders of modern technology, "The vast TV audience of the U.S. and Canada will see it through the same TV eye but filmed from the screen in London and flown over the Atlantic in under eight hours by jet bombers."

Opposite A mother dressed up as a waitress serves refreshments at a post-coronation street party in the East End of London (June 13, 1953).

Left Princess Elizabeth, in the coronation coach, en route to Westminster Abbey to be crowned Queen Elizabeth II (June 2, 1953).

Below Queen Elizabeth II, wearing the Imperial State crown, returns to Buckingham Palace from Westminster Abbey, following her coronation (June 2, 1953).

"All these millions from Hamburg to Hollywood will see her coach jingle through rejoicing London *this very day.*"

1954

THE PACEMAKERS

Roger Bannister always acknowledged that like the ascent of Everest with which his feat is often compared, the first sub-four-minute mile was a team effort. Bannister's pacemakers were Chris Brasher, who later instigated the first London Marathon, and Chris Chataway. Brasher set the pace for the first two laps of the four-lap race, at 57.7 seconds and 60.6 seconds—on target for the record but slowing. A tactical error meant that Chataway now had to run past Bannister to take the lead (Bannister should have run in third place), and the next lap took 62.4 seconds. They were now 0.7 seconds too slow, but Chataway took Bannister to within 260 yds /238 m of the finish, from where Bannister's famous surge took him across the line with 0.6 seconds to spare.

Roger Bannister's four-minute mile

Running a mile in less than four minutes was once considered impossible, but in May 1954 Roger Bannister proved that it could be done.

The four-minute mile was the "Everest target" of athletics—not only was it once considered impossible, but it would bring lasting fame to whoever was the first to achieve it. During the first half of the 20th century, breaking "the four-minute barrier" became an increasingly intense obsession for middle-distance runners. During World War II, Swedish athletes broke the world mile record six times in three years, reducing the time from 4 minutes 6.4 seconds to a tantalizingly close 4 minutes 1.3 seconds, a record that would stand for nine years. Then, on May 6, 1954, at the Iffley Road Stadium in Oxford, English medical student Roger Bannister did what so many others had dreamed of doing —he broke the four-minute barrier.

BREAKING THE BARRIER

It was Bannister's second attempt at the elusive target, and he knew it might be his last. He ran the first half mile in 1 minute 58.3 seconds, which meant that the four-minute mile was still within reach. The next quarter mile took 1 minute 2.4 seconds—too slow. But on the last lap Bannister powered away from the field and broke the tape, eyes closed, in a time of 3 minutes 59.4 seconds. History had been made, and although Australian John Landy broke Bannister's world record just weeks later, no one could take away Bannister's achievement of being the first person to run a mile in less than four minutes.

Bannister always acknowledged that the first sub-four-minute mile was a team effort.

Opposite British athlete Roger Bannister shakes hands with Prime Minister Winston Churchill outside Downing Street in London as pacemakers Chris Brasher (left) and Chris Chataway look on. Churchill is to present the team with checks for the Save Our Churches campaign.

Left The moment of glory—Roger Bannister breaks the tape at the end of his historic sub-four minute mile.

Where were you when?

Now I have broken the four-minute mile it will be done again—it is like breaking the sound barrier of sport. ... This is the happiest day of my life. I never really expected to break four minutes.

—Roger Bannister, quoted in the *Daily Sketch*, May 7, 1954

I was prepared to bet my shirt Bannister would do it.

—Gunder Hägg, previous world record holder, in reply to a cable sent by the *Daily Sketch* newspaper on May 7, 1954

The atmosphere was now electric, the fans ecstatic as Bannister surged into the lead with 250 yards left. His long legs whipping the track from under him, he entered the home straight. His face was strained as he dragged every ounce of energy from his tiring body, but he never lost speed or balance before breaking the tape and collapsing into the arms of Stampfl [his coach] *and an official.*

—Terry O'Connor, sports journalist, recounting "a historic event I was privileged to witness in person"

1955

BLACKBOARD JUNGLE

Ironically, the film *Blackboard Jungle* was intended as a moralistic tale rather than a rebellious one. Based on a novel by Evan Hunter, it tells the story of a young teacher trying to cope with life at a tough New York school where his pupils beat him up and, in one scene, smash his collection of jazz records. However, most people were too busy dancing to the soundtrack to take much notice of the narrative. The film was most popular in America, where it made $1 million, but the infamous riots broke out mainly in Britain, where groups of Teddy Boys (teenage gangs whose behavior was already the subject of tabloid fascination and questions in parliament) were regularly arrested for damaging cinemas, leading to the film being banned in many towns.

Above Bill Haley and his Comets: promotional poster, with Bill Haley, and his trademark kiss curl, far right (January 1957).

Opposite German teenagers cheer on Bill Haley and the Comets at a rock 'n' roll concert in the Berlin Sportspalast.

Bill Haley rocks around the clock

Bill Haley did not invent rock 'n' roll, but he did introduce it to millions of teenagers in the film *Blackboard Jungle*.

The 1950s was the decade in which youth stopped respecting age and started questioning its values instead. It was a rebellion informed by literary antiheroes such as Holden Caulfield in J. D. Salinger's *The Catcher in the Rye* and screen rebels such as Marlon Brando and James Dean; a rebellion that found an outlet in a "new" form of music—rock 'n' roll. This "new" music emerged in the early 1950s, when white musicians began playing rhythm and blues, bringing to the mainstream an existing musical form previously disparaged as "race music." Bill Haley, often credited with inventing rock 'n' roll, was in the vanguard of this musical revolution, but he was by no means its first performer.

ROCK AROUND THE CLOCK

Despite the fact that Bill Haley and the Comets were billed as "The Nation's Rockingest Rhythm Group," their single "Rock Around the Clock" flopped when it was first released in April 1954. However, the flop was merely a false start—it went to No.1 on both sides of the Atlantic and sold more than 22 million copies after film director Richard Brooks used the song over the opening credits of his movie *Blackboard Jungle*, which created a social phenomenon on its release in 1955.

In cinemas across the globe, teenage audiences jumped out of their seats and danced in the aisles when they heard the opening song, often ripping out the seats to make space. The damage to cinemas—and the ensuing confrontations between teenagers and police—made the film notorious for rabble-rousing and gave "Rock Around the Clock" its legendary status as the song that popularized rock 'n' roll.

"One-two-three o'clock, four o'clock rock..."

Where were you when?

"One-two-three o'clock, four o'clock rock!" ... The effect of those words shouted to a deafening, pistol-cracking beat unlocked the floodgates of a generation's self-awareness. It was a crude sound. It was a young sound. And once again, it was a sound stolen by white musicians from blacks. It expressed very forcibly the contempt of teenage minds for middle-aged, middle-class, middle-of-the-road music. Above all, it vibrated with highly charged adolescent sexual energy.

—Peter Lewis, journalist and scriptwriter, in his book *The Fifties*

1955

MICKEY MOUSE

Walt Disney's most famous cartoon character, and his first big success, was Mickey Mouse, who first appeared on November 18, 1928, in the feature-length cartoon *Steamboat Willie* at the Colony Theater in New York. Although this cartoon was famous as Disney's first feature and for the first appearance of Mickey Mouse, it was not the first Mickey Mouse cartoon to be produced. *Plane Crazy* was made earlier, but since it was a silent cartoon, it was sidelined in favor of *Steamboat Willie*, which had sound. Among Disney's last words, spoken to his wife during his fatal illness, were, "Fancy being remembered around the world for the creation of a mouse!"

"I could never convince the financiers that Disneyland was feasible, because dreams offer too little collateral."

Disneyland opens

Walt Disney realized his own dreams, as well as those of millions of children, when he opened his Disneyland theme park in July 1955.

During his childhood Walt Disney's strict Presbyterian parents were continually telling him that play and leisure were a waste of time, but in adulthood he made childhood fantasy his way of life. During the 1930s, after establishing a Hollywood cartoon studio and making his break with *Steamboat Willie* (see opposite), Disney began to consider setting up an eight-acre "magical park" next to his Burbank studios for the use of his employees and their families. World War II prevented him from doing so, and by the time peace came, his plans had grown enormously. He now saw it as his life's mission to create a themed fantasyland "where the parents and the children could have fun together," although he had difficulty realizing his mission because, he said, "I could never convince the financiers that Disneyland was feasible, because dreams offer too little collateral."

THE DREAM BECOMES REALITY

Having eventually raised the necessary $17 million, Disney bought a 160-acre site in Anaheim, California, and construction began in July 1954, just a year before opening, on the five individually themed zones that would make up the Magic Kingdom of Disneyland: Main Street, U.S.A., which, Disney said, "turned back the clock to the days of grandfather's youth"; Frontierland, celebrating "the pioneering spirit of our forefathers"; Adventureland, "an exotic tropical place"; Tomorrowland, looking at "the marvels of the future"; and Fantasyland, complete with castle and fantasy village, where "classic stories of everyone's youth become realities for youngsters—of all ages—to participate in."

With the Magic Kingdom attracting more than 5 million visitors a year, Disney proved that dreams can create collateral, and while it was criticized for its sanitized view of life, Disneyland proved so successful that the Disney Corporation went on to open three more theme parks, in Florida (1971), Tokyo (1983), and Paris (1992).

Opposite Walt Disney poses in front of a backdrop that includes his most famous creation, Mickey Mouse.

Left A crowd of children rushes through the gate of Sleeping Beauty's Castle in Disneyland.

Where were you when?

Plastic crocodiles snapped. Lions roared. Tigers growled. The shore was lined with tropical flowers. Wild birds cried from the treetops. This happy world of wonders within a troubled world came to life with magic wandlike suddenness when Walt Disney stepped off the Santa Fe and Disneyland train. From there, Disney strolled to the Town Square at the head of Main Street, U.S.A. His dedication address was simple: "All who come to this happy place—welcome," he said.

—Los Angeles Times, July 18, 1955

1955

DEAN'S FILMS

James Dean's first film, *East of Eden*, was based on the John Steinbeck novel of the same name, about two teenage boys vying for the love of their father; in the film Dean played the rejected "bad" son, Cal. Next came Dean's best film, *Rebel Without a Cause*, often imitated, never bettered, in which Dean played Jim—an alienated teenager whose rebellion against his middle-class parents and the world of adult values ends in tragedy when he tries to protect his friend from being shot by the police. His third and last film, *Giant*, was released posthumously in 1956 and effectively saw him playing two roles as Jett Rink: first the downtrodden outcast and then, after Rink strikes oil, the victim "turned" millionaire.

Above The crumpled remains of "Little Bastard," the Porsche Spyder in which James Dean died, being transported on the back of a breakdown truck.

Opposite James Dean leans against his trailer on the set of his third and last film, *Giant*.

James Dean dies in car crash

James Dean made only three films before he died in 1955, but they were enough to ensure his status as a legend of the silver screen.

James Dean had a fascination with death, violence and speed. He was drawn to the stories of men who risked their lives, whether in war or in dangerous sports such as his own hobby, motor racing, and once said, "Death is the only thing left to respect. The one inevitable, undeniable truth." And it was his own untimely death, en route to a motor race, that sealed his image as a global icon of youth rebellion in the mold of his second screen role, the disillusioned teenager Jim in *Rebel Without a Cause*.

THE CRASH

On the afternoon of September 30, 1955, Dean left Los Angeles for a race meeting at Salinas Airport, California. He had originally intended to tow his Porsche 550 Spyder to the race, but at the last minute he decided to drive it there instead, taking his mechanic, Rolf Wütherich, as passenger. Just outside a hamlet named Cholame, he approached a Y junction at an estimated 85 mph and collided head-on with a Ford Tudor driven by student Donald Turnupseed, who had not seen Dean's speeding silvery-gray car in the dusk.

DEAD ON ARRIVAL

Turnupseed escaped with minor injuries, and Wütherich, who had been thrown from the Porsche, survived with several broken bones. But Dean, 24, was pronounced dead on arrival in the hospital after being trapped in the smashed Porsche, which one witness described as looking "like a crumpled pack of cigarettes."

> "Death is the only thing left to respect. The one inevitable, undeniable truth."

Where were you when?

Suddenly the phone rang and I heard George say, "No, my God, when? Are you sure?" He stopped the film and turned on the lights, stood up and said to the room, "I've just been given the news that Jimmy Dean has been killed." There was an intake of breath. No one said anything. I couldn't believe it; none of us could.

—Elizabeth Taylor, actress and co star

1955

RIOTS AT LITTLE ROCK

In May 1955, following its ruling in the 1954 case of *Brown* v. *The Board of Education* (of Topeka, Kansas), the U.S. Supreme Court ordered the desegregation of American public schools "with all deliberate speed." The consequent outrage among whites, and the equal determination of blacks to see the ruling enforced, resulted in riots at Central High School in Little Rock, Arkansas, in September 1957. Whites demonstrated against desegregation and state governor Orval Faubus deployed the state National Guard to prevent black children from entering the school; President Dwight D. Eisenhower then overruled Faubus, sending in 1,000 U.S. paratroopers to enforce the court order and keep the peace.

Another significant outcome of the boycott was the emergence of a new civil rights leader: Martin Luther King, Jr.

Rosa Parks rides in the front of the bus

The arrest of Rosa Parks for sitting in the front of a bus triggered a boycott that kick-started the modern U.S. civil rights movement.

In more enlightened times, toward the end of the 20th century, South Africa's policy of apartheid was condemned around the world, but in 1950s America a similar policy was enshrined in law under another name: segregation, a.k.a. Jim Crow. The quest for racial equality in the United States dates back to the abolition of slavery in the 19th century, but the emergence of the civil rights movement as an organized political force did not occur until the 1950s. It began with a 1954 Supreme Court ruling that racial segregation in schools was unconstitutional (see left) and gained momentum with the Montgomery Bus Boycott of 1955–56, following the arrest of black seamstress Rosa Parks for sitting at the front of a segregated bus.

THE MONTGOMERY BUS BOYCOTT

On December 1, 1955, 43-year-old Rosa Parks was arrested in Montgomery, Alabama, for refusing a bus driver's order to give up her seat to a white man and move to the back of the bus. Three days later she was fined $14 after telling the court that she had kept her seat "because my feet hurt," triggering a 381-day boycott of the Montgomery's City Lines buses by the city's black population. City Lines lost 65 percent of its revenue through the boycott and was eventually forced to integrate seating, promise courteous treatment to black passengers and begin hiring black drivers—a success that one journalist called "the birth of the Negro revolt." Another significant outcome of the boycott was the emergence of a new civil rights leader who had recently arrived in Montgomery as the new Baptist minister: Martin Luther King, Jr.

Right Federal troops escort a racist student from Little Rock Central High School, Arkansas, where white students tried to prevent the lawful entry of black students to the school (September 1957).

Where were you when?

Rosa Parks: *"Why do you push us around?"*
Officer: *"I don't know, but the law is the law and you're under arrest."*

—Rosa Parks, in her book *Quiet Strength*, with Gregory J. Reed, 1994

The advice I would give any young person is, first of all, to rid themselves of prejudice against other people and to be concerned about what they can do to help others. And of course, to get a good education and take advantage of the opportunities that they have.

—Rosa Parks

Above Having been arrested for sitting in the front of a segregated bus a year earlier, Rosa Parks legally sits in the front of a bus in Montgomery, Alabama, after the Supreme Court ruled segregation illegal (December 1956).

The fairy-tale marriage lasted for 26 years, but sadly, the prince and princess did not live happily ever after. On the night of September 13, 1982, Princess Grace suffered a stroke and lost control of her car, which veered off the road and plunged into a ravine close to where she had filmed a car chase in *To Catch a Thief* more than a quarter of a century earlier. First reports stated that Grace's passenger, her youngest daughter, Stephanie, had escaped with minor injuries and that Princess Grace was in a stable condition. Unfortunately, this was not the case: Princess Grace was in a critical condition and died the next day, while Princess Stephanie's injuries were so severe that she was unable to attend her mother's funeral.

Below Actress Grace Kelly leaving a Hollywood studio lot for the last time before her marriage.

Opposite Grace Kelly and Prince Rainier III of Monaco praying during their wedding ceremony at Monaco Cathedral (April 19, 1956).

Grace Kelly marries Prince Rainier

After a match made in Cannes came the fairy-tale wedding of Hollywood film star Grace Kelly to her handsome prince, Rainier of Monaco.

Like most fairy-tales the story of Grace Kelly and Prince Rainier involved a beautiful girl falling in love with a handsome prince who whisked her away from her everyday life to live in a royal palace. But unlike most fairy tales, the heroine's everyday life was not one of drudgery or hardship: Grace Kelly was the well-educated daughter of a self-made millionaire who had been allowed to follow her dreams by pursuing an acting career. She proved to be a phenomenal Hollywood success, and it was through Hollywood that she met her prince. Having visited Monaco in 1954 to film Alfred Hitchcock's *To Catch a Thief*, she met its ruler, Prince Rainier, the following year while promoting the film at the Cannes Film Festival.

THE WEDDING

"The prince and the showgirl" immediately fell in love with each other and married just over a year later, on April 19, 1956, in a celebration described as "one of the most lavish, most highly attended and most reported-on events of the decade." More than 1,200 guests attended the wedding, and thousands more watched on television, as America's filmocracy rubbed shoulders with dignitaries from 25 nations and the queen of Hollywood became the crown princess of Monaco, transformed in a moment from Grace Kelly into Her Serene Highness Princess Grace. And in a twist on the fairy tale, shortly after the wedding and at Rainier's insistence, Princess Grace gave up her day job with some reluctance, announcing her retirement from film.

"One of the most lavish, most highly attended and most reported-on events of the decade."

16

Where were you when?

After a courtship of less than two weeks, Rainier and Kelly announced their engagement. Before marrying, though, she had to fulfill her contract with MGM by starring in High Society. *The star and the prince were married in a three-hour public wedding at Monaco's Cathedral of St. Nicholas. The ceremony was watched by 30 million television viewers.*

—*LA Times* report

1956

ED SULLIVAN

Edward Vincent Sullivan was a newspaper reporter before becoming a celebrated broadcaster, having risen through the ranks from cub reporter for the *Port Chester Daily Item* to syndicated gossip columnist for the *New York Daily News*, a post he held from 1932 until his death in 1974. His first experience as a presenter was as a theatrical master of ceremonies, which led to his own radio show, *Ed Sullivan Entertains*, in 1942. Then came the job that was to make him an American institution, when he was made host of the television variety show *Toast of the Town*, which ran from 1948 until 1971, for most of that time under its new name, *The Ed Sullivan Show*.

Above Backstage before his second appearance on *The Ed Sullivan Show*, Elvis Presley checks his hair while Sullivan (r) talks to Presley's manager, Colonel Tom Parker (October 28, 1956).

Right Female fans gaze up adoringly as Elvis makes his first appearance on *The Ed Sullivan Show* (broadcast September 9, 1956).

Elvis on *The Ed Sullivan Show*

Elvis Presley provoked moral outrage with his TV performances, but eventually even Ed Sullivan had to bow to his popular appeal.

In January 1956 Elvis Presley's first nationally released single, "Heartbreak Hotel," went to No.1 in the American pop chart, and soon it was No.1 across the world—"the King" had arrived. Later that year, Elvis made a television appearance on the *Milton Berle Show*, confirming his nickname "Elvis the Pelvis" with a hip-gyrating performance of "Hound Dog" that was considered so outrageous in its overt sexuality that it drew more than 700,000 letters of complaint.

Top variety-show host Ed Sullivan swore that he would never have such an obscene act on his Sunday night variety show, but he changed his mind when Presley appeared on the rival *Steve Allen Show* and reduced Sullivan to 15 percent of the ratings. A three-show deal was duly struck, and on September 9, 1956, Elvis made his first appearance on *The Ed Sullivan Show*, breaking all ratings records with an audience of 50 million, or 82 percent of the American viewing public.

"SINGULARLY DISTASTEFUL"

Once again, Elvis lived up to his nickname, with a provocative, gyrating, sneering, grunting performance that electrified his teenage audience and again outraged the moral majority. One critic wrote, "He moved as if he was sneering with his legs," while *The New York Times* complained, "He injected movements of the tongue and indulged in wordless singing that was singularly distasteful."

Again the complaints poured in, and Sullivan's producers famously decided that for Presley's appearance on January 6, 1957, he would be filmed only from the waist up. At the end of that show, Sullivan calmed some of the outrage, putting his own reputation on the line by saying, "I wanted to say to Elvis Presley and the country that this is a real decent fine boy, and we've never had a pleasanter experience on our show with a big name than we've had with him. You're thoroughly all right." (*See also "The Death of Elvis," p. 168.*)

Where were you when?

I was twelve or thirteen years old and I saw Elvis on The Ed Sullivan Show *on our black-and-white 14-inch table-model TV. At the time, my father owned a store and one of the waitresses who had a license was going to the next city to see Elvis in* Love Me Tender. *She offered to take me with her, but my father was reluctant. He acquiesced, and of course I saw* Love Me Tender. *I was hooked. When I graduated from high school, as a present, my father bought me a hi-fi, which really is a record player with speakers and also the album* GI Blues. *I still have that album. It was my very first, and of course, many have been added since.*

—Priscilla LeBlanc, Ohio

1956

Opposite Two Hungarians walk past the mutilated bodies of Hungarian state secret policemen, whose corpses, strewn with unread Soviet propaganda, have been dumped in the street outside their former headquarters.

The Hungarian Uprising

When the Hungarian people rose up against Soviet oppression, the USSR sent in troops to crush the democratic process.

On October 23, 1956, Hungarian workers and students demonstrating for democratic reform and the withdrawal of Soviet troops from their country pulled down a giant statue of former Soviet leader Joseph Stalin in the center of the capital, Budapest. The following day, the demonstrations escalated into civil war as anti-Soviet protesters rallied around deposed liberal prime minister Imre Nagy (see below), and the pro-Soviet government appealed to the USSR to send more troops to crush the insurrection.

Many Hungarian soldiers ignored government instructions to support the Soviet troops and instead joined the fight on the side of the protestors. After three days of running battles in the streets, Nagy formed a new government and managed to restore calm, securing an assurance of Soviet withdrawal and promising democratic reform in Hungary.

"HELP HUNGARY"

On October 29 the Soviet tanks left Budapest, but on November 1, three days after this surprise withdrawal, Soviet reinforcements in the form of more than 75,000 troops and 2,500 tanks crossed the border into Hungary. Nagy immediately withdrew Hungary from the Warsaw Pact and, as the leader of a newly independent and neutral state, appealed to the United Nations for help. But help was slow in coming. The United Nations was debating the Suez Crisis (see p. 84), and when a resolution calling for the USSR to withdraw was eventually tabled, on November 4, the Soviet delegate simply vetoed it. At 4:00 A.M. the same day, Soviet tanks once again entered Budapest.

As the Soviet forces crushed every pocket of resistance with tanks, aircraft and artillery, the day's events were relayed to the world by radio and teleprinter. The United Nations again called on the USSR to withdraw from Hungary, but meanwhile, the teleprinter messages had grown more and more desperate, and Budapest's Freedom Radio had fallen silent after broadcasting one last message: "Help Hungary. Help. Help. Help. Hear this tortured appeal. The shadows are deepening over Hungary. Extend your brotherly hand. Save us."

IMRE NAGY

Nagy was born in Hungary but took Soviet citizenship in 1918 after being interned in Siberia during World War I, escaping during the Russian Revolution and then joining the Bolshevik forces. He returned to Hungary briefly in 1919 and then again in 1944. In 1953 he was made prime minister and introduced liberal reforms that were popular with the people, but which saw him forced from office as a "right deviationist" and then expelled from the Communist Party. Restored to power during the civil unrest of 1956, he appeared to have defeated the Soviets but was subsequently executed for his part in the Hungarian Uprising. After Hungary's declaration of independence from the USSR in 1989, Nagy was reburied in Budapest as a national hero.

Where were you when?

[I was ordered] to lead a formation of five tanks against insurgents in the Eighth and Ninth districts. Once I arrived there, it quickly became clear to me that those who were fighting for their freedom were not bandits, but loyal sons of Hungary. As a result, I informed the minister of defense that I was going over to the insurgents.

—Colonel Pal Maleter, Hungarian army

As I moved deeper into the city, every street was smashed. Hardly a stretch of tramcar rails was left intact. ... Hundreds of yards of paving stones had been torn up, the streets were littered with burned-out cars. Even before I reached the Duna Hotel, I counted the carcasses of at least 40 Soviet tanks.

At the corner of Stalin Avenue, two monster Russian T-54 tanks lumbered past, dragging bodies behind them, a warning to all Hungarians of what happened to the fighters.

—Noel Barber, correspondent for the *Daily Mail* newspaper

1956

The Suez Crisis

Egypt's seizure of the Suez Canal and Anglo–French–Israeli collusion over military intervention created political crisis in 1956.

The Suez Crisis erupted over control of the Suez Canal but was really the outer expression of far more complex world power struggles. British troops had protected the neutrality of the Anglo–French-owned canal for nearly 70 years, but in June 1956 Britain handed that responsibility over to Egypt under the terms of a treaty signed 20 months earlier. Eleven days after the handover Colonel Gamal Abd al-Nasser was elected president of Egypt, and a month after that, infuriated by the refusal of both the United States and Britain to help finance the Aswan High Dam, Nasser declared, "May you choke to death on your fury!" Two days later he seized control of the Suez Canal in direct breach of the 1954 treaty.

Britain and France favored military action to regain control of the canal, but U.S. secretary of state John Foster Dulles, hoping for a peaceful solution, suggested trying to persuade Nasser to accept the control of a 22-nation Suez Canal Users' Association. When Nasser refused, Britain and France entered secret discussions with Israel about how military intervention could be engineered without the appearance of collusion or of an Anglo–French attack on Egypt. The solution was for Israel to invade Egypt and advance toward the canal so that after issuing an ultimatum to both Israel (who had already agreed to comply) and Egypt to withdraw from the canal zone, Britain and France could take bilateral military action, ostensibly to protect the canal.

INTERNATIONAL HUMILIATION

Israel attacked on October 29, a 12-hour ultimatum was issued on October 30, and Anglo–French aerial bombardment began on October 31, all to the fury of the United States and the outrage of the British parliamentary opposition. Anglo–French ground forces then began fighting for control of the canal zone, but on November 6 the United Nations approved a U.S. proposal to demand a cease-fire and that British and French troops be replaced by a UN peacekeeping force. The outcome of the fiasco was international humiliation for Britain and France, the eventual downfall of British prime minister Anthony Eden and, according to historian Christopher Lee, the exposure of the supposed Anglo–American "special relationship" as a myth—or, at least, as a one-sided affair.

TIMELINE

11/17/1869 The Suez Canal is opened.

1875 The British government purchases 44 percent of shares in the canal.

1888 The Suez Canal Convention lays down rules governing the operation of the canal and guarantees free passage through the canal.

06/13/56 The last British troops leave the canal zone, handing control to Egypt.

07/26/56 The Egyptian government nationalizes the canal, a direct breach of a 1954 agreement.

10/29/56 Israel makes a preemptive strike in Sinai.

10/31/56 Britain and France bombard the canal zone and invade in early November.

11/56 Britain, France and Israel are forced to withdraw and let troops take over.

04/57 The canal reopens after the removal by UN forces of ships that had been sunk by the Egyptians as a blockade to canal traffic.

06/67 The canal is closed during the Arab–Israeli Six-Day War (a.k.a. June War) and does not reopen until 1975.

Where were you when?

We didn't have to do any fighting at all. As soon as the Egyptians saw us, they scarpered. We found one camp all abandoned, filled with food and clothing. We had a great time.

—David Gibbon, British soldier

This is not one of those problems which admits of debate followed by debate followed by debate. We went down and offered a most sensible, reasonable, just and generous settlement of this dispute. It was rejected.

—Robert Menzies, Australian prime minister and leader of the Five Nations Committee convened to settle the dispute, as quoted in *The Evening News*

"May you choke to death on your fury!"

Opposite Egyptian president Gamal Abdel Nasser arriving back in Cairo from Alexandria following his announcement that he had "taken over" the Suez Canal Company.

Left Aerial view of the Suez Canal, its entrance blocked by ships scuttled on Nasser's orders (November 11, 1956).

Below British prime minister Anthony Eden shows the strain during the Conservative Party conference in Llandudno, Wales. Three months later he resigned over the Suez Crisis (November 1956).

THE SUEZ CANAL

The 106-mile Suez Canal was built by a French-led international consortium and opened in 1869, linking the Mediterranean, at Port Said, to the Red Sea at Suez. Its economic importance lies in the fact that it provides the shortest sea route eastward from Europe by removing the necessity of sailing around Africa and the Cape, reducing freight and, thereby, import/export costs. At the time of the Suez Crisis, Britain owned 44 per cent of the Suez Canal Company, and some 5,000 British-owned ships, representing about 33 per cent of all traffic, passed through the canal each year.

1960-1969

1960

1912 The South African Native National Congress (later the African National Congress, or ANC) is founded to organize nonviolent resistance to white power.

1944 Nelson Mandela joins the ANC.

06/55 The Congress Alliance of some 3,000 delegates from all over South Africa adopts as its policy document the Freedom Charter, outlining plans for a nonsegregated, nonracist South Africa.

1956 The ANC adopts the Freedom Charter as its central policy document.

03/21/60 At a demonstration in Sharpeville, police open fire on unarmed protesters, killing some 70 people and wounding 180.

03/25/60 In the aftermath of the Sharpeville massacre, the South African government outlaws all non-white political organizations, including the ANC. The ANC responds by forming a military wing, Um-khonto we Sizwe (Spear of the Nation), and conducting a campaign of industrial and economic sabotage.

02/90 Black political parties are once again legalized in South Africa.

12/93 South Africa's apartheid constitution is finally dissolved (see p. 221).

05/94 The ANC wins South Africa's first multi racial election.

The Sharpeville Massacre

A demonstration in the township of Sharpeville, South Africa, turned into a massacre when police opened fire on unarmed protesters.

The Sharpeville Massacre was not only a human tragedy but also a milestone in South African history, provoking widespread international condemnation of the country's policy of apartheid, or racial segregation. Apartheid was formalized in law by the National Party, which came to power in 1948, and was reinforced over time by further legislation, including "pass laws" requiring non-whites to carry identification papers (pass books). On March 21, 1960, the recently formed Pan-Africanist Congress (PAC) called for a campaign of civil disobedience against the pass laws, asking non-whites to leave their pass books at home and surrender to the police, thus overwhelming the system and making it unworkable.

THE MASSACRE

In the township of Sharpeville, some 15,000 demonstrators gathered that day outside the police station, where they were confronted with a cordon of 75 armed police. Stones were thrown, the crowd rushed forward, and the police opened fire on the unarmed protesters, killing some 70 people (reports of the death toll vary from 56 to 69) and injuring some 180. Any question that the police were even partially justified by the threat of a large and angry crowd is totally undermined by the statement of police commander D. H. Pienaar, who said afterward, "It started when hordes of natives surrounded the police station. If they do these things, they must learn their lesson the hard way."

In the aftermath, instead of addressing the issue, South Africa's Nationalist government intensified the cause for complaint by banning all non-white political organizations. The only positive thing to come out of so many deaths was that the world had to take notice. Political decrial, trade embargoes and sports boycotts all ensued, and South Africa quit the British Commonwealth the following year after open condemnation from other members. However, although South Africa was increasingly isolated by its racist policies, apartheid was not finally eradicated until 1993 (see p. 221).

Where were you when?

People were running in all directions. Some couldn't believe that people had been shot, they thought they had heard firecrackers. Only when they saw the blood and dead people, did they see that the police meant business.

—Tom Petrus, *My Life Struggle*

It was like a world war battlefield, with bodies strewn all around.

—Unnamed South African policeman

APARTHEID

The Afrikaans word *apartheid* literally means "apart-hood" or "apartness," and was the name given to a policy of racial segregation and oppression enshrined in a number of Apartheid Laws passed by the Nationalist government from 1948 onward. White domination had been common practice in South Africa since the arrival of Dutch and British settlers in the 17th and 18th centuries, and some separatist laws were already in place. However, the Apartheid Laws turned separation into "a complete political, social and economic system" of white supremacy, with no representation for non-whites in the central parliament and complete segregation of land, housing, labor, education, transport, and public services.

Above The aftermath of the Sharpeville Massacre (March 21, 1960).

Opposite A family tends the grave of one of the many victims of the Sharpeville Massacre.

1960

LOCKHEED

Lockheed, the company that built the U-2 reconnaissance plane, has a long history of high-altitude expertise. Air pressure is much lower at high altitudes, limiting the height at which aviation pioneers could fly, and one early American pilot, Wiley Post, was instrumental in developing pressure suits for high-altitude flights in his famous Lockheed Vega, named *Winnie May*. Two years after Post's death in 1935, Lockheed perfected the first fully successful pressurized cabin, flight-tested in May 1937 in the Lockheed XC-35. Lockheed then went on to build some of the world's most famous high-altitude planes, including the world's first Stealth bomber, the SR-71 Blackbird, and the U-2, or, to give the plane its full title, the Lockheed U-2 Dragon Lady.

Below A U-2 spy plane at Edwards Air Force Base, United States.

Opposite Gary Powers in the dock during his trial at the Hall of Columns, Moscow.

Gary Powers's U-2 spy plane is shot down

In May 1960 an American spy plane was shot down over the USSR, and two years later its pilot was exchanged in a Berlin spy swap.

The cold war between the West and the Soviet bloc, which had been threatening to heat up since the end of World War II, almost came to a thermonuclear boil during the 1960s. In secret, each side was spying on the other, while in public their leaders attended summit meetings aimed at maintaining the uneasy peace. But in May 1960 the covert was made public, embarrassing U.S. president Eisenhower and leading to the collapse of a summit meeting in Paris that same month.

On May 1 a Soviet surface-to-air missile brought down an American U-2 "high-altitude reconnaissance aircraft" (spy plane) piloted by Gary Powers, which had been flying over Soviet missile sites and armaments factories at almost twice the height of a conventional airliner. The Americans denied that the plane was on a spying mission, saying, implausibly, that it must have strayed off course while carrying out weather research and that the cameras on board were for photographing clouds—a story later contradicted by an announcement that America must guard itself against attack.

SPY SWAP

During his trial Powers apologized to the Soviets and said that he was acting on the orders of the CIA. On August 19 he was convicted of espionage and sentenced to 10 years' detention—three in prison and the remainder in a labor camp—but in the end he served only 18 months of his sentence. A measure of Powers's true importance to the United States was that on February 10, 1962, after months of secret negotiations, the Americans exchanged Powers for one of the most senior Soviet agents to have been apprehended in the United States, Colonel Rudolph Abel. In a scene reminiscent of countless espionage novels and films, agents of the two superpowers swapped their spies on a bridge in Berlin.

Where were you when?

I must tell you a secret. When I made my first report, I deliberately did not say that the pilot was alive and well... and now just look how many silly things they [the Americans] have said.

—Nikita Khrushchev, Soviet leader, May 7, 1960

1960

TIMELINE

1919 Austrian scientist Ludwig Haberlandt begins researching the idea of an oral contraceptive.

1939 American scientist Russell Marker begins researching ways of extracting progesterone from plants.

10/05/51 Continuing Marker's research, Austrian-American scientist Carl Djerassi and others file the first patent (granted 1956) for a method of synthesizing progesterone.

1951 At the behest of the Planned Parenthood Movement, American endocrinologist Gregory Pincus and gynecologist John Rock begin researching a contraceptive pill.

1953 Polish-American scientist Frank Colton files patents for another method of synthesizing progesterone, also based on Marker's research.

1954 Pincus and Rock begin clinical trials of their pill, developed using Colton's method of synthesis.

1956 Pincus and Rock begin large-scale field trials of their pill, in Puerto Rico and Haiti.

10/18/60 *Enovid 10*, the first-approved contraceptive pill, goes on sale in the United States.

01/30/61 The Pill goes on sale in Britain as *Conovid*.

Above American social reformer Margaret Sanger, founder of the birth control movement (c.1915).

The Pill goes on sale

The sixties was the decade of cultural, social and sexual revolution, the last of these being made possible by the contraceptive pill.

Among other things, the Swinging Sixties were characterized by hippiedom, flower power and free love, all of which provoked outrage among the moral majority. At the start of the decade, love was made much freer than it had been previously through the introduction of the contraceptive pill, something that had been unthinkable earlier in the century, socially if not scientifically—social reformer Margaret Sanger was imprisoned in 1916 for founding America's first birth-control clinic, but just three years later Austrian scientist Ludwig Haberlandt was testing hormone-based contraceptives on rabbits and later predicted that his research would lead to an oral contraceptive pill.

THE PILL BECOMES A REALITY

Three decades after her imprisonment, Margaret Sanger was still campaigning for better birth control, encouraging scientific research into a contraceptive that would be "harmless, entirely reliable, simple, practical, universally applicable, and aesthetically satisfactory to both husband and wife." Haberlandt's ideas had initially proved impractical, largely because of the difficulty of isolating the hormone progesterone, but by the 1950s scientists had found ways of synthesizing progesterone, enabling endocrinologist Gregory Pincus and gynecologist John Rock to realize Sanger's dream by developing the first oral contraceptive.

SEX SHOULD BE DONE FOR PLEASURE

The Pill, as it almost immediately became known, was first sold commercially in 1960 in America and went on sale in Britain in January 1961. It may not have actually caused the sexual revolution of the 1960s, but it certainly arrived in the right social climate to facilitate it, and now, at last, people were able to live out the philosophy of progesterone synthesist Carl Djerassi: "Sex should be done for pleasure; reproduction for reproduction." Religious leaders and moral guardians disagreed, as noted by writer Irene Thomas: "Protestant women may take the pill. Roman Catholic women must keep taking *The Tablet* [Catholic newspaper]."

Where were you when?

When the Pill went on sale in our shop, it was after all the talk in the newspapers and lots of information from the drug companies. The way everyone was talking, you would think it would sell out in minutes. But it didn't. I had the boys coming in for their usual, of course, but no girls. I think in those early months they were too worried about what people would say, especially in a small town like ours.

—Roger Montgomery, then an assistant in a chemist shop in Gloucestershire, England

YAMS AND THE PILL

One of the obstacles to developing an oral contraceptive was the difficulty of isolating progesterone, a problem solved by research professor Russell Marker's discovery that progesterone could be synthesized from a chemical contained in a certain type of inedible Mexican yam. A further complication was that the body did not readily absorb the hormone (synthetic or natural) if taken orally, but two scientists, Carl Djerassi and Frank Colton, independently found the solution. Both used their more easily absorbed synthetic progesterone to treat menstrual problems, and it was not until Margaret Sanger encouraged Rock and Pincus to develop the Pill that anyone thought of using synthetic progesterone as a contraceptive.

Above Dr. John Rock, codeveloper of the Pill, lights his pipe and smiles—perhaps at the irony of the fact that the 17 children gathering on the porch behind him are his grandchildren.

1961

EARLIER MANNED SPACEFLIGHTS

Yuri Gagarin made the first *successful* manned spaceflight, but he was not actually the first man in space. At least four cosmonauts allegedly lost their lives in unsuccessful space shots between 1957 and 1960, some of them tracked into space by the USAF Air Research and Development Command. The first of them was Alexis Ledovski, who reached a height of 200 miles before communication was lost; it is not known whether he then cleared Earth's gravity and was lost in space, or if his craft burned up on reentry to the Earth's atmosphere. The legacy of cold war secrecy means that the fates of Ledovsky and fellow cosmonauts Serentsy Schiborin, Andrei Mitkov and Ivan Kachur have never been officially confirmed.

Below Russians gather in Moscow's Red Square to honor Yuri Gagarin's achievement.

Opposite Gagarin on the cover of *Time* magazine (April 21, 1961).

Yuri Gagarin is the first man in orbit

In April 1961 the space race began in earnest when the USSR succeeded in making the first successful manned spaceflight.

The space race was not just a race for national pride, as the race to the North and South poles or to the top of Everest had been: It was also a vitally important aspect of the Cold War, providing a measure of each side's technological advancement at a time when the stakes for world peace had never been higher. Thus the Soviet Union's achievement in making the first successful manned spaceflight was a double blow for the United States and stung U.S. president John F. Kennedy into announcing the moon race the following month (see p. 133).

THE HISTORIC FLIGHT

On the morning of April 12, 1961, Major Yuri Alexeyevitch Gagarin was driven by bus to the launchpad at Baikonur, Western Siberia, where he reputedly urinated on the right rear wheel of the bus—establishing a tradition followed by cosmonauts ever since—before climbing aboard the spacecraft *Vostok I*. At 9:07 a.m. *Vostok* was launched to a height of some 195 miles before going into orbit around the Earth at a speed of 17,500 mph. Among the first words spoken from space was Gagarin's observation: "The sky looks very, very dark and the Earth bluish." Gagarin completed one orbit before the braking rockets were fired, bringing *Vostok* back to Earth near Saratov, central USSR, after a flight of 108 minutes.

As well as proving that a human being could survive weightlessness and the G-forces associated with launch and reentry ("I feel well. I have no injuries or bruises"), the flight also made Gagarin an international superstar. He told Soviet leader Nikita Khrushchev, "I could see seas, mountains, big cities, rivers and forests," and three months later he told his story to Queen Elizabeth and Prince Philip over lunch at Buckingham Palace before being fêted by the British public in London and Manchester. In the United States, NASA chief James Webb described the flight as "a fantastic, fabulous achievement."

Where were you when?

In my orange flight suit I approached a woman and a little girl with a calf, who began to run away. I called out, "Mother, where are you running? I am not a foreigner." She asked then if I had come from space, and I replied, "As a matter of fact, I have!"

—Yuri Gagarin, speaking to the press, 1962

"The sky looks very, very dark and the Earth bluish."

TWENTY-FIVE CENTS

APRIL 21, 1961

MAN IN SPACE

TIME

THE WEEKLY NEWSMAGAZINE

RUSSIA'S
YURI GAGARIN

VOL. LXXVII NO. 17

1961

TIMELINE

07/17/45–
08/02/45 At the Potsdam Conference The victorious powers divide Germany into four zones of occupation.

05/23/49 The western sector of occupied Germany becomes the Federal Republic of Germany, and the eastern sector subsequently becomes the German Democratic Republic.

06/20/49 The United States, Britain, France, and the USSR sign a Four-Power Agreement governing the status of Berlin, which includes a clause ensuring the right to free circulation throughout the city.

08/13/61 The East German authorities use barbed wire to close the border between East and West Berlin.

08/17/61 The United States, Britain, and France demand that the USSR ends "illegal restrictions" in Berlin.

08/02/61 The East Germans replace the barbed wire with a 5 ft./1.5 m-high concrete wall. The Berlin Wall is later fortified to become twin 13 ft./4 m-high walls with a no-man's land between them.

The Berlin Wall goes up

In August 1961 the metaphorical Iron Curtain became a physical reality in the city of Berlin with the erection of the Berlin Wall.

In 1946, although he was not the first to use the phrase, former British prime minister Winston Churchill famously described the division between the Communist East and the free West of Europe by saying, "An iron curtain has descended across the Continent." Until 1961 a chink of light shone through the Iron Curtain in the divided city of Berlin, where the right of free circulation between East and West was guaranteed under the terms of an agreement signed in 1949 by the United States, Britain, France and the USSR. However, in the intervening years an increasing number of refugees (some 2.5 million in total) had fled the political, social and economic hardships of Communist East Germany via West Berlin, an exodus that was detrimental both to Communist pride and to the East German economy. The totalitarian answer was to prevent people from leaving by building a wall.

THE WALL RISES

In the early hours of August 13, 1961, East German soldiers used rolls of barbed wire to seal the border, train service between the two halves of the city was canceled, and some 50,000 East Berliners who worked in West Berlin were simply told they would not be returning to work. Building materials that had been stored close to the border were brought out of hiding, and construction of a wall began immediately to replace the barbed wire.

Protests on both sides of the wall were to no avail, as were the demands of the Western powers for the USSR to end the "illegal restrictions." The wall rose inexorably higher, and by August 20 the city was divided not by barbed wire but by a 5 ft./1.5 m-high reinforced concrete wall. The Western powers stationed tanks and troops along the wall, but the East Germans simply added tank traps and built higher, until East and West Berlin were divided by twin 13 ft./4 m-high walls with a no-man's land between them, a hated symbol and instrument of oppression that remained in place for 28 years before it was finally torn down in 1989 (see p. 216).

Where were you when?

Elements of two, possibly three, Soviet divisions stationed outside Berlin were at the outset deployed in small tank and infantry groups. These elements have been withdrawn. The East German army units are still there. The East German population, cowed by the show of Soviet and East German force, is generally taking a cautious line on developments.

—Oleg Penkovskiy, Soviet diplomat, quoted in a CIA report a week after the wall was erected

ICH BIN EIN BERLINER

On June 26, 1963, U.S. president John F. Kennedy made a morale-boosting visit to the divided city of Berlin, reassuring West Berliners that the United States would risk war if necessary to protect their freedom and telling them, "All free men, wherever they may live, are citizens of Berlin. And therefore, as a free man, I take pride in saying *Ich bin ein Berliner* [I am a Berliner]." He went on to criticize the Communist regime by announcing, "There are those who say, in Europe and elsewhere, 'We can work with the Communists.' Let them come to Berlin. And there are even a few who say that it's true that Communism is an evil system, but it permits us to make economic progress. Let them come to Berlin."

Above U.S. president Kennedy visits the Berlin Wall. Kennedy's famous phrase "*Ich bin ein Berliner*" had an unintended dual meaning: "Berliner" was the German nickname for a jam doughnut (June 1963).

Opposite For some, East–West relations continued despite the presence of the wall.

1962

MARILYN'S MARRIAGES

Marilyn Monroe married three times, twice famously and once not. Her first marriage was to merchant seaman Jimmy Dougherty in June 1942, soon after her 16th birthday—a short-lived partnership that Monroe later described as "a sort of friendship with sexual privileges." Twelve years later she married baseball legend Joe DiMaggio, but DiMaggio's jealousy and Marilyn's flirtations were not a good combination and the marriage lasted just nine months. Her third husband was one of America's leading intellectuals, playwright Arthur Miller—a pairing variously referred to by the press as "the playwright and the showgirl" (after her film *The Prince and the Showgirl*), "the owl and the pussycat," and "the hourglass and the egghead."

Opposite The price of fame: Marilyn Monroe hemmed in by press, paparazzi, police and the public.

Below Marilyn's bedroom, photographed five days after her death (August 9, 1962).

The death of Marilyn Monroe

Marilyn Monroe, described by *The Times* newspaper as "not so much a Hollywood legend as *the* Hollywood legend," died on August 5, 1962.

In July 1962 Marilyn Monroe was sacked from the set of the film *Something's Got to Give* for persistent absence. To the public she was still Hollywood's greatest star and one of the world's most desirable and highly paid women, but in private, things had fallen apart—her marriage to third husband, Arthur Miller, had ended in divorce; her latest film, *The Misfits*, had flopped at the box office (though it achieved cult status after her death); and now she had lost the opportunity to show that *The Misfits* was a temporary aberration. The trajectory that had taken Monroe from poor orphan to "the most potent star attraction in the American cinema" had passed its zenith, and the plunge back down to Earth was a rapid one.

THE OVERDOSE

At about 8:00 p.m. on August 4, Marilyn's friend Peter Lawford spoke to her on the telephone and was so worried by her tone that he asked her lawyer, Mickey Rudin, to check on her. Rudin phoned at 9:30, but Marilyn's housekeeper, Eunice Murray, told him that everything was fine; Marilyn was resting in her room. In fact, she was probably already dying.

At about 3:00 a.m. Murray woke sensing something wrong and noticed that Monroe's light was still on. The bedroom door was locked, so Murray went outside, reached through the window grille to part the curtains, and saw Marilyn lying facedown on the bed with one hand on the telephone and a near-empty bottle of sleeping pills beside her. Murray had already phoned Marilyn's psychiatrist, Ralph Greenson, who arrived at 3:40 A. M., closely followed by her doctor, Dr. Engelberg, who pronounced Monroe dead at the scene. Conspiracy theories have persisted ever since that her apparent suicide was in fact murder, with Marilyn's well-known sleeping problems providing the perfect cover for anyone intent on ending her life.

Where were you when?

Marilyn Monroe committed suicide yesterday. The usual overdose. Poor silly creature. I am convinced that what brought her to that final foolish gesture was a steady diet of intellectual pretentiousness pumped into her over the years by Arthur Miller and "The Method."

—Noël Coward, diary entry for August 6, 1963

When Marilyn died, many of the news reports mentioned that she had been found in the nude. I remember talking about it on my way to school with my friends; we were all more shocked by what she wasn't wearing than by her death, as in those days it was really quite racy to sleep with nothing on.

—Marie Clayton, London

1962

Dr. No, the first Bond movie

The world premiere of *Dr. No*, on October 5, 1962, marked the start of a celluloid phenomenon that would continue into the 21st century.

In modern movie parlance it would be called a sleeper. Few people had great expectations of *Dr. No* even as a one-off success, let alone the first of a series that would run for more than 40 years—although the producers were clearly aiming high and considered the likes of Cary Grant and Richard Burton to play the lead role of secret agent 007. In the end, they cast relative unknown Sean Connery in the role that would make him an international star, and in 1962 he became the first of several actors to utter the immortal words, "The name's Bond. James Bond."

THE BOND FRANCHISE

Dr. No established the formula for the entire series of film adaptations of Ian Fleming's Bond stories: a cocktail (shaken, not stirred) of Bond girl, Bond villain, Bond car, dinner suits, guns, and gadgets, all brought together in what one critic described as "a gleeful blend of sex, violence, and wit." This first film was made on a low budget—director Tony Richardson described co-producer Harry Saltzman as a "sublime hustler ... what we didn't know was that he hadn't a bean"—but still compares well with the later big-budget extravaganzas. One scene in particular captures the essence of Bond and provides one of cinema's most memorable moments: when Ursula Andress, as Bond girl Honey Ryder, emerges from the waves in her white bikini in a sixties homage to Botticelli's *The Birth of Venus*.

Most critics agree that the first three Bond movies, *Dr. No*, *From Russia with Love,* and *Goldfinger*, were as good as any that followed ("the later films got bigger, but not better"), but for those who don't remember the first Bond movie or even the first Bond, their personal first is often their favorite. To date, the most prolific Bonds have been Sean Connery and Roger Moore, with seven films each, the most persistent villain has been Blofeld, with three appearances, and Bond's favorite car, with three appearances, has been the Aston Martin DB7.

Where were you when?

I remember watching the first TV broadcast of this in the late 1970s. Unfortunately, for Dr. No the editors had to condense the film to fit the one-and-a-half-hour format, with the result that the introduction scene of Sean Connery at the Le Cercle club, the death of Professor Dent, and the scene where Bond crawls through Dr. No's ventilation pipes were completely deleted.

—James Berando, Washington

THE FIRST JAMES BOND FILM ADVENT

IAN FLEMING'S

Dr. No

007

IAN FLEMING

The world's most famous secret agent was created in 1953 by Ian Fleming for his first novel, *Casino Royale*. Fleming's varied education and career gave him plenty of background material—he had trained at Sandhurst military academy and studied languages at Munich and Geneva universities before working for four years in Moscow as a foreign correspondent for Reuters, for six years as a banker and stockbroker, and for the duration of World War II as a senior intelligence officer in the Royal Navy. Fleming wrote 12 novels and seven short stories featuring James Bond, the last of them being *The Man with the Golden Gun*, which was published in 1965, the year after his death.

Above Ursula Andress and Sean Connery in *Dr. No* (1962).

Opposite The first James Bond film adventure! Ian Fleming's *Dr. No* (1962).

"The name's Bond. James Bond."

1962

TIMELINE

04/17/61 1,500 Cuban exiles, armed and trained by the CIA, are landed at Cuba's Bay of Pigs.

04/20/61 The 1,200 surviving invaders surrender to Castro's forces.

10/16/62 U.S. president John F. Kennedy is given evidence that the USSR is building missile sites in Cuba.

10/22/62 Kennedy demands that the USSR dismantle the sites and announces that the United States will enforce a "quarantine zone" around Cuba, blockading the import of military hardware.

10/24/62 The U.S. quarantine goes into force at 10:00 A.M.

10/26/62 Kennedy receives a message from Soviet leader Khrushchev agreeing to withdraw if the United States guarantees not to invade Cuba.

10/27/62 Kennedy receives a message from Khrushchev agreeing to withdraw if the U.S. removes missiles from Turkey. Kennedy agrees to the first compromise and ignores the second.

10/28/62 Khrushchev signs an agreement to dismantle the bases.

11/20/62 Having verified that the bases have been dismantled, Kennedy lifts the blockade.

Above A crowd gathers in a television shop to watch President Kennedy's address on the Cuban Missile Crisis.

The Cuban Missile Crisis

When the United States discovered that the USSR was building missile sites in Cuba, the world was brought to the brink of nuclear war.

The world has probably never come closer to all-out nuclear war than it did in October 1962. The United States's ill-conceived Bay of Pigs invasion (see opposite) gave the USSR the opportunity to build missile sites in Cuba, within firing distance of the U.S. mainland. U.S. president John F. Kennedy naturally demanded that the sites be dismantled, and for a week the world held its breath as Kennedy and Soviet leader Khrushchev metaphorically stared each other out. Khrushchev blinked first, the missile sites were dismantled, and the world stepped back from the nuclear brink.

The crisis began with increased Soviet shipping to Cuba in July and August 1962, traffic that U.S. intelligence incorrectly believed was carrying defensive weaponry in fulfilment of Khrushchev's promise to lend "all possible aid" to Cuba in the wake of the Bay of Pigs invasion. It was not until October 16 that Kennedy was made aware of the true situation, when a U-2 spy plane (see p. 90) provided photographic evidence that the Soviets were building offensive missile sites on Cuba, just 90 miles from the U.S. coast.

BLOCKADE

Kennedy immediately convened a 15-man Executive Committee, which spent five days debating what to do, and on October 22 he announced to the world that the USSR had made "a deliberately provocative and unjustified change in the status quo which cannot be accepted by this country." Then Kennedy executed his political masterstroke: Instead of an air strike or ground invasion, which some advisers had wanted but which would inevitably have led to war, he announced a naval blockade of Cuba and demanded that the USSR dismantle its missile sites. The blockade was to take effect from 10:00 A.M. on October 24, at which time some 20 Soviet ships were steaming toward the area, the two closest ones escorted by a submarine. If the ships ran the blockade or the submarine torpedoed the American ships, nuclear holocaust would be only the press of a button away. But at the last minute the ships stopped dead in the water and then turned around.

Where were you when?

The Cuban Missile Crisis was a flash point of the Cold War and a dangerous time. We had to stand them down. The job of the air force was to make sure the president's threat had teeth. You can't deter with smoke and mirrors. You have to back it up with real capability.

—General Russell E. Dougherty, Pentagon Air Force Nuclear Planner

We're eyeball to eyeball, and I think the other fellow just blinked.

—Dean Rusk, U.S. Secretary of State

Kennedy had won the first hand, but the game of nuclear poker was not over. The USSR continued building the missile bases, using the equipment that had been delivered before the blockade took effect, and the Executive Committee continued to press Kennedy to destroy them with an air strike. Once again, Kennedy tried persuasion first, sensing that Khrushchev was ready to back down. On October 26 Khrushchev offered to withdraw if the U.S. agreed to lift the blockade and guaranteed not to invade Cuba, but the following day, he raised the price, saying that Kennedy must also withdraw U.S. missiles from Turkey.

In an extremely skilled piece of diplomacy, Kennedy agreed to the first compromise but ignored the second. On October 28 Khrushchev accepted Kennedy's terms, announcing that he had given "a new order to dismantle the arms which you describe as offensive, and to crate them and return them to the Soviet Union." The sites were duly dismantled, the blockade lifted, and the Cuban Missile Crisis was over.

Above Soviet freighter *Polzunov* (top of picture), loaded with nuclear missiles removed from Cuban soil, is escorted out of Cuban waters by American destroyer *Vesole*.

At the last minute the ships stopped dead in the water.

Below Cuban soldiers pose with their artillery after repelling the Bay of Pigs invasion.

THE BAY OF PIGS INVASION

Unhappy with Cuban prime minister Fidel Castro's Communist sympathies, U.S. president Eisenhower's administration planned to depose Castro by arming and training some 1,500 Cuban exiles and then delivering them to the Bay of Pigs, on Cuba's south coast, in the hopes of creating an insurrection that would topple Castro and his government. When John F. Kennedy became president in January 1961, he gave the go-ahead for the "émigré invasion," which took place that April, and had to take responsibility when it not only failed in its objective but also made Castro even more pro-Soviet, giving the USSR the opportunity to build the missile bases that led to the Cuban Missile Crisis the following year.

1963

TIMELINE

"I have a dream…"

During the March on Washington in August 1963, civil rights leader Martin Luther King, Jr made his most famous speech.

The March on Washington was one of the greatest moments of the American civil rights movement and the largest political demonstration in U.S. history to that date. More than 200,000 people, black and white, gathered in Washington, D.C., for a peaceful one-day rally at the Lincoln Memorial, where the Reverend Martin Luther King, Jr., captured the imagination of the world with a speech that resonates to this day, "I have a dream that one day this nation will rise up and live out the true meaning of its creed: 'We hold these truths to be self-evident, that all men are created equal.'" More than 40 years later King's dream of racial equality is yet to be fully realized, but August 28, 1963, stands out as a significant milestone on the road to equal rights.

THE MARCH

Demonstrators converged on Washington from all around the United States, most of them by coach, some 30,000 in 21 specially chartered trains, and an intrepid few on foot. Some walked the 230 miles from New York, and three students traveled 700 miles from Alabama by walking and hitchhiking. As they arrived, the participants gathered at the Washington Monument, where they were entertained by singers including Joan Baez, Bob Dylan and the trio Peter, Paul and Mary, who were then at No.2 in the U.S. charts with their version of Dylan's protest anthem "Blowin' in the Wind." At about midday the demonstrators began to march toward the Lincoln Memorial, where three hours of speeches were televized by America's big-three television networks and broadcast around the world via the recently launched Telstar communications satellite.

THE SPEECH

Finally, Martin Luther King, Jr., stepped up to make the closing address, an oration that would become one of the most famous speeches in history. He began by saying, "I am happy to join with you today in what will go down in history as the greatest demonstration for freedom in the history of our nation." And he ended, "When we allow freedom to ring, when we let it ring from every village and every hamlet, from every state and every city, we

Where were you when?

As the sun came up, you could see the whole freeway. All lanes completely jammed with buses. That's the moment we knew this march would be a big success.

—Bruce Hartford, student, remembers the start of his day in Washington, D.C.

It was a hot summer day and the March on Washington was being broadcast on TV. My mother told me never to forget this day. She said it was history in the making.

—Mark Preston, Oregon

will be able to speed up that day when all God's children, black men and white men, Jews and Gentiles, Protestants and Catholics, will be able to join hands and sing in the words of the old Negro spiritual: '*Free at last! Free at last! Thank God Almighty, we are free at last!*' "

Fearing violence and rioting, the authorities had canceled all police leave and placed the military on standby, but the day passed peacefully, with most of the demonstrators dispersing soon after King's address. That speech and the peaceful deportment of the demonstrators legitimized the goals of the civil rights movement in the minds of many Americans and was instrumental in the passing by Congress of the Civil Rights Act of 1964, outlawing segregation of public facilities and discrimination by employers on the grounds of race, religion, gender, or nationality of origin.

Opposite Leaders of the March on Washington: (l-r) Matthew Ahmann, Floyd McKissick, Martin Luther King, Jr., Rev. Eugene Carson Blake, and an unidentified marcher.

Below Martin Luther King, Jr., waves to supporters gathered on the Mall, Washington, D.C., during the March on Washington (August 28, 1963).

THE MARCH ORGANIZERS

The March on Washington was the brainchild of labor union leader and civil rights activist A. Philip Randolph, who in 1941 had organized an earlier march on Washington to demand equal employment opportunities and racial desegregation in the armed forces. That march achieved its goal without anyone taking to the streets, having been called off when President Franklin Roosevelt agreed to establish the Fair Employment Practices Committee. As in 1941, Randolph turned to fellow activist Rustin Bayard to help organize the 1963 march, and together they formed a coalition to make the march as effective as possible, eliciting the support of various disparate civil rights groups, including Martin Luther King, Jr.'s, Southern Christian Leadership Congress.

"We hold these truths to be self-evident, that all men are created equal."

1963

TIMELINE
(NOVEMBER 22)

11:37 John F. Kennedy and his party land in Air Force One at Love Field Airport, seven miles northwest of downtown Dallas.

12:29 JFK smiles and waves to the crowd as his open limousine turns onto Elm Street.

12:30 As the motorcade passes the Texas School Book Depository, JFK and state governor John Connally are both hit by rifle fire. The presidential limousine speeds toward Parkland Memorial Hospital.

12:32 A police patrolman races toward the room from where the shots were fired. On the way, he sees a man in the cafeteria later identified as Lee Harvey Oswald.

1:00 Kennedy is pronounced dead.

1:40 A shop manager reports that he has seen a suspicious character entering the Texas Theater.

1:50 Oswald is arrested in the Texas Theater.

Above Millions of Americans heard the news of President Kennedy's death at 1:35 P. M. from then fledgling newscaster Walter Cronkite (November 22, 1963).

Right JFK and his wife, Jackie, arrive at Love Field, Dallas, Texas, on the fatal day (November 22, 1963).

The assassination of President John F. Kennedy

Millions of people worldwide remember the shock of hearing the news, making this the archetypal "where were you when" event.

Partly because it happened live on television, partly because of the conspiracy theories that have rumbled on for more than 40 years since, and partly because it was such a devastating shock that a young, popular president and family man could be gunned down in his prime, the assassination of John F. Kennedy is burned into the consciousness of millions of people of more than one generation.

DALLAS, TEXAS

Having won a very close election against Richard Nixon in 1960, Kennedy's hopes of winning a second term in 1964 with a large enough mandate to push through major civil rights reforms were brutally ended when he was assassinated on November 22, 1963. Kennedy was sitting next to his wife, Jackie, in an open car, smiling and waving to the cheering crowds as the presidential motorcade passed through the streets of Dallas, Texas. Then shots rang out, the president slumped forward, and a secret serviceman scrambled aboard the limousine—too late to save the life of Kennedy, who, half an hour later, was pronounced dead from shots to the neck and head.

Fifty minutes after the shooting, police arrested ex–U.S. marine Lee Harvey Oswald, who had been seen fleeing the Texas School Book Depository from where the fatal shots were allegedly fired, and later charged him with the murder. But two days later, before he could be brought to trial, Oswald was himself assassinated (see sidebar, p. 108), fueling rumors that have persisted ever since that he was part of a wider conspiracy.

(continued on next page)

Where were you when?

This monstrous act has taken from us a great statesman and a valiant man.

—Sir Winston Churchill, British prime minister

I was eight years old, and my parents let my sister and I forgo school and go downtown to see the president. I can't remember exactly where we stood, but it was only four or five blocks from the "grassy knoll." Kennedy passed by, and my sister commented, "They were moving too fast." No more than 10 minutes later we were astonished to hear that Kennedy had been shot.

—John Truss, Texas

1963 (Kennedy assassination cont.)

THE ASSASSINATION OF LEE HARVEY OSWALD

Millions of Americans wanting to see the man accused of shooting Kennedy tuned in to watch live on television as Oswald was taken through the underground parking garage of Dallas police headquarters to be transferred to the county jail. Suddenly a large man stepped forward, pushed a revolver into Oswald's ribs, and fired a single, fatal shot while the escorting officers looked on in disbelief. Oswald died almost instantly, and his assassin, strip-club owner Jack Ruby, offered no resistance when arrested. Ruby may have satisfied a public desire for revenge, but he prevented the truth from being firmly established and justice from taking its course—a course that may well have ended in the same way, with the death of Oswald.

New York World-Telegram

PRESIDENT SHOT DEAD

Cut Down By Sniper In Dallas

EXTRA

Where were you when?

The minute the third shot was fired, I screamed, hoping the policeman would hear me, to ring the Texas Book Depository because it had to come from there. Being directly across the street from the building made it much more clear to those standing there than the people who were on the side of the street where the building was.

—Phil Willis, in evidence to the Warren Commission

The assassination of John F. Kennedy is burned into the consciousness of millions of people of more than one generation.

Opposite top Assassin Lee H. Oswald just before his assassination.

Above "President Shot Dead": commuters read about the assassination.

Right Members of the Kennedy family at JFK's funeral: (l–r) brother Edward; daughter, Caroline; wife, Jackie; brother, Robert; and son, John.

1963

Beatlemania

Beatlemania started with a television appearance on *Sunday Night at the London Palladium* and soon became a global phenomenon.

The Beatles already had a huge following in the clubs of Liverpool and Hamburg by the time they signed a recording contract in 1962, and within a year of releasing their first single, "Love Me Do," that club following had been turned into a national phenomenon. On October 13, 1963, after three No.1 singles, the Beatles topped the bill on the British television show *Sunday Night at the London Palladium* and drew an estimated 15 million viewers for a performance that was almost completely drowned out by screams of the live audience—a hysterical and soon typical reaction that the media named Beatlemania.

The symptoms of Beatlemania, which mainly affected teenage girls, were a tendency to block streets by gathering in large crowds near theaters, television studios, or airports; a high incidence of screaming, crying, and hysterical wailing; uncontrollable clutching of the face and hair; fainting; and occasional loss of bladder control.

BEATLEMANIA CROSSES THE ATLANTIC

If the Beatles had ever worried about "breaking" the American market, those fears were laid to rest when, with "I Want to Hold Your Hand" at No.1 on the U.S. charts, they arrived in New York on February 7, 1964, to be greeted by the now familiar sight of some 3,000 screaming, fainting girls. They made three consecutive appearances on *The Ed Sullivan Show* (see p. 81), the first of which was watched by a record 73 million people, and two months later "Can't Buy Me Love" became the first single to simultaneously top the UK and U.S. charts. Beatlemania had crossed the Atlantic, and with the phenomenon also beginning to affect Australia and Europe, it soon took over the world.

> **...a performance that was almost completely drowned out by screams of the live audience.**

THE BEATLES SPLIT

In April 1970 came the news that Beatles' fans had long dreaded—Paul McCartney made the divorce of the Fab Four official by issuing a High Court writ to dissolve "the business carried on as the Beatles and Co." The Beatles had not recorded together since their famous session on the roof of Apple Records in January 1969, but the announcement still came as a shock. Many commentators consider the split to be the result of the void left by the death of the Beatles' manager, Brian Epstein, in 1967, while others blame Lennon's relationship with Yoko Ono and McCartney's with Linda Eastman for shifting the focus of pop music's greatest songwriting partnership. Any lingering hopes of a reunion were finally dashed by the death of John Lennon in 1980 (see p. 186).

Where were you when?

When the Beatles came to Adelaide, Mum and Dad (60ish) and I rushed to Anzac Highway, along with hundreds of youthful fans, to see their motorcade pass by. My boyfriend Pete laughed and thought us slightly mad, but somehow the Beatles were different and we were swept up in the moment.

—Joan Patton, Adelaide, Australia

When Beatlemania launched itself upon the British pop music scene, I was working with Eden Kane as his tour manager. Some weeks later we were sitting in the car and a Beatles record came on the radio. Eden thought for a moment and then said, "Well, I guess that's it for us." He was so right!!

—Malcolm Cook, Norfolk, England

Above (L-R) Paul McCartney, Ringo Starr, George Harrison and John Lennon fly the flag as they board their plane at London Airport (February 8, 1964).

Opposite Beatlemania affected toddlers as well as teenagers: a four-year-old's impression of the Beatles.

1964

JUNE 12 · 1964 · 25¢

TIMELINE

1945–1954 Communist-led guerrillas known as the Viet Minh fight to free Vietnam from French colonial rule (known as the Indochina War).

05/07/54 The French are defeated at Dien Bien Phu and withdraw from Vietnam.

07/20/54 Under the terms of the Geneva Agreements, Vietnam is divided along the 17th parallel between Communist North Vietnam and U.S.-backed South Vietnam.

1955 North Vietnam and South Vietnamese Communist rebels (the Viet Cong) begin a guerrilla war to overthrow the South Vietnamese government and reunite the country.

05/11/61 U.S. president John F. Kennedy sends 400 Special Forces troops to carry out covert operations in North Vietnam, Laos and Cambodia.

08/02/64 North Vietnamese torpedo boats attack the destroyer U.S.S. *Maddox*.

08/07/64 Congress approves the Gulf of Tonkin Resolution and the United States officially enters the Vietnam War.

(For the conclusion of the war, see "The fall of Saigon," p. 156).

The United States enters the Vietnam War

Having been politically involved in Vietnam since World War II, the United States officially entered the Vietnam War in August 1964.

American involvement in Vietnam began during World War II with U.S. support for a Communist-led Vietnamese nationalist group, the Viet Minh, in its guerrilla war against a common enemy: Japan. After the war, however, when France sent troops to reestablish colonial rule in Vietnam, allegiances had shifted. America's enemy was now Communism, and the United States therefore gave financial aid to the French-backed regime in southern Vietnam rather than continuing to support the Communist Viet Minh in the north.

In May 1954 the Viet Minh succeeded in defeating the French after a siege at Dien Bien Phu, and in July the country was partitioned between Communist North Vietnam and pro-Western South Vietnam. Believing that if one state fell to Communism others would inevitably follow—creating a domino effect and the threat of worldwide Communism—the United States made a commitment to defend the "territorial integrity" of South Vietnam and duly sent military advisers to train and assist the South Vietnamese army.

Over the next decade North Vietnamese troops, together with South Vietnamese Communist rebels known as the Viet Cong, began a guerrilla war to overthrow the South Vietnamese government and reunite the country. The first U.S. casualties of that war were two military advisers killed in a battle between Viet Cong and the South Vietnamese army on July 8, 1959, at Bien Hoa. U.S. involvement increased significantly on May 11, 1961, when President John F. Kennedy dispatched Special Forces troops to conduct covert military operations in North Vietnam, Laos, and Cambodia, and then again in 1964, when his successor, President Johnson, sanctioned further covert operations.

THE TONKIN GULF RESOLUTION

Then came the event that gave Johnson, who was accused of being "soft on Communism," the opportunity to refute that accusation by entering the war officially. On August 2, 1964, three North Vietnamese torpedo boats attacked the destroyer U.S.S. *Maddox* in the Gulf of Tonkin, off the northeast coast of Vietnam. They inflicted no damage, but as a result of the

THICH QUANG DUC

In June 1963 the world watched in horror as, in Saigon, Buddhist monk Thich Quang Duc doused his body in gasoline and set fire to himself in front of U.S. television cameras in protest at the treatment of Buddhists by the U.S.-backed South Vietnamese regime. By pledging in 1954 to defend South Vietnam from Communism, the United States had also reluctantly committed itself to supporting the country's unpopular, corrupt leader Ngo Dinh Diem. Although the United States had tacitly accepted irregularities such as Diem's refusal to hold an agreed referendum on reunification, Quang Duc's self-immolation prompted them to warn Diem to mend his ways. When Diem failed to do so, the United States supported a military coup against Diem, who was replaced by Lt Gen. Nguyen Van Thieu.

attack, Congress approved the Tonkin Gulf Resolution, which historians have since described as "the functional equivalent of a declaration of war."

After the attack on U.S.S. *Maddox* and retaliatory strikes by U.S. forces, Johnson made an announcement clearly aimed at keeping China and/or the USSR out of the conflict: "To anyone who may be tempted to support or widen the present aggression, I say this: There is no threat to any peaceful power from the United States. But there can be no peace by aggression and no immunity from reply. The world must never forget that aggression unchallenged is aggression unleashed. We in the United States have not forgotten. That is why we have answered aggression with action." With these words, Johnson gave notice to the American people of a war that would last in excess of 10 years more (see p. 156) at the price of some 47,000 American lives and some 1 million Vietnamese lives.

"The world must never forget that aggression unchallenged is aggression unleashed."

Where were you when?

I was to see that sight again, but once was enough. Flames were coming from a human being; his body was slowly withering and shriveling up, his head blackening and charring. In the air was the smell of burning human flesh; human beings burn surprisingly quickly. Behind me I could hear the sobbing of the Vietnamese who were now gathering. I was too shocked to cry, too confused to take notes or ask questions, too bewildered to even think…. As he burned, he never moved a muscle, never uttered a sound, his outward composure in sharp contrast to the wailing people around him.

—David Halberstam, *New York Times* reporter

Above The coffins of soldiers killed in Vietnam arrive home in the United States (undated).

Opposite The Vietnam War features on the cover of *Life* magazine (June 12, 1964).

1965

THE NAME

Over the years, Robert Allen Zimmerman has given interviewers many different stories concerning his choice of the pseudonym Bob Dylan. In his autobiography *Chronicles: Volume One,* he explains that he was going to call himself Robert Allyn, changing the spelling of his middle name from Allen because "it looked more exotic, more inscrutable." Then he read some poems by Dylan Thomas. "Dylan and Allyn sounded similar. Robert Dylan. Robert Allyn. I couldn't decide—the letter D came on stronger. But Robert Dylan didn't look as good as Robert Allyn.... Bob Dylan looked and sounded better than Bob Allyn. The first time I was asked my name in the Twin Cities, I instinctively and automatically without thinking simply said, 'Bob Dylan.'"

Above Bob Dylan gives a press conference in London (undated).

Right Dylan, with electric guitar, onstage at the Olympia in Paris, France, during the controversial world tour of 1965–66 (1966).

Dylan goes electric

When folk musician Bob Dylan began recording and performing with an electrically amplified backing band, folk purists were outraged.

Bob Dylan never wanted to be the spokesman of a generation or the champion of folk music: "As far as I knew, I didn't belong to anybody then or now.... Being true to yourself, that was the thing." And in 1965, to the dismay of the self-appointed protectors of folk, being true to himself meant going electric. His so-called betrayal of folk music began with the crossover album *Bringing It All Back Home*, released on March 22, half of which was acoustic and half electric—a change in outlook that was confirmed and reinforced by his first all-electric album, *Highway 61 Revisited*, which was released on August 30 the same year.

FOLK ROCK

In his live performances Dylan introduced his new folk-rock sound in the same way as he had on *Bringing It All Back Home*—by dividing each concert in half. He played an acoustic solo set in the first half and then announced, "It used to be like that: now it goes like this," before launching into an energetic, passionate electric set with the Canadian rock group later known as The Band. It was live onstage that Dylan learned what his so-called fans thought of his change of direction. He was booed at the 1965 Newport Folk Festival and throughout his world tour of 1965–66, most infamously at the Trade Hall in Manchester, England, where one purist yelled "Judas" from the auditorium. (This did not occur at London's Albert Hall as popular mythology has it, although it does appear on a bootleg album somewhat inaccurately entitled *Live at the Royal Albert Hall*.) In the press Dylan responded by saying that the music was more important than the boos and that his true fans were those who understood what he was doing—and 40 years later his continuing success proves him right.

"It used to be like that: now it goes like this."

Where were you when?

We'd go back to the hotel room, listen to a tape of the show and think, "Shit, that's not so bad. Why is everybody so upset?"

—Robbie Robertson, guitarist with The Band

After three acoustic numbers following the bluegrass opener, I thought the whole evening was going to be unplugged, but then in the shadows, when the lights dimmed between songs, we could see the electric guitars being handed from the wings where they were racked like rifles at a stockade.

—Jeff Doran, Nova Scotia

1965

GREAT NORTHEAST BLACKOUT #2

Those whose only knowledge of the Great Northeast Blackout was the stories they had been told about it were able to experience something similar for themselves on August 14, 2003, when eight U.S. states and the Canadian province of Ontario lost power in an outage that affected some 50 million people. Power was lost at about 4:00 P.M. after one power station became overloaded. It then created a domino effect across the outdated grid system, blacking out the Canadian state of Ontario and the U.S. states of Connecticut, Massachusetts, Michigan, New Jersey, New York, Ohio, Pennsylvania, and Vermont.

The Great Northeast Blackout

During rush hour one November evening in 1965 the biggest power failure in U.S. history blacked out eight U.S. states and parts of Canada.

At approximately 5:15 P.M. on the evening of November 9, 1965, a 230-kilowatt transmission relay failed in the power grid supplying New York City, blacking out the city and overloading the interstate electricity grid. The lights went out in NYC, followed over the next few minutes by those in New York State, Connecticut, Massachusetts, New England, New Hampshire, Rhode Island, Vermont, parts of Pennsylvania and parts of Ontario, Canada. The blackout caused chaos, particularly in the biggest city, New York, but it also brought out an oft-hidden sense of community among city dwellers, leading the Great Northeast Blackout to become a semilegendary event.

THE CHAOS AND THE CALM

The most immediate and obvious effect of the blackout, which occurred at the height of the rush hour, was the chaos to commuters. Millions of car drivers were delayed as traffic signals failed, some 800,000 people were trapped on the New York subway, and thousands more were stranded in their office buildings or, worse, trapped in the elevators.

But for many New Yorkers who were not trapped or in a hurry, the blackout created an air of calm not often felt in the city that never sleeps. Thousands who did not usually travel on foot walked across the bridges in the dark to avoid the gridlocked traffic, while thousands more simply went to the nearest restaurant and ate by candlelight, sharing tables and conversation with strangers. There was a rare sense of shared experience as people helped each other in the dark, shared flashlights and candles and gathered on Broadway and in Times Square to marvel at the moonlit city.

Left New Yorkers sitting on 8th Avenue during the East Coast blackout (August 14, 2003, see left).

Opposite Commuters walk through New York's Grand Central Terminal, lit only by floodlights, during the Great Northeast Blackout which affected parts of Canada and the northeastern United States (November 9, 1965).

Where were you when?

In the midtown Manhattan restaurant where I was pleasantly marooned with about twenty-five others, I had drinks and a fine dinner by candlelight. A transistor radio was placed on the bar, and we alternately listened to it and then, conversationally table-hopping, talked the news over with new friends nearby. Occasionally we looked out the window at the crowds passing (the prostitutes working that street were among the first to procure flashlights), and every hour or so I went out and walked over to Broadway, then a great dark way lit only by a stream of headlights and here and there a candle flickering in a high window. Back in the restaurant, as the news announcements made it clear that getting home would be impossible, I felt cozily snowbound, a man who had to make the best of it in ridiculously easy circumstances.

—Loudon Wainwright III, singer-songwriter, in *Life* magazine

THE SWINGING SIXTIES

The 1960s are remembered as the decade of peace, love and harmony, epitomized by the Woodstock Festival that took place in upstate New York as the "Swinging Sixties" drew to a close. But to remember that alone is to remember the decade with rose-tinted hindsight. In fact, for the first half of the 1960s, most people were preoccupied by the Cold War, particularly when the Cuban Missile Crisis brought the world to the brink of nuclear war in 1962 and for the second half by the Vietnam War. As an antidote to these threats to civilization, a strong peace movement evolved during the 1960s, neatly dovetailing with the alternative youth culture that emerged in America as the baby-boom generation came of age—a combination that soon became an international phenomenon, summarized as "Flower Power" and encapsulated in the slogan "Make love not war."

SWINGING LONDON

In Britain 1961 marked the first time since 1938 that teenagers had been able to find their own way to adulthood, at their own pace, without conscription for National Service providing the standard rite of passage—something that sparked off a youth revolution to match the American "youthquake" of the late 1950s. By the mid-1960s the established American youth culture was cross-fertilizing with the emerging British one in the form of the "British invasion" of the United States led by the Beatles. Appropriately, then, the arrival of the "swinging" aspect of the sixties was announced by an American journalist writing in and about Britain. In spring 1966 *Time* magazine ran a front-page headline that read, "London. The Swinging City"—an epithet that would later be applied to the entire decade. In his article, *Time*'s London correspondent, who had seemingly been indulging in some alternative substances himself, wrote, "In this century every decade has its city.... Today it is London, a city steeped in tradition, seized by change, liberated by affluence, graced by daffodils and anemones, so green with parks and squares that, as the saying goes, you can walk across it on the grass. In a decade dominated by youth, London has burst into bloom. It swings, it is the scene."

London, of course, had benefited hugely from a pop culture whose spiritual home was Liverpool (home of the Beatles *et al.*), but the epitome of swinging Britain was genuinely London's: Carnaby Street, whose street sign became the capital's most popular postcard and which earned itself a place in the *Oxford English Dictionary* as a noun meaning "fashionable clothing for young people." And while London was swinging, San Francisco was turning on, tuning in and dropping out—far from the boutiques of Carnaby Street, the Haight-Ashbury district of San Francisco was nurturing the hippie subculture characterized by peace, free love, self-expression and a belief in Eastern wisdom.

THE SUMMER OF LOVE

In 1967, the year after *Time*'s "swinging" coinage, popular youth culture became steeped in the Haight-Ashbury hippie outlook during what was dubbed "The Summer of Love." The year began with a "Be-In" in Golden Gate Park, San Francisco, in January, billed as the "Gathering of the Tribes," and continued in June with the first major open-air pop festival, at Monterey, California. Some observers described the gatherings as a diluted, commercialized form of hippiedom for America's middle classes, but they set the tone for the Summer of Love, and in August were copied in Britain, with a "Love-In" in Hyde Park, London, and the three-day "Festival of the Flower Children" on Lord Bedford's estate at Woburn Abbey, Bedfordshire.

The summer's anthems were provided by Scott McKenzie, with "If You're Going to San Francisco (Wear Some Flowers in Your Hair)"; Procol Harum, with "Whiter Shade of Pale"; and, of course, the Beatles, with the album *Sgt. Pepper's Lonely Hearts Club Band* and the singles "All You Need Is Love" and "Strawberry Fields"—and the hippie theme was then continued into the autumn with the premier in October of the musical *Hair* off Broadway.

October also saw the year's largest antiwar demonstration: a march on the Pentagon at which organizers and political activists Jerry Rubin and Abbie Hoffman had promised they would levitate the Pentagon building 300 ft./90 m into the air. The march provided some of the 1960s' most iconic images—of young girls placing flowers in the barrels of soldiers' guns—but did not succeed in lifting the Pentagon or in stopping the war in Vietnam. Flower power, it seemed, had its limits.

Opposite "London: The Swinging City": the cover of *Time* magazine (April 1966).

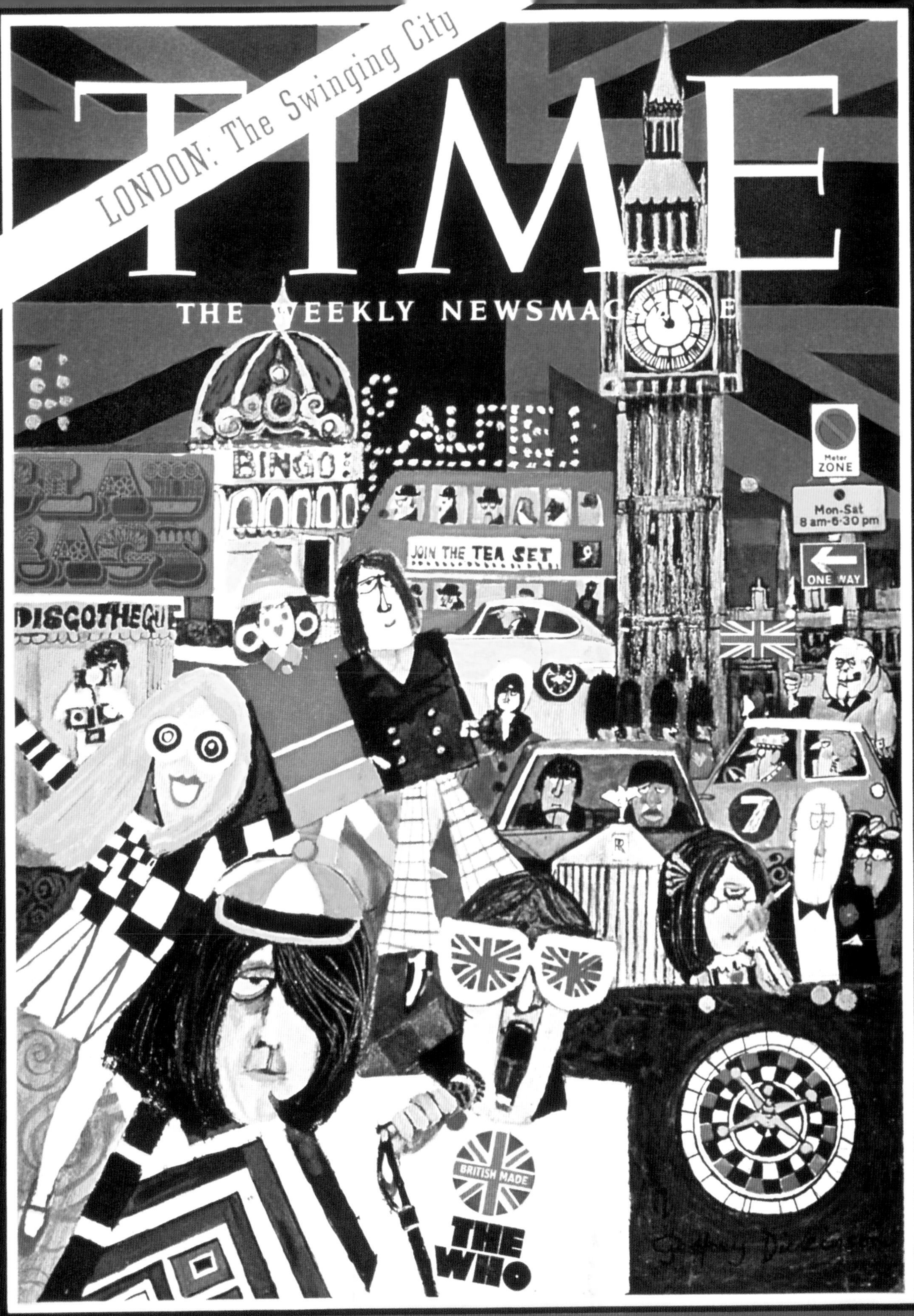
LONDON: The Swinging City
TIME
THE WEEKLY NEWSMAG
BINGO
ALFIE
Meter
ZONE
Mon-Sat
8 am-6.30 pm
ONE WAY
JOIN THE TEA SET
DISCOTHEQUE
7
BRITISH MADE
THE WHO

VOL. 87 NO. 15

1967

The 1967 World's Fair was originally scheduled to take place in the USSR to celebrate the 50th anniversary of the Russian revolution, but when the Soviets dropped out, Canada took over in such style that Montreal's Expo '67 is remembered as one of the most successful ever World's Fairs. Themed as "Man and His World," the exposition was presented in five main sections—Man the Creator, Man the Explorer, Man the Producer, Man the Provider, and Man & the Community—and featured 90 national and corporate pavilions. Montreal hosted 50,306,648 visitors, including Queen Elizabeth II, U.S. president Lyndon B. Johnson, Princess Grace of Monaco, Jacqueline Kennedy, and Charles de Gaulle.

Canadian centennial

The 100th anniversary of Canadian Confederation fell on Dominion Day, July 1, 1967, but the centennial party lasted all year.

On July 1, 1867, the British North American colonies of New Brunswick, Nova Scotia, and the Province of Canada (comprising present-day Ontario and Quebec) were unified as the Dominion of Canada. A century later a much larger confederation celebrated the birth of its national identity in such style that some historians feel Canada never again reached such heights of optimism and self-confidence, while others remember 1967 as the year that provided the impetus for full constitutional independence in 1982 (see p. 232).

The celebrations, organized by a Centennial Commission led by John Fisher, aka Mr. Canada, fell into two main categories: "monumental" and "active." The former ensured a legacy of lasting memorials in the form of public buildings, the greatest of which was the National Arts Centre in Ottawa, while the "active" celebrations ranged from the educational to the bizarre.

CENTENNIAL TRAIN

Active celebrations included a group of touring museums known as the Centennial Train and Caravans, which attracted 10 million visitors to learn about Canadian history and culture; nationwide performance arts events commissioned and organized by umbrella organization Festival Canada; the Centennial Tattoo, a military extravaganza that toured Canada's major cities; and Toronto's Caribana festival, which is now an annual event. For all this, though, the undisputed jewel in the crown was the enormously successful Expo '67 in Montreal (see sidebar).

To the good-natured delight of spectators watching a children's display outside the Canadian pavilion, blustery weather causes a mix-up in the spelling of "Canada" (1967).

The monorail exits Buckminster Fuller's famous geodesic dome (the U.S. pavilion) at Expo '67.

All children born in 1967 were dubbed Centennial babies, with the first baby to be born on Dominion Day designated the National Centennial Baby—she was none other than Pamela Anderson, who later went on to achieve fame as a model and actress. But perhaps the most poignant symbol of the lasting pride instilled by the Centennial celebrations was the simplest: The Centennial Flame, which was lit at midnight on December 31, 1966, and initially intended to be kept alight for exactly 12 months, still burns to this day.

Where were you when?

As we enter our centennial year we are still a young nation, very much in the formative stages. Our national condition is still flexible enough that we can make almost anything we wish of our nation. No other country is in a better position than Canada to go ahead with the evolution of a national purpose devoted to all that is good and noble and excellent in the human spirit.

—Prime Minister Lester B. Pearson, 1967

1967

THE FIRST KIDNEY TRANSPLANT

The kidney was the first of the vital organs to be successfully transplanted. On June 17, 1950, U.S. surgeon Richard Lawler transplanted a kidney from a patient who had died of liver disease into the body of 44-year-old Ruth Tucker, who was suffering from a kidney disorder that had already killed her mother, sister and uncle. Tucker's kidney was removed, and when her blood vessels and ducts were connected to those of the donor kidney, the new organ changed color from a moribund bluish brown to a healthy reddish brown, indicating a successful transplantation. Tucker survived for five years, but eventually complications set in and she died when the transplanted kidney failed.

The first human heart transplant

On December 3, 1967, South African heart surgeon Dr. Christiaan Barnard performed the first successful human heart transplant.

In all walks of life, once a goal becomes physically or technically achievable, a race develops among those eminent in that field to be the first to achieve it. After pioneering work by U.S. cardiac surgeon Dr. Norman Shumway, who carried out the first heart transplant (in a dog) in 1958, the race was on among cardiac experts to transplant a human heart. The next landmark was also achieved in the United States, where, in January 1964, Dr. James D. Hardy became the first surgeon to implant a heart in a human: 58-year-old Boyd Rush. The intended donor, dying of brain damage, was still alive when Rush's heart failed, so instead Rush was given the heart of a chimpanzee. He survived for just three hours.

SIX-HOUR OPERATION

Three years later the honors went to South Africa, where a team of 30 doctors and nurses, led by Dr. Christiaan Barnard, carried out what is usually cited as the first successful human heart transplant. The donor was 25-year-old traffic victim Denise Ann Darvall, and the recipient was 55-year-old wholesale grocer Louis Washkansky. The five-hour operation, carried out at the Groote Schuur Hospital in Cape Town, was deemed a success because the implanted heart functioned fully, but unfortunately, Washkansky died just 18 days

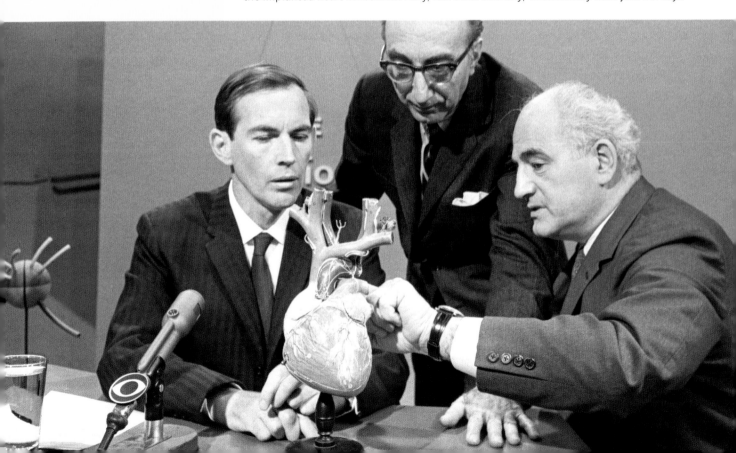

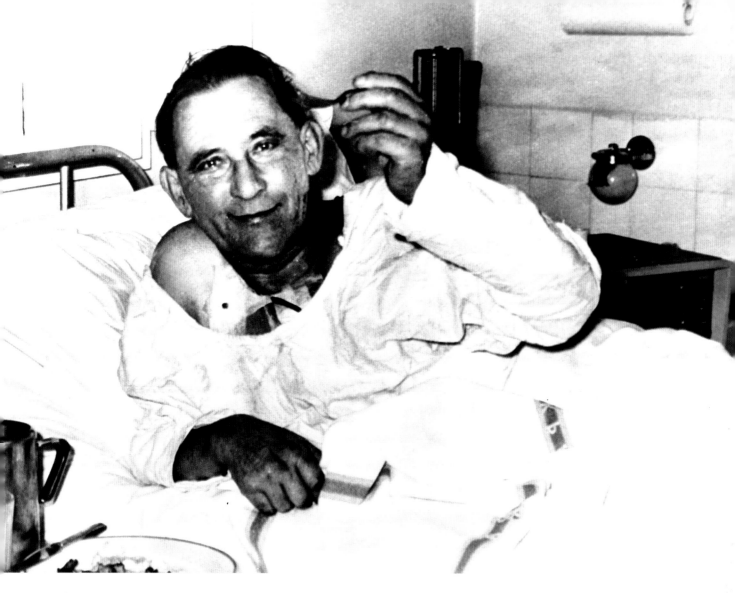

later of pneumonia, seemingly because the drugs he was taking to prevent his immune system rejecting the donor heart left him susceptible to infection.

But if there was any doubt that credit should go to Barnard, he removed that doubt by performing a second human heart transplant on January 2, 1968—this time the recipient, Philip Blaiberg, survived for 594 days (approximately a year and a half). Barnard went on to improve treatment and techniques to the point where more than half his patients survived for more than five years after surgery.

Above Louis Washkansky recovers in Groote Schuur Hospital after undergoing the world's first successful heart transplant, performed by Dr. Christiaan Barnard (December 1967).

Opposite Dr. Christiaan Barnard (l) talks to U.S. heart surgeons Dr. Michael DeBakey and Dr. Adrian Kantrowitz on the set of the television program *Face the Nation*, where the three discussed their achievements in pioneering heart surgery (December 24, 1967).

Where were you when?

The heart transplant wasn't such a big thing surgically. The technique was a basic one.

—Dr. Christiaan Barnard, *Time* magazine, September 3, 2001

My uncle had just had a heart attack, and I remember my mum crying all the time. When I heard of the transplant, I was thinking how wonderful it would be if Dr. Barnard could operate on Uncle Dennis.

—Sally Green, Norwich, Norfolk

1968

RIOTS

Martin Luther King, Jr., would not have wanted to be associated with the five days of rioting that followed his death. Some 2,000 homes and shops were ransacked and more than 5,000 fires started, some of them within 300 yds/275 m of the White House. More than 70,000 troops and National Guardsmen were called out to quell the rioters, some 24,000 people were arrested, and 40 were killed. Historians have since pointed out that just as a great statesman cannot achieve world peace, but one zealot can start a war, so Martin Luther King, Jr., "could not eliminate racial prejudice, but a sordid drifter, shooting King down from ambush, could cause a dozen cities to burn."

The assassination of Martin Luther King Jr.

The murder of civil rights leader Martin Luther King, Jr., by a white assassin on April 4, 1968, triggered race riots across the United States.

After the March on Washington (see p. 104), Martin Luther King, Jr., began to widen the scope of his campaigns from racial equality to the fight against poverty in general, whether black or white. In April 1968 he traveled to Memphis, Tennessee, to support a dustmen's strike, and it was there, at the Lorraine Motel, that he was shot dead as he leaned over a balcony and spoke what were to be his last words to his friend Jesse Jackson: "Be sure to sing 'Precious Lord' tonight, and sing it well."

The assassin escaped in a white Ford Mustang, and just over two weeks later the FBI announced that its prime suspect was James Earl Ray, alias Eric Galt. Two months after that, on June 7, Ray was arrested at Heathrow Airport in London, using the alias Ramon George Sneyd, and extradited to the United States. He pleaded guilty and was sentenced to 99 years' imprisonment but died in 1998 shortly after telling a television interviewer, "I was not the trigger man. I didn't know anything about the killing."

THE FUNERAL

When news of the assassination was broadcast, riots broke out in more than 100 American cities and on U.S. Army bases in Vietnam (see left), but at King's funeral in Atlanta, Georgia, on April 9 the emphasis was not on violence but on remembering a man of peace. More than 150,000 people, including Jacqueline Kennedy and U.S. vice president Hubert

Humphrey, followed King's coffin through the streets as it was drawn to his burial place on a wooden farm cart pulled by two mules. The humility reflected in the choice of a plain cart and mules was consistent with U.S. radical journalist I. F. Stone's assessment of King's place in history: "He stood in the line of saints which goes back from Gandhi to Jesus; his violent end, like theirs, reflects the hostility of mankind to those who annoy it by trying hard to pull it one more painful step up the ladder from the age to the angel."

Below Martin Luther King Jr.'s widow and daughter, Coretta and Yolanda, en route to King's funeral, with other mourners reflected in the car window (April 9, 1968).

Where were you when?

Four cars of policemen passed me—flying. And then somebody hollered across the street, "King has been shot." ... I got right behind the police cars and I went...and the blood and everything was still there.

—Jerry Fanion, Shelby County human relations director

There were only a few whites living in the block; but I felt little tension or hostility. I mainly noted the black smoke drifting down from H Street, four blocks away. Kathy was out back working in our foot-wide strip of garden, listening to reports of looting and arson on a portable radio as a black fog settled in.

—Sam Smith, from *Multitudes: An Unauthorized Memoir*

Opposite A federal trooper patrols the streets of Washington, D.C., during the riots that broke out after Martin Luther King, Jr.'s, assassination (April 6, 1968).

Opposite King lies mortally wounded on the balcony of the Lorraine Motel, while his companions point to the source of the gunshots (April 4, 1968).

1968

TIMELINE

Student protests in Paris

Student protests in Paris during May 1968 escalated into a general strike that threatened to bring down the French government.

Charles de Gaulle's right-wing presidency of France, which began in 1958–59, has been described as "haughty and autocratic in style, more concerned with gloire and grandeur than the everyday problems of ordinary lives." This did not sit well with the post war baby-boom generation who was then reaching university age, or with an increasingly discontented workforce, and de Gaulle was narrowly reelected in 1965 only after a second vote. Despite this indication of his decline in popularity, the sudden explosion of discontent into violence in May 1968 took both sides by surprise.

The protests began peacefully enough in March with a sit-in at the University of Nanterre. The sit-in was triggered by the arrest of six students at an anti-Vietnam demonstration (see p. 112), but it was really a protest directed at the outdated, authoritarian nature of the education system. Sit-ins were also staged at other campuses and lasted until the first week of May, when the students were forcibly evicted by the police, whose heavy-handedness led to the worst street violence in France since World War II.

THE MAY RIOTS

Students barricaded the streets with cars and threw bricks, paving stones and Molotov cocktails (gasoline bombs) at riot police, who, rather than calming the situation, inflamed it further with their indiscriminate and ferocious violence. French workers then called a one-day general strike in support of the students, and this was followed by a number of snap strikes that eventually saw up to 10 million workers, including professionals, taking industrial action in protest at their own grievances, which included low state salaries,

The Communist Party pledged to "eliminate the government."

Where were you when?

We were driving home at the end of our honeymoon and arrived in Paris to spend a romantic night before crossing the Channel, to find ourselves in the midst of the student riots in Paris. We had never seen such large numbers of police dressed in full riot gear—helmets, padded jackets, riot shields, and, of course, clubs—phalanxes of them looking very menacing and barring the way to huge numbers of people, not all students, shouting and throwing anything to hand. Many of the streets were blocked off, and all the bridges seemed to be closed. We didn't really know what was going on until we arrived back in England.

—Andrew and Hannah Alers-Hankey, London

discrimination in employment, outdated organization of the medical profession and censorship in journalism.

De Gaulle was forced to take drastic action, particularly when the Communist Party pledged to "eliminate the government." After confirming that he had the support of the French military, he announced that he would not resign, dissolved the National Assembly, and called a general election. Over the next month he managed to persuade the so-far silent majority that he was the only barrier to a left-wing dictatorship, and on June 30 he won the election with a landslide victory. Seemingly more secure than before the riots, he resigned the following year after his proposals for a Senate were rejected in a referendum.

Above French students hurl cobblestones at riot police in the rue St. Jacques, Paris, while police reply with tear gas (May 1968).

Below French president General Charles de Gaulle (r) in a determined mood during a television interview conducted by French journalist Michel Droit in the immediate aftermath of the riots (June 7, 1968).

CHARLES DE GAULLE

Like all strong, expressive leaders, Charles de Gaulle provoked extreme reactions both among his supporters and his detractors. After taking an active part in both World Wars, he became a popular post war leader as prime minister and later president, ensuring France's international importance but upsetting many of his international counterparts in the process (not least by blocking Britain's entry into the European Community and publicly rebuking the United States for its involvement in Vietnam). However, as times changed, his lack of popularity with many at home was demonstrated by the May riots of 1968 and by the reaction of left-wing leader François Mitterand, who said of de Gaulle's refusal to resign after the riots, "The voice we have just heard is that of dictatorship."

1968

01/05/68 Alexander Dubcek is elected as the leader of the Czech Communist Party.

03/23/68 Dubcek is summoned to an emergency Warsaw Pact meeting to try to bring him into line.

05/68 The USSR begins moving troops up to the Czech border.

07/29/68– 08/01/68 Dubcek meets with Soviet leader Leonid Brezhnev and other Communist bloc leaders at the village of Cierna nad Tisou. The USSR agrees to allow Czechoslovakia its own "road to Socialism," and the Czechs give assurances of "Socialist solidarity."

08/02/68– 08/21/68 Tanks from the USSR and the Warsaw Pact countries of East Germany, Poland, Hungary and Bulgaria cross the Czech border.

08/21/68 Dubcek and other Czech leaders are arrested and taken to Moscow.

08/27/68 Dubcek is returned to Czechoslovakia, having been forced to capitulate to Soviet demands. Senior Soviet politicians, backed by the presence of Soviet troops, oversee the "normalization" of Czechoslovakia.

10/16/68 The Czech government is forced to sign a treaty accepting that Warsaw Pact troops will remain in Czechoslovakia, beginning a period of occupation and repression that will last until 1989 (see p. 216).

Soviet invasion of Czechoslovakia

In August 1968 seven months of liberal reform in Czechoslovakia gave way to 20 years of Soviet occupation and repression.

The year 1968 began well for Czechoslovakia. On January 5, after 20 years of hard-line Communist rule as part of the Soviet bloc, its liberal Communist leader, Alexander Dubcek, was elected as the first Slovak to lead the Czech Communist Party. In a series of reforms that became known as the Prague Spring, he immediately began relaxing the most oppressive aspects of Communist rule by freeing political prisoners, lifting press censorship and allowing greater freedom of speech on television and radio. Dubcek called it "Socialism with a human face," but the Soviet leadership in Moscow was not impressed.

INVASION

On August 1, 1968, the USSR promised to allow Czechoslovakia its own "road to Socialism" (see Cierna nad Tisou *below*), but with tanks and troops massed on the border, it was a transparently false promise. Just three weeks later, on the night of August 20–21, Dubcek's worst fears were realized: Tanks from the USSR and four Warsaw Pact countries rolled across the Czech border, airborne troops were flown into Czech air bases, and by August 22 more than half a million Warsaw Pact troops had overrun the country. Czechs blockaded the streets, stood in front of the tanks and fought pitched battles, attacking the tanks with improvised weapons and their bare hands, but it was a war that could not be won. The Prague spring had given way to a harsh Soviet winter that was to last for more than 20 years.

Rather than replacing Dubcek, the Soviets simply made him the puppet leader of a now occupied country. Soviet ministers were sent to oversee the "normalization" of Czechoslovakia, censorship was reimposed, opposition parties abolished and oppression reestablished. Meanwhile, the Soviet press reported that the Czech leadership had asked the USSR "to render the fraternal Czechoslovak people urgent assistance" and that the Czech people were grateful for "the timely arrival of Soviet troops."

CIERNA NAD TISOU

On July 29, 1968, the Soviets summoned the Czech leadership to a meeting in the border village of Cierna nad Tisou in an attempt to bring Dubcek and his colleagues into line. But the Czech leaders lived up to the trust of the people, tens of thousands of whom had signed a petition, saying, "You are writing a fateful page in the history of Czechoslovakia. Write with deliberation, but, above all, courage. We trust you." On August 1 Dubcek won an assurance that Czechoslovakia would be allowed to pursue its own "internal reforms," a diplomatic victory that the official Soviet newspaper *Pravda* called "a crushing blow" for the Czechs. Having lost the diplomatic battle, the USSR delivered its crushing blow in the form of an invasion three weeks later.

Where were you when?

*I got a phone call from my aunt in Prague, which was odd, as she was not due to call for some time.
She said that the local radio was reporting the Russians were invading. She asked if I, living in Britain,
knew anything about what was going on. I tuned my radio to the BBC news, but then the line went dead.
I heard later the Russians had cut all the telephone wires.*

—Jan Macik, Surrey, England

Above Prague residents stand atop an overturned van with their national flag while others surround Soviet tanks during the invasion that crushed the Prague Spring (August 21, 1968).

Opposite Alexander Dubcek (2nd from left) and Soviet leader Leonid Brezhnev (3rd from left) arrive in Cierna nad Tisou for a meeting to discuss the Czechoslovakian situation (August 1968).

1968

THE FOSBURY FLOP

Along with Beamon's long jump, the Mexico City Olympics was also famous for Dick Fosbury's high jump. Until the 1968 Games, all high jumpers dived forward over the bar, but Fosbury, who had failed to gain the requisite height with the conventional technique, invented a revolutionary and controversial new style: He dived backward over the bar, flipping his legs up at the last moment. Fosbury won gold, but his coach warned: "Kids imitate champions, but if they imitate Fosbury, he will wipe out an entire generation of high jumpers because they will all have broken necks." Despite this, the Fosbury Flop, as it was known, soon became the standard technique for the high jump.

Above Multiple exposure of Dick Fosbury employing the revolutionary Fosbury Flop at the Mexico City Olympics (1968).

Opposite As he leaps into history, Bob Beamon looks shocked by his sudden ability to fly (October 18, 1968).

Bob Beamon's long jump

At the 1968 Mexico City Olympics, Bob Beamon managed a feat often described as one of the greatest sporting achievements of all time.

Most of the headlines were variations on the same theme: "Beamon leaps into history." And it truly was a historic leap. Having fouled two jumps in the qualifying round, U.S. athlete Bob Beamon defied all expectations, and seemingly gravity itself, with his first jump of the final. A gasp went around the stadium as he leaped almost clear out of the pit, but there was a delay before the actual distance was announced because, as Beamon remembers, "The electronic measuring device could only measure up to twenty-eight feet. They had to go find a manual tape to measure this distance."

Twenty minutes later the result was finally displayed on the scoreboard: 8.90 meters. Beamon only understood imperial measurements and asked his team mate, bronze medallist Ralph Boston, "What does it mean?" When Boston told him it meant 29 feet 2½ inches, Beamon collapsed.

THE JUMP IN CONTEXT

One historic May afternoon in 1935, Jesse Owens smashed the world long-jump record with a distance of 26½ feet (8.13 m). In the 33 years since, the world record had been improved by just 9 inches (23 cm), but on October 18, 1968 Bob Beamon advanced it by an additional 20 inches (53 cm) in a single jump. Detractors claim that his feat was assisted by the altitude of Mexico City, but this objection is irrelevant in the light of the fact that the silver and bronze medal distances were either side of 26¾ feet (8.17 m), both outside the previous world record, and fully 2 feet 3 inches (71 cm) behind Beamon.

The joint holder of the previous world record, Igor Ter-Ovanesyan, said, "Compared to this jump, we are as children" and he was right. It would be another 23 years before Beamon's remarkable record was broken.

Where were you when?

I felt very peaceful and calm. My body was never more relaxed. There was no sound. I felt alone. I could not feel my legs under me; I was floating. I shook my arms and hands to loosen up. I took the first step on the runway. After that, it was all automatic; instinct took over and lifted me from the white board. All I heard was the pumping of my heart. I landed with such impact that I continued to jump like a kangaroo hopping out of the sandpit.

—Bob Beamon, as quoted in *The British Sunday Times Great Sporting Moments*

1969

TIMELINE

10/04/57 The USSR launches *Sputnik I* as the first man-made satellite.

11/03/57 Laika becomes the first dog in space, in *Sputnik II* (see p. 134).

07/29/58 America's National Aeronautics and Space Administration (NASA) is founded.

09/14/59 The Soviet probe *Luna II* is the first spacecraft to impact the moon.

04/12/61 Soviet cosmonaut Yuri Gagarin makes the first successful manned spaceflight (see p. 94).

05/25/61 U.S. president Kennedy announces the *Apollo* space program.

06/02/66 The American probe *Surveyor 1* is the first spacecraft to make a controlled landing on the moon.

12/21/68– The United States's *Apollo 8*
12/27/68 achieves the first manned flight around the moon.

07/16/69 The United States's *Apollo 11* leaves Earth.

07/20/69 U.S. astronauts Armstrong and Aldrin walk on the moon at 10:45 P.M. EDT (July 21 GMT).

07/24/69 *The Apollo 11* mission is completed with a successful splashdown after 8 days 3 hours and 19 minutes.

Above (l-r) Neil Armstrong, Michael Collins and Edwin "Buzz" Aldrin two months before their historic flight to the moon (May 1, 1969).

Right *Apollo 11* lifts off from Pad 39A, Cape Kennedy (Kennedy Space Center) at 09:32 A.M. (July 16, 1969).

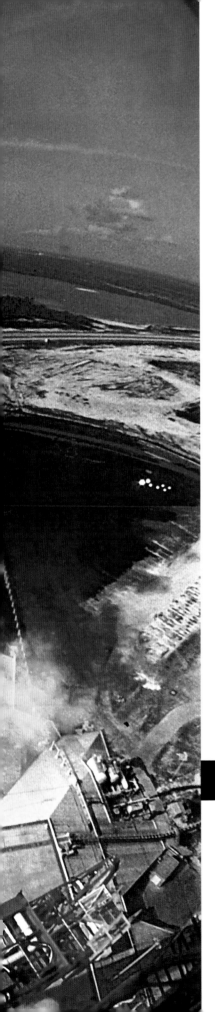

Man walks on the moon

The first manned moon landing was so significant that it was watched on television by a fifth of the world's population.

On May 25, 1961, U.S. president John F. Kennedy launched the Apollo space program by swearing that America would land a man on the moon by the end of the decade. Kennedy did not live to see his dream become a reality, but unless the conspiracy theorists are to be believed in their claim that the entire Apollo program was a hoax, his goal was achieved on July 20, 1969, five months inside his deadline.

Apollo 11 left Earth on July 16 and traveled the 240,000 miles (386,000 km) to the moon in three days. Apollo then made 13 orbits of the moon before the landing module Eagle, carrying Neil Armstrong and Edwin "Buzz" Aldrin, separated from the mother ship Columbia, piloted by Michael Collins, to make the final descent to the surface. After a tense 12 minutes and 36 seconds, having overridden the computer to avoid a boulder-filled crater and make a manual landing, Armstrong announced, "The Eagle has landed."

MANKIND'S FIRST STEPS ON THE MOON

After a meal of bacon squares, peaches, biscuits and fruit juice, Armstrong and Aldrin prepared to become the first human beings to walk on the moon. Back on Earth, some 350 million people sat watching their televisions as Armstrong announced, "The hatch is coming open." He then stood "on the porch" before descending the ladder and making mankind's most famous single footstep, off the ladder and onto the lunar surface, with the immortal words, "That's one small step for man, one giant leap for mankind."

That night, crime rates in New York dropped so low that one police chief requested a moonwalk every night; while in London thousands gathered to watch on a big screen in Trafalgar Square, and in Rome the pope performed a blessing as he watched. And on the moon, Armstrong and Aldrin took a phone call from U.S. president Nixon, who told them, "Because of what you have done, the heavens have become part of man's world."

(continued on next page)

Where were you when?

I was leaning against a wall…or maybe it was leaning against me. I concentrated on the smallest thing—like the numbers on the screen. I cried…it seemed like forever…tears of relief.

—Mrs. Joan Aldrin, astronaut's wife, Houston, Texas

I was five years old when the images were first shown in England on the following morning's news. My mother called me into the living room and said, "Watch this—this is history in the making." I was never the same after that. At forty, I still consider it to be one of the most formative events of my life.

—Oliver Keenes, Surrey, England

DOG IN SPACE

Before humans ventured beyond Earth's atmosphere, a succession of animals was sent into space, mainly dogs and monkeys. The first dog in space was a Soviet stray named Laika, who was nicknamed "Muttnik" by the American press after traveling to an altitude of nearly 2,000 miles in the Soviet satellite *Sputnik II*. Sputnik's telemetry system failed during the flight, so nobody knows exactly what happened to Laika, but there are various theories that she suffocated when the oxygen ran out, died of heat exhaustion or died after eating poisoned meat from *Sputnik's* automatic feeder. For many years the Kremlin maintained that Laika had survived the journey, but that was impossible—the capsule burned up on reentry to Earth's atmosphere in April 1958.

Where were you when?

When we actually descended the ladder, it was found to be very much like the lunar gravity simulations we had performed here on Earth. No difficulty was encountered in descending the ladder.

—Neil Armstrong, writing in 1994 on the NASA website

"Because of what you have done, the heavens have become part of man's world."

HORNET + 3

Opposite top A packet of Russian cigarettes depicting the Sputnik space satellites and Laika, the first dog in space (September 18, 1958).

Left U.S. president Richard Nixon and the *Apollo 11* astronauts exchange "A-OK signs" through the window of the Mobile Quarantine Facility on board the U.S.S. *Hornet* (July 24, 1969).

Above Buzz Aldrin stands beside the Stars and Stripes, close to the lunar module in the moon's Sea of Tranquility (July 20, 1969).

1969

Woodstock

One of the defining moments of the sixties was the legendary pop festival that ran from August 15 to 17, 1969, in Woodstock, upstate New York.

With its back-to-nature resonances of livestock and forestry, Woodstock is the perfect title for this archetypal music festival. Woodstock is now synonymous with love, peace and the zenith of sixties hippiedom, but these things came close to being known by the altogether less peaceful name of Wallkill, which is where organizers had originally planned to hold the festival until objections from local residents threatened to sink the entire project. Then, at the last minute, Max Yasgur rescued it by allowing his farm in Woodstock to be used by what he described as "the largest group of people ever assembled in one place."

THE ISLE OF WIGHT FESTIVAL

Britain's smaller-scale equivalent of Woodstock was the annual Isle of Wight festival, inaugurated in 1968. On August 31, 1969, just two weeks after Woodstock, the second Isle of Wight Festival attracted some 150,000 music fans and was headlined by one of Woodstock's notable absentees—Bob Dylan, who was playing one of his first concerts after three years of semiretirement following a motorbike accident. The following year it was headlined by one of Woodstock's notable highlights, Jimi Hendrix, as one of his last concerts before his death on September 18 that year.

Above Singer Roger Daltrey performing with the Who at the Isle of Wight Festival (August 1969).

Where were you when?

We were driving home at the end of our honeymoon and arrived in Paris to spend a romantic night before crossing the Channel, to find ourselves in the midst of the student riots in Paris. We had never seen such large numbers of police dressed in full riot gear—helmets, padded jackets, riot shields, and, of course, clubs—phalanxes of them looking very menacing and barring the way to huge numbers of people, not all students, shouting and throwing anything to hand. Many of the streets were blocked off, and all the bridges seemed to be closed. We didn't really know what was going on until we arrived back in England.

—Andrew and Hannah Alers-Hankey, London

THREE DAYS OF PEACE, MUSIC... AND RAIN

Officially known as the Woodstock Music and Art Fair, this pop extravaganza was billed as "Three Days of Peace and Music," and it attracted somewhere between 300,000 and 500,000 people to see bands including Sly and the Family Stone: The Who: Jefferson Airplane: Joan Baez: Joe Cocker: Crosby, Stills, Nash and Young: Mountain: Santana: and Jimi Hendrix, whose spaced-out rendition of "The Star-Spangled Banner" served as the weekend's anthem to alternative America.

The other musical highlight was the crowd singing "Let the Sunshine In" during a thunderstorm on the Sunday afternoon. The quagmire created by the rain, together with a lack of sanitation and insufficient food and drink, could have caused serious problems, but extra supplies were delivered by helicopter. In true hippie style, people remained peaceful and harmonious, allowing host Max Yasgur to delightedly sum it all up by telling the crowd, "I think you people have proven something to the world. That half a million kids can get together for three days and have fun and music, and have nothing but fun and music."

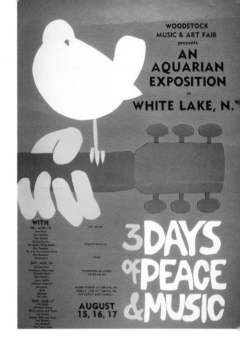

"I think you people have proven something to the world. That half a million kids can get together for three days and have fun and music, and have nothing but fun and music."

Above Santana onstage at Woodstock in front of a crowd of several hundred thousand people.

Top 3 DAYS OF PEACE & MUSIC: poster for the Woodstock Music and Art Fair.

1970-1979

1970

APOLLO 13: THE MOVIE

In 1995, a quarter of a century after the real thing, the drama of the *Apollo 13* mission was re-created for the big screen with Hollywood stars Tom Hanks as Jim Lovell, Bill Paxton as Fred Haise, Kevin Bacon as John Swigert and Ed Harris as mission controller Gene Kranz. The screenplay was based on astronaut Jim Lovell's book *Lost Moon*, but reviews were mixed, one of the problems being that everyone knew the outcome before the film began. The BBC said, "There are no great surprises in this film.... But you are left with a tear in your eye at the end and full of admiration at the bravery of the astronauts. A definite feel-good movie," while *Rolling Stone* called it "a triumph of stirring storytelling and heart-stopping suspense."

Apollo 13 crisis

The *Apollo 13* drama unfolded like the plot of a Hollywood movie, complete with happy ending, and duly reached the big screen in 1995.

After two successful missions with *Apollo 11* (see p. 133) and *Apollo 12*, NASA was beginning to make moon landings look easy. On April 11, 1970, the *Saturn V* rocket that would carry *Apollo 13* into space lifted off just as the others had done, and for 56 hours *Apollo 13* hurtled toward the moon just as the others had done. Then disaster struck—an oxygen tank in the service module exploded, and seconds later came the famous transmission, "OK, Houston, we have a problem" (sometimes reported as "We've *had* a problem"). In an instant the mission changed from the third lunar landing to an epic struggle to save the lives of astronauts James (Jim) Lovell, Fred Haise and John Swigert. To make matters worse, *Apollo* could not simply turn around; it had to continue into space and orbit the moon before limping home.

SAFE RETURN

NASA later determined that months before the mission, wires leading to a fan thermostat in the oxygen tank had been tested at too high a voltage, burning the insulation and causing a short circuit when the fan was activated. The resulting spark caused an explosion that destroyed the tank, blew off one side of the service module and disabled the other oxygen tank. The tanks held oxygen both for breathing and for the electrical power systems, and Houston soon calculated that there would not be enough oxygen to get the astronauts back to the earth.

The only hope was for all three astronauts to transfer to the lunar landing module, which had its own oxygen supply but was designed for only two astronauts, and to save oxygen by shutting down the command and service modules until they were needed for the descent to Earth. This they did, and finally, after three and a half days of tension and anxiety followed avidly by the world's media, the command module splashed down in the Pacific with all three astronauts safe and well.

"OK, Houston, we have a problem."

Where were you when?

My family lived in Suffolk, England, close to the USAAF airbases at Woodbridge and Bentwaters. The return of the crippled spacecraft dominated the news, and as it got closer to Earth, American planes and helicopters were in the air continually, heightening the tension. NASA didn't know where Apollo 13 *might land, and they were patrolling the North Sea in case it splashed down there. It was like the whole world stopped and looked up; everyone was willing the astronauts home.*

—Roddy Langley, London

Above Astronauts and flight controllers anxiously watch the monitors in the Mission Control Center during the *Apollo 13* crisis (April 14, 1970).

Opposite After splashing down in the Pacific, the *Apollo 13* astronauts emerge from the capsule to await the recovery helicopter.

1970

FLQ

Formed in February 1963 in the wake of the upsurge of separatism initiated by the Quiet Revolution (see p. 232 Quebec referendum), the Front de Libération du Québec (FLQ) was an extreme group of socialists and nationalists committed to realizing independence for Quebec— through violence if necessary. As well as independence, the FLQ manifesto also called for a Marxist insurrection, the overthrow of the Quebec government, and the establishment of a workers society. Between 1963 and 1970 the FLQ perpetrated some 200 acts of violence, including the bombing of the Montreal Stock Exchange on February 13, 1969. By 1970, after seven years of violence, 23 FLQ members were in prison. Those who were released formed part of the ransom demands after the kidnappings that precipitated the October Crisis.

The body of Pierre Laporte is discovered in the trunk of a car in Montreal, Canada (October 19, 1970).

The October Crisis

In October 1970 Canada was subject to emergency war measures after Quebec separatists kidnapped a British diplomat and a Quebec politician.

During the 1960s the separatist cause in Quebec took two main paths: the peaceful, which saw the rise to power of the Parti Québécois in 1976; and the violent, which included the formation of the extremist Front de Libération du Québec (FLQ; see sidebar). In 1970 the FLQ's actions provoked a national crisis when on October 5 an FLQ unit kidnapped British trade commissioner James Cross in Montreal and then five days later another unit kidnapped Quebec's vice-premier and Labour and Immigration Minister, Pierre Laporte, also in Montreal. Ransom demands included the release of 23 "political prisoners" (FLQ members convicted of acts of violence), $500,000 in gold, the broadcast and publication of the FLQ Manifesto, and safe passage for the kidnappers to Cuba or Algeria.

WAR MEASURES

As the tension mounted, troops were sent to guard the federal government in Ottawa, and in Quebec the provincial government formally requested the intervention of the Canadian army to support police in maintaining order. Then, on October 16, Prime Minister Pierre Trudeau (at the request of the premier of Quebec and Mayor of Montreal) declared a state of insurrection, outlawing the FLQ and controversially invoking the emergency War Measures Act, thus curtailing civil liberties throughout the country.

The following day, Laporte's body was found in the trunk of a car at St. Hubert Airport near Montreal; his kidnappers and murderers were arrested during November and December and later brought to justice. On December 3, after police had discovered where Cross was being held, he was released unharmed in return for safe passage for his kidnappers to Cuba, where the Federal Justice Minister said they would remain in exile for life—though in fact they later returned to Canada and served time for kidnapping.

"THE NIGHTMARE IS OVER"

On the day of Cross's release, Trudeau announced, "The nightmare is over," but federal troops were not withdrawn from Quebec until three weeks later, on December 24. The imposition of the War Measures Act (previously invoked only during the two World Wars)

Where were you when?

I am speaking to you at a moment of grave crisis, when violent and fanatical men are attempting to destroy the unity and the freedom of Canada. One aspect of that crisis is the threat which has been made on the lives of two innocent men. These are matters of the utmost gravity.

—Pierre Trudeau, announcing the invocation of the War Measures Act

We are going to win because there are more boys ready to shoot members of Parliament than there are policemen.

—Michel Chartrand, labour leader and FLQ supporter, speaking at the height of the crisis received widespread public and cross-party support at the time but has since been criticized as an overreaction. This criticism, made with the knowledge of the limited capabilities of the FLQ, is somewhat unfair on Trudeau, who was acting after a decade of increasing violence, at a time when the FLQ claimed to have "100,000 revolutionary workers, armed and organized."

The crisis is unlikely to be repeated, because it led separatists to favor political action over violence (see p. 232 Quebec referendum), and the War Measures Act has been replaced by the less draconian Emergencies Act of 1988. However, it continues to resonate through Canadian politics and popular culture, being the subject of the 1994 film *Octobre* and the film *October 1970*.

A patrol of four soldiers with semi-automatic rifles and a machine gun marches past Montreal City Hall (October 16, 1970).

1972

TIMELINE

08/28/72 Mark Spitz wins the 200-m butterfly in a world record 2 minutes 0.7 seconds. The United States wins the 4x100-m freestyle relay, in world-record time of 3 minutes 26.42 seconds.

08/29/72 Spitz wins the 200-m freestyle in a world record 1 minute 52.78 seconds.

08/31/72 Spitz wins the 100-m butterfly in a world record 54.27 seconds. The United States wins the 4x200- m freestyle relay, in world record time of 7 minutes 35.78 seconds.

09/03/72 Spitz wins the 100-m freestyle in a world record 51.22 seconds.

09/04/72 The United States wins the 4x100-m medley relay, in world record time of 3 minutes 48.16 seconds.

Above Mark Spitz with five of his gold medals. He took two days off before winning two more (August 31, 1972).

Right Spitz leads the 200-meters butterfly (August 1972).

Opposite Australian swimmer Shane Gould during a training session at the Munich Olympics (August 1972).

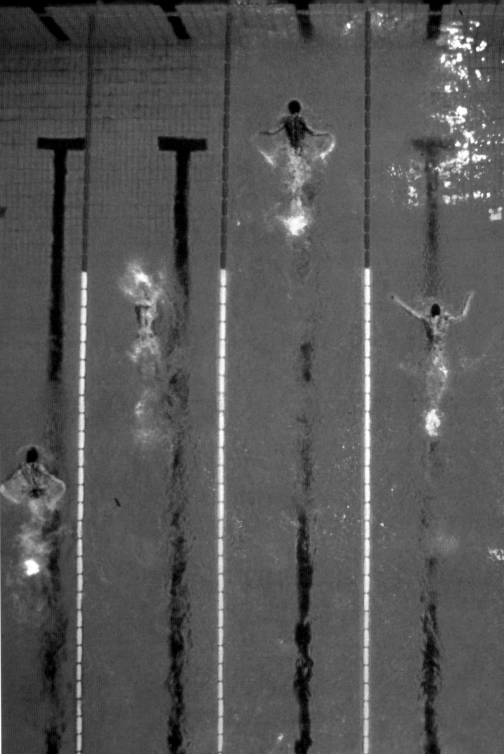

Where were you when?

That picture with my teammates holding me high above them I enjoy more than the one that was taken with the seven gold medals around my neck. Having a tribute from your teammates is a feeling that can never be duplicated.

—Mark Spitz, speaking after the event

I am trying to do the best I can. I'm not concerned with tomorrow, but with what goes on today.

—Mark Spitz

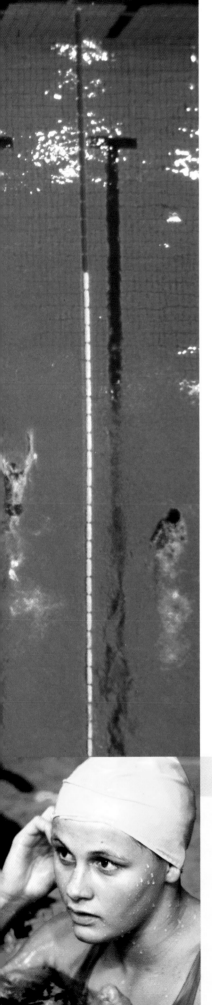

Mark Spitz's seven gold medals

Seven gold medals and seven world records in a single Games is more than any other athlete in any sport has achieved before or since.

The first week of the 1972 Olympic Games in Munich was completely dominated by American swimmer Mark Spitz, with an achievement of such magnitude that it has not been bettered in more than 30 years since. Spitz arrived in Munich with something to prove, having disappointed himself and his fans at the 1968 Mexico City Olympics by winning "only" four medals—two gold, one silver and one bronze—after having set himself a target of five golds.

FIVE GOLD MEDALS AND FIVE WORLD RECORDS

In Munich, Spitz made no mistake. On the third day of the Games, he won his first event, the 200-m butterfly, in a time nearly 1 second faster than his own world record. Later that afternoon he won his second gold in the 4x100-m freestyle relay, in which the Americans beat the world record by more than 2 seconds. The following day, Spitz won the 200-m freestyle, knocking half a second off his own world record, and then he had a day off before taking two more golds: the 100-m butterfly, in which he narrowly beat his own world record by 0.29 seconds, and the 4x200-m freestyle relay, in which the United States beat the world record by nearly 7 seconds.

"CHICKEN"?

Spitz had now achieved the five golds he had wanted from Mexico, and he told his coach that he would save himself for the 4x100-m medley relay by not swimming in the 100-m freestyle—which just happened to be against his archrival Jerry Heidenreich. His coach told him it was both events or neither, and asked if he wanted people to call him "chicken." Spitz duly entered the 100 m and beat Heidenreich by 0.43 seconds before completing his haul the next day with gold and a world record in the 4x100-m medley relay, truly living out his father's maxim "Swimming isn't everything—winning is."

SHANE GOULD

Australian swimmer Shane Gould has been dubbed "the female Mark Spitz" for her performance in the Olympic pool at Munich. At the age of 15, she shrugged off the barracking of the American team—who wore T-shirts proclaiming "All that glitters is not Gould"—to win three golds and set three world records (in the 200-m freestyle, 400-m freestyle and 200-m individual medley), as well as winning silver in the 800-m freestyle and bronze in the 100-m freestyle. By the end of the year, she was the holder of the women's world record for every freestyle distance from 100 m to 1,500 m , but she turned professional in 1973, ruling herself out of the following Olympic Games.

1972

TIMELINE

09/17/70 King Hussein of Jordan declares martial law and orders his forces to eject Palestine Liberation Organization (PLO) guerrillas from the country.

09/27/70 PLO leader Yasser Arafat signs a truce with King Hussein after the PLO is evicted from its Jordanian strongholds in a 10-day conflict known to the PLO as Black September.

09/05/72 At 5:10 A.M. members of PLO suborganization Black September storm the Israeli compound in the Olympic Village in Munich, taking 10 hostages, one of whom escapes.

09/05/72 AFTERNOON After negotiating with West German chancellor Willy Brandt, the terrorists and their hostages are flown to Furstenfeld military airfield, 25 miles from Munich.

09/05/72 MIDNIGHT The terrorists are ambushed by German police as they take their hostages toward a waiting aircraft. All the hostages and four of the terrorists are killed; one terrorist escapes and three are captured.

09/08/72 The Israeli air force bombs 10 guerrilla bases in Lebanon in revenge for the events in Munich.

10/29/72 Black September terrorists hijack a Lufthansa airliner and successfully demand the release of the three terrorists being held for the Munich hostage-taking.

Israeli athletes murdered at the Olympics

The 1972 Munich Olympics was forever tainted by the deaths of 11 athletes after a terrorist attack on the Israeli compound.

The Munich Olympics provided its share of great sporting memories—Mark Spitz (see p. 146), Olga Korbut, Shane Gould—but all of them were overshadowed by the events that took place on September 5, away from the sporting arena. At 5:10 A.M., despite the presence of 250 plainclothes police officers stationed there in response to a warning that there might be trouble, eight members of the Black September terrorist organization (see opposite) burst into the Israeli compound within the Olympic Village, firing submachine guns. Wrestling coach Moshe Weinberg was killed instantly, and weightlifter Yosef Romano died later of injuries sustained while holding a door shut so that his teammates could escape out the window.

FAILED RESCUE ATTEMPT

The terrorists took 10 hostages, one of whom managed to escape, and demanded the release of 200 Palestinians held in Israeli prisons. West German chancellor Willy Brandt flew to Munich to negotiate in person with the terrorists, arranging for them to be taken by helicopter to a military airfield from where, he told them, they would be flown by plane to an Arab country. But that night, as the terrorists and their hostages crossed the tarmac toward the waiting plane, German police opened fire in a woefully inept rescue attempt that resulted in all nine hostages being killed. Four terrorists were also killed, one escaped, and three were captured, only to be released just over a month later in exchange for hostages taken in the hijacking of a Lufthansa airliner. The Games were suspended on the morning of September 6 for a memorial service in the Olympic Stadium. They were resumed later the same day with the agreement of most nations, including Israel, although some individual athletes withdrew and the Israeli team no longer took part.

Where were you when?

Shortly after we arrived at the airport perimeter, we heard gunfire, but the guards assured everyone that it was just the troops inside clearing their weapons now that the hostage-taking was over safely. Then came the awful news that an attempt to rescue the hostages had been botched. The hostages were dead, as were five of the gunmen and a policeman.

—Brian Williams, Reuters report, July 9, 1972

BLACK SEPTEMBER

The title of the terrorist organization whose members attacked the Israeli compound derives from the name given to the events of September 1970, when the Palestine Liberation Organization (PLO) was expelled from Jordan. Concerned by the increasing power of the PLO, which had taken control of much of northern Jordan, as well as by the risk of reprisals for PLO attacks mounted from his country, King Hussein ordered his forces to eject PLO guerrillas and leaders. Military action led to a bloody 10-day civil war that became known to the PLO, which had been driven from its strongholds, as Black September. (*See also: "Entebbe Hostage Crisis," p. 164.*)

Above One of the masked terrorists in the Munich Olympic Village (September 5, 1972).

Opposite Munich's 740-acre Olympic park, as seen from the Olympic tower (1972).

1972

TIMELINE

Summit Series 1972

9.02.72 Montreal, Game 1:
USSR 7–Canada 3

9.04.72 Toronto, Game 2:
Canada 4–USSR 1

9.06.72 Winnipeg, Game 3:
Canada 4–USSR 4

9.08.72 Vancouver, Game 4:
USSR 5–Canada 3

9.22.72 Moscow, Game 5:
USSR 5–Canada 4

9.24.72 Moscow, Game 6:
Canada 3–USSR 2

9.26.72 Moscow, Game 7:
Canada 4–USSR 3

9.28.72 Moscow, Game 8:
Canada 6–USSR 5

Above Paul Henderson waves to the welcoming crowd in Toronto on Team Canada's return from Moscow (September 1972).

Paul Henderson scores for Canada

One sports writer described the reaction to Henderson's legendary goal as "reminiscent of the celebrations at the end of World War II."

It has been called the most famous goal in the history of hockey—an unforgettable moment that came in the dying seconds of a series that could not have been better scripted had it been a feature film.

Canada had withdrawn from amateur international ice hockey competition in 1970, so fans were delighted when the NHL organized the eight-game Summit Series in 1972, pitting Canada's best professionals against the USSR. But the Canadian players and fans alike were in for a shock—the Soviets won two and tied one of the first four games, which were all played on Canadian soil. Morale did not improve after the first of four return games in Moscow, in which Team Canada watched a 4–1 lead evaporate into a 5–4 defeat.

THE GOAL HEARD AROUND THE WORLD

Team Canada was now trailing 1–3–1 with only 3 games to go—they would have to win all three to win the series and salvage any national pride. Paul Henderson scored winning goals for Canada in Games 6 and 7, getting the nation firmly behind the team and setting up a dream finale that few Canadians missed: Game 8 was broadcast live during the afternoon of September 28, when most schools canceled classes and many companies suspended business—and those that didn't found themselves facing record levels of absenteeism.

It has been said that all Canadians of a certain age remember that roller-coaster ride of a game. The Soviets built up a 5–3 lead by the end of the second period, and Canada tied the score halfway through the third. But a tie would not be enough. Only a win would do, and as the seconds ticked away, it looked as if the series would end in a tie. And then Paul Henderson came off the bench. With less than a minute to go, he missed one chance and came back for another. His shot was blocked but rebounded straight back to him, and this time, with just 34 seconds of the series left to play, he made sure of it—or, in the immortal words of commentator Foster Hewitt: "Here's a shot. Henderson makes a wild stab for it and falls. Here's another shot. Right in front. They Score!! Henderson has scored for Canada!"

Where were you when?

I found myself with the puck in front of the net. Tretiak made one stop and the puck came right back to me. There was room under him, so I poked the puck through. When I saw it go in, I just went bonkers.

—Paul Henderson, scorer of the winning goal

The Canadians battled with the ferocity and intensity of a cornered animal.

—Anatoli Tarasov, Soviet coach

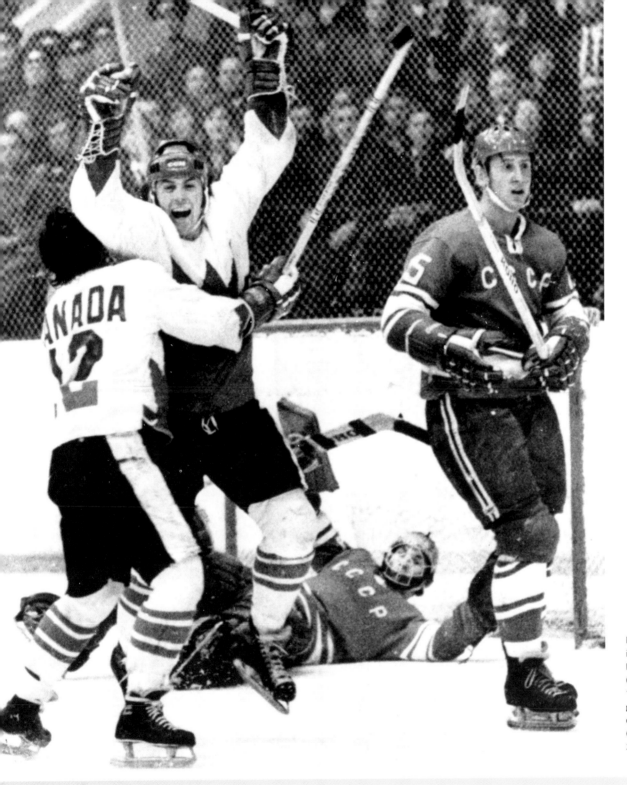

Paul Henderson is congratulated by Yvon Cournoyer (12) after scoring "the most famous goal in the history of hockey" (September 28, 1972).

TEAM OF THE CENTURY

It took remarkable resilience for a team that was booed off the ice after Game 4 in Vancouver to come back and win the series, and that resilience has become a part of Canadian folklore. The goal itself has been described as something that transcended sport and has come to symbolize what it means to be Canadian, while a Canadian Press millennium survey named 1972 Team Canada as the Team of the Century and voted Henderson's winning goal 8th in a poll of Top Canadian News Events of the 20th Century. In December 1999, on the eve of the new millennium, 1972 Team Canada was inducted into the Hockey Hall of Fame in Toronto as the greatest team of the century.

THE RISE OF THE WOMEN'S MOVEMENT

After winning the right to vote—which in France, Italy and Ireland did not occur until after World War II—the next step for feminists was to fight for equal rights and opportunities in all areas of life. A new wave of organized women's rights movements, a.k.a. Women's Liberation movements ("women's lib"), began to emerge in many countries during the 1960s and made great headway during the 1970s—particularly in Switzerland, which in 1971 became the last Western nation to grant women the right to vote in federal elections.

BETTY FRIEDAN, GLORIA STEINEM, AND GERMAINE GREER

One of the triggers for this resurgence of feminism was the publication of *The Feminine Mystique*, by American feminist Betty Friedan, in 1963, analyzing the ways in which postwar American society had stifled women by pressuring them to return to traditional prewar roles. Three years later, in 1966, Friedan co founded America's National Organization of Women (NOW) in order to fight gender discrimination in employment opportunities, wages, contraception and abortion. And four years after that, she went on to lead the National Women's Strike for Equality on August 26, 1970, when some 50,000 women gathered in New York to mark the 50th anniversary of the implementation of the 19th Amendment to the U.S. Constitution—the amendment that gave American women the right to vote.

Another prominent figure in the rise of the American women's movement during the 1970s was Gloria Steinem, who got the decade off to a flying start by co founding the Women's Action Alliance in 1970, the National Women's Political Caucus in 1971 and becoming founding editor of *Ms.* magazine in 1972. And as the 1970s began, the cause was also being taken up in Britain, where Australian feminist Germaine Greer published *The Female Eunuch* (1970), attacking the misrepresentation of female sexuality in male-dominated Western society and representing marriage as a legalized form of slavery for women.

LEGAL LANDMARKS

The 1970s was a decade when women's movements on both sides of the Atlantic achieved landmark legal rulings that made equal opportunities a realistic possibility rather than just an ideological pipe dream. In Italy women won the right in 1970 to sue for divorce and, in 1972, to use birth control legally for the first time. On February 9, 1970, British Parliament passed unopposed a bill to give women equal pay by 1976, and on March 6 the following year, women kept up the pressure with Britain's largest-ever Women's Liberation march, which saw 4,000 women marching across London from Hyde Park to Downing Street.

In 1972 their North American sisters achieved two notable landmarks. Canada's largest women's organization, the National Action Committee on the Status of Women, was founded that year, and in the United States an Equal Rights Amendment to the Constitution (ERA) was passed by both Congress and the Senate. Unfortunately for its supporters, at the deadline for its ratification, a decade later, only 30 of the necessary 38 states were in favor of its adoption (5 more had

Feminist campaigners invade the Royal Albert Hall, London, and disrupt the Miss World contest, which they claimed to be demeaning to women, by firing ink at spectators and letting off stink bombs (November 21, 1970).

Protesters on Britain's largest-ever Women's Liberation march (March 6, 1971).

withdrawn their support) and the amendment lapsed.

The two main problems in canvassing support for the ERA were the same problems facing feminism in general: opposition from conservative thinkers outside the women's movement and disagreements among activists within it. Supporters of the amendment claimed that it would provide a constitutional guarantee of equal treatment for women, while opponents argued that it would introduce unwanted responsibilities (such as the requirement to serve in the military) and the removal of various benefits (such as the right to financial support from their husbands). Meanwhile, conservative men opposed it because they saw it as undermining their role, and conservative women opposed it because they felt that feminism denigrated the roles of wife and mother.

The most significant legal landmark of all for the U.S. women's movement was also one of the most controversial:

the U.S. Supreme Court ruling in the case of *Roe* vs. *Wade*, which was passed on January 22, 1973. The ruling resulted in the liberalizing of the abortion laws on the basis of personal liberty and the right to privacy, giving women the right to choose, and it still divides America to this day. Abortion was legalized in France in 1975 and in Italy in 1977.

Although full equality of opportunity has still not been achieved in all quarters, the women's rights campaigns of the 1970s and since have had an enormous positive effect on society's attitudes to women.

And, of course, the decade ended with Britain becoming the first European country to elect a female prime minister— Margaret Thatcher—to the inevitable jibes that she succeeded only by behaving like a man.

1974

TIMELINE

06/17/72 Five men carrying photographic and electronic surveillance equipment are arrested while committing a burglary at Democratic headquarters in the Watergate building, Washington, D.C.

01/30/73 Two former aides to the Campaign to re elect the President (CREEP) are convicted of conspiring to spy on the Democratic Party headquarters.

05/17/73 A U.S. Senate select committee (the Ervin Committee) begins hearings into the Watergate burglary and the activities of CREEP.

05/22/73 President Richard Nixon admits concealing evidence of wrongdoing but denies knowledge of illegal activities at the time they took place.

06/25/73– In testimony to the Ervin Committee,
06/29/73 Nixon's former legal counsel, John Dean, directly contradicts Nixon's statement of May 22.

07/16/73 A former White House aide reveals that all conversations in the White House have been recorded at Nixon's request. Nixon subsequently refuses several court orders to release the tapes.

10/20/73 Sixteen impeachment resolutions are raised in the House of Representatives after Nixon orders the removal from office of a special prosecutor for refusing to do a deal over the White House tapes.

07/27/74 The House Judiciary Committee votes in favor of the first article of impeachment against Nixon for obstructing the Watergate investigation; further charges are approved over the next three days.

08/05/74 Nixon is forced to release transcripts of three self-incriminating conversations relating to the burglary.

08/08/74 Nixon resigns to avoid impeachment.

09/08/74 Nixon's successor, Gerald Ford, issues him with an unconditional pardon for crimes committed in office.

ALL THE PRESIDENT'S MEN

Watergate was a triumph of investigative journalism for which Carl Bernstein and Bob Woodward won every major journalistic award, including a Pulitzer Prize for their coverage in the *Washington Post*. They were an unlikely partnership—Bernstein, a school dropout who had worked his way up from copy boy and had already spent six years at the *Washington Post*; and Woodward, a Yale graduate who gave up studying law to be a journalist and had only recently arrived at the *Post*. In 1974, after Nixon's resignation, they completed *All the President's Men*, a bestseller based on their investigation, and two years later a feature film of the book was released, starring Dustin Hoffman as Bernstein and Robert Redford as Woodward.

The Watergate scandal

The Watergate scandal ended on August 8, 1974, when Republican Richard Nixon became the first U.S. president to resign from office.

The scandal began on June 17, 1972, with a break-in at the Democratic Party headquarters at the Watergate Building in Washington, D.C., and might have ended soon afterward were it not for the tenacity of investigative journalists Carl Bernstein and Bob Woodward of the *Washington Post*. Five burglars were arrested carrying photographic and electronic surveillance equipment, and evidence linked them to Nixon's Campaign to Re elect the President (CREEP). The trial of the burglars was conveniently delayed until after the presidential election, which resulted in a landslide victory for Nixon, but the implications of foul play (that the burglars were in fact spying on the Democrats) did not go away, because by then Bernstein and Woodward had published evidence that the burglary was part of an illegal "dirty tricks" campaign by the White House.

RESIGNATION

Another 18 months of journalistic revelations resulted in court hearings and then a Senate select committee inquiry that implicated the White House in the original burglary, the obstruction of justice in the subsequent investigation and the use of illegal and unethical activities against opponents.

It transpired that Nixon had ordered the automatic recording of all conversations in the White House, but citing executive privilege, he refused several court orders to hand over the tapes until finally forced to do so on August 5, 1974. Here was conclusive evidence that Nixon had been personally involved in a scandal that Senate committee chairman Sam Ervin described as the theft of "not the jewels, money or other property of American citizens, but something much more valuable—their most precious heritage—the right to vote in a free election." Knowing that he would be highly unlikely to avoid conviction if impeached, Nixon resigned the presidency.

Where were you when?

I was eleven at the time. I vividly remember a cartoon in the newspaper, drawn by Gerald Scarfe, showing a monstrously slack-jawed President Nixon holding an H-bomb and saying, "If I go, I'll take you all with me!" I cut the cartoon out and kept it for years.

—Thomas Keenes, London

Left The Watergate building, Washington, D.C.

Above left Nixon leaving the White House following his resignation over the Watergate scandal, somewhat incongruously smiling and giving his trademark gesture of raised hands with V's-for-victory.

1974

DARWIN'S EARLIER CYCLONES

Darwin was founded under the name Palmerston by settlers from South Australia in 1869, and within a decade the fledgling town had experienced nature's destructive potential. Cyclonic storms wreaked substantial damage in 1878 and again in 1881, but these were completely overshadowed by the cyclone that hit Palmerston on January 6, 1897, killing 15 people, destroying more than half the port's fleet of pearling luggers—and moving one Christian preacher to claim it as "a gentle reminder from Providence that we are a very sinful people." Major cyclones again hit Darwin (the town was renamed in 1911) in 1917 and 1937. According to Aboriginal belief, natural forces are provoked by human actions, and many of the local Larrakia people consider the cyclones to have been caused by white settlers incurring the wrath of Nungalinya, or Old Man Rock, just off the coast.

Cyclone Tracy

Australian newspaper *The Age* described Cyclone Tracy as a "disaster of the first magnitude...without parallel in Australia's history."

Paradoxically, Cyclone Tracy was both predictable and a complete shock. Darwin had been hit by major cyclones in 1897 and 1937 (see sidebar), so according to the 40-year cycle, Darwin was due for another hit. But after several false alarms—including Cyclone Selma, which threatened Darwin earlier the same month but then dissipated—nobody was too worried when the Bureau of Meteorology announced at 10.00 A.M. on December 20, 1974, that a tropical depression over the Arafura Sea had been upgraded to cyclone status and code-named Tracy.

SANTA NEVER MADE IT INTO DARWIN

For several days Tracy moved southwest on a course that would take it well north of Darwin, but early on December 24 it rounded Cape Fourcroy, where it changed direction and began to head directly toward the city. By late afternoon on Christmas Eve, heavy, low clouds had gathered over Darwin, causing squalls of rain and gusting winds; by 10.00 P.M. the gusts were growing stronger and buildings were sustaining damage, and at midnight the cyclone struck with its full force, battering the city for nearly seven hours, destroying some 70 percent of the buildings (estimates vary), leaving 20,000 people homeless, and killing 65 people—49 on land and 16 at sea.

Over the next few days almost 80 percent of Darwin's 48,000 population was evacuated, and for the next six months people were allowed access to the city only with an official permit. In February 1975 the Darwin Reconstruction Commission was formed and challenged with rebuilding the city within five years. The damage had been so severe that the commission even discussed rebuilding the city in a new location, but remarkably, by 1978 Darwin's population had recovered to pre-Tracy levels.

The impact of Cyclone Tracy was so great that it extended beyond news reports and the mammoth reconstruction effort to find a place in Australian popular culture: in 1986 the disaster was the subject of a television mini-series and, in the immediate aftermath, a pop song was recorded by Bill Cate to raise money for the relief effort, entitled "Santa Never Made It into Darwin."

Opposite The aftermath: a house on the outskirts of Darwin, completely destroyed by Cyclone Tracy (December 25, 1974).

Where were you when?

There's no choice but to evacuate Darwin. There's nothing left here to stay for. The city has been almost completely wrecked and the unanimous opinion of the people is that it should be bulldozed and rebuilt.

—Major General Alan Stretton, director-general of the Natural Disasters Organization, as quoted by the BBC

You started to almost think that it would never happen to Darwin even though we had cyclone warnings on the radio all the time. Most of the people who had lived here for quite some time didn't really believe the warnings.

—Barbara James, Darwin resident, interviewed by journalist Bill Bunbury for his book *Cyclone Tracy, Picking Up the Pieces*

1975

TIMELINE

04/07/68 U.S. president Johnson orders a reduction in the bombing of North Vietnam.

05/10/68 Peace talks begin in Paris between the United States and North Vietnam.

12/31/70 Congress repeals the Tonkin Gulf Resolution (see p. 112), giving U.S. president Richard Nixon no further authority to widen the scope of the war. Nixon nonetheless orders further offensives.

01/27/73 A cease-fire agreement is signed at the Paris Conference.

01/75 North Vietnamese and Viet Cong begin a new offensive on South Vietnam.

04/23/75 U.S. president Gerald Ford announces that America's involvement in the Vietnam War is at an end. U.S. forces begin the final evacuation of American personnel and South Vietnamese civilians by airplane.

04/28/75 North Vietnamese forces cut off Saigon from the rest of South Vietnam and shell the airfield, putting an end to the airlift.

04/29/75 As the North Vietnamese and Viet Cong close in on Saigon, U.S. forces begin the final massive helicopter evacuation from the U.S. embassy.

04/30/75 The last U.S. troops leave the embassy. Saigon is captured and South Vietnam surrenders.

1976 The Socialist Republic of Vietnam is proclaimed.

The fall of Saigon

The fall of Saigon marked the definitive end of the Vietnam War, but it was not the result that the United States had been hoping for.

The end of the Vietnam War was as complex and drawn out as its beginning (see p. 112). In April 1968, U.S. president Lyndon Johnson began seeking a diplomatic solution to the conflict, ordering a reduction in the saturation bombing of North Vietnam so that peace talks could begin in Paris the following month. However, the difficulty of negotiating a settlement (see "The Paris Peace Talks," below), together with renewed U.S. aggression from Johnson's successor President Nixon in the name of "peace with honor," meant that a peace treaty was not signed until nearly five years later, in January 1973.

The terms of the treaty did not make for lasting peace. U.S. combat troops were withdrawn in exchange for a release of prisoners, but North Vietnamese and Viet Cong troops were allowed to remain in South Vietnam, leaving the south in much the same position as it had been 10 years earlier: under threat of a Communist takeover.

THE WAR ENDS IN FAILURE

Perhaps not surprisingly, in January 1975, two years after the U.S. withdrawal, the North Vietnamese and the Viet Cong launched a new offensive against South Vietnam. This time the United States refused to send troops to the aid of the South. Instead, in April all remaining U.S. personnel were withdrawn in a weeklong airlift, culminating in a desperate two-day helicopter evacuation from the roof of the U.S. embassy in Saigon as the Communist forces approached the city.

The last U.S. troops to be evacuated had to barricade the doors to the roof, and as they were taken aloft, the embassy was sacked by South Vietnamese civilians and troops enraged at being abandoned. The same day, North Vietnamese tanks rolled into the city, and South Vietnam officially surrendered to the North, to be reunified the following year as the Socialist Republic of Vietnam. The war ended with the Communist takeover—the very thing that the United States had fought for more than a decade to prevent.

Left During the Paris Peace Talks, U.S. secretary of state Henry Kissinger (l) laughs with North Vietnamese delegate Le Duc Tho (r).

Opposite An American helicopter evacuates foreign nationals from a Saigon rooftop for transportation to waiting U.S. Navy ships (April 1975).

THE PARIS PEACE TALKS

The peace talks began on May 10, 1968, but immediately foundered on the issues that had started the war in the first place: the United States insisted on the withdrawal of North Vietnamese troops from South Vietnam and a guarantee that the existing South Vietnamese government remain in place, while the North Vietnamese wanted the country reunified, and the Viet Cong demanded their right to representation in the government of the South. Eventually, both sides agreed to allow the South to choose its own government, and the United States agreed not to demand the withdrawal of Communist forces from the South in return for the North not insisting on reunification. However, U.S. withdrawal enabled the North to achieve reunification by force two years later.

Where were you when?

Later I was told that every chopper participating in the evacuation had eight to ten bullet holes.... Nobody was hit. I was the last marine out.... When we got on those birds, all we had was what was on our backs. We were told a couple of days before the evacuation to crate up our gear for shipment home, but we don't think any of it got out. I was in my gear for almost a week. When we got to Manila, we changed clothes, given one hundred dollars [sic] and I bought some civilian clothes. We showered and shaved aboard the ship. ... Let me say this. The primary mission of the MSG [Marine Security Guard] is the protection of classified material. Our secondary mission is the protection of American lives. I believe we did it all.

—Marine Sgt. John J. Valdez, as quoted in *Leatherneck Magazine*, May 1975

"Peace with honor."

1975

VENERA AND *VIKING*

On June 8, 1975, a month before the historic ASTP (*Apollo-Soyuz* Test Project), the USSR launched the *Venera 9* interplanetary probe toward Venus. *Venera* later became the first artificial satellite of Venus and released a data capsule that made a successful landing on the planet's surface, transmitting 53 minutes of data including television pictures. Not to be outdone, on August 20 the United States launched the interplanetary probe *Viking 1* toward Mars. Once in orbit around the red planet, *Viking* released a module that successfully landed on September 3, 1976, and sent back the first pictures of the Martian surface.

United States and the USSR meet in space

In an act of cold war détente, U.S. and Soviet spacecraft docked in orbit, and for two days the crews moved between both craft.

It would have been unthinkable earlier in the cold war, but in 1972 the United States and the USSR agreed to a joint space mission as part of a détente package aimed at improving relations between the two nations. The *Apollo-Soyuz* Test Project (ASTP) took three years to prepare, and then, on July 15, 1975, the two craft left Earth, bound for their rendezvous in space. Two days later *Apollo* and *Soyuz* were guided gently toward each other in orbit 140 miles above the Atlantic and successfully docked. The commanders—astronaut Tom Stafford and cosmonaut Alexei Leonov—exchanged greetings, each in the other's language, and reached through the hatches between the two craft for a historic handshake.

COME OVER TO OUR PLACE

Over the next two days the six crew members moved freely between the two spacecraft, conducting joint experiments, sharing their meals and making combined television broadcasts to those watching on Earth. On July 19 the new friends and ambassadors said good-bye to one another, closed the hatches and undocked. They then took up separate orbits, the Soviets returning to Earth on July 20; the Americans remained in space four days longer, splashing down in the Pacific on July 24.

...joint experiments, shared meals and combined television broadcasts

Left The first color photograph taken on the surface of the planet Mars, by the *Viking 1* probe (July 21, 1976).

Opposite Soviet commander Alexei Leonov (l) and his American counterpart, Thomas Stafford (r), shake hands through the hatch connecting *Soyuz* and *Apollo* as they orbit somewhere over West Germany (July 17, 1975).

Where were you when?

*High above the French city of Metz, the two commanders shook hands. There were no grand speeches, just a friendly greeting from men who seemed to have done this every day of their lives. In the background was a hand-lettered sign in English—*Welcome aboard Soyuz.

—Official NASA statement 1975

I remember being amazed that they could get these two spacecraft to dock with each other when they can't even design a flat-pack kitchen with parts that fit together.

—Joshua Tetley, Ackworth, England

1975

THE DEATH OF HAILE SELASSIE

On August 27, 1975, two months before the death of Franco, another head of state died: Emperor Haile Selassie I of Ethiopia (formerly Abyssinia). In 1916, as Ras (Prince) Tafari, Selassie had led a successful revolution and was made regent and heir to the throne. He became emperor in 1930 and came to be viewed as the Messiah by the adherents of Rastafarianism, who consider Ethiopia the Promised Land. Selassie was exiled to England after the Italian conquest of Ethiopia (1935–36) but returned in 1941 after the country was liberated by the British. He helped to form the Organization of African Unity (OAU), but there was considerable opposition to his reign, and in 1974 he was deposed, amid accusations of corruption, and died the following year in suspicious circumstances.

The death of Franco

The death of the fascist dictator General Franco on November 20, 1975, paved the way for a new liberal democracy in Spain.

General Francisco Franco came to power as dictator of Spain in 1939, following victory in the Spanish Civil War (1936–39), which was achieved through his military skill, the lack of intervention by other European democracies and his close alliance with the fascist regimes of Germany and Italy. Franco kept Spain out of World War II because German dictator Adolf Hitler was not prepared to meet his demand to cede France's North African territories to Spain, and after the war the Spanish parliament declared Franco head of state for life. In 1949 he declared Spain to be a monarchy—although without a monarch—and in 1954 he decided that his heir would be Juan Carlos, the grandson of Spain's last ruling king, a decision that he made public in 1969.

DEMOCRATIC CONSTITUTION

Franco had decreed that on his death the Spanish monarchy would return, but he hoped that it would be on his terms, as a continuation of his regime. He forced Juan Carlos to publicly swear that as king, he would uphold the principles of Francoism, ensured that the establishment machinery around Juan Carlos was staunchly Francoist, and left a posthumous message warning the Spanish people to be vigilant against "the enemies of Spain and Christian civilization": in other words, the enemies of Francoism—Socialists, Communists and liberals.

After a long illness, Franco died in Madrid on November 20, 1975. Juan Carlos duly ascended the throne, but he proved to have very different ideas about the future of Spain from those of Franco. In July 1976 he appointed as prime minister Adolfo Suarez, who had worked for Franco but shared Juan Carlos's view that Spain should move toward democracy. A referendum showed that 90 percent of the Spanish people agreed with them, and in 1978 Spain adopted a democratic constitution, removing the last significant vestiges of Franco's dictatorship within three years of his death.

Below Crowds in Madrid read the news of Franco's death (November 1975).

Opposite Franco's funeral procession en route to the Valley of the Fallen in Madrid (November 1975).

Where were you when?

He had come to be regarded not so much as a man, but as an enduring symbol of authoritarianism.... The olive-colored flesh sagged in folds from his face, his palsied right hand trembled continuously, and the speech—once shrill and demanding—was slurred and frequently unintelligible.

—*Time* Magazine, November 3, 1975

1976

TIMELINE

1962 Britain and France join forces to create a supersonic passenger aircraft.

03/02/69 The French-built prototype Concorde 001 makes a successful test flight at Toulouse.

04/09/69 The British-built prototype Concorde 002 makes a successful test flight at Filton Airfield, Bristol.

01/21/76 The world's first supersonic passenger flights begin with simultaneous takeoffs by British Airways and Air France from London to Bahrain and Paris to Rio de Janeiro, respectively.

05/24/76 British Airways and Air France begin supersonic transatlantic passenger services from London and Paris to Dulles Airport, Washington, D.C.

11/22/77 British Airways and Air France inaugurate supersonic passenger services to New York City.

1978 The 16th and last production Concorde is completed.

04/20/79 The last Concorde makes its first flight.

07/25/00 Concorde suffers its first and last accident when an Air France Concorde crashes in Gonesse, France, shortly after takeoff from Charles de Gaulle Airport, with the loss of 114 lives.

05/03 Air France retires the last of its Concordes.

10/24/03 The last commercial flight of Concorde takes place as British Airways retires the last of its fleet.

The first supersonic passenger flight

Concorde, one of the world's best-loved and most immediately recognizable aircraft, went into passenger service in January 1976.

In 1976 Concorde took passenger air travel to new heights—and new speeds. The world's first supersonic passenger jet flew half as high again as the Boeing 747 and nearly three times as fast, with a maximum speed of more than twice the speed of sound. With jet travel now readily available to the masses, Concorde also provided the world's traveling elite with a new exclusivity—at least on the restricted number of routes flown by this famous delta-winged, slender-fuselaged, droop-snooted aircraft.

WHITE ELEPHANT

After more than a decade of joint Anglo–French development, including the longest period of preservice testing of any commercial aircraft, Concorde finally went into passenger service on January 21, 1976. Air France and British Airways Concordes made simultaneous takeoffs from Paris to Rio de Janeiro and London to Bahrain, respectively, and transatlantic services followed four months later amid talk of orders in the hundreds from airlines all around the world. However, only 16 Concordes were eventually built, due to political and environmental objections that were not helped when the lawyer hired to secure landing rights publicly admitted, "Concorde is noisy as hell."

The cost of developing and producing Concorde had spiraled from an estimated $300 million in 1962 to an actual $3,500 million by the time the last one was completed in 1978. Given the lack of orders for production aircraft, and the small number of routes that the noisy beast was allowed to fly, this money (amounting to $230 million per aircraft) was never going to be recouped, making this undeniably great technological achievement something of a white elephant—but what an elegant elephant.

Left The British prototype of the Anglo–French Concorde outside its hangar at Filton, Bristol, surrounded by the British Aircraft Corporation employees who helped to build it.

Opposite Spectators wave Union Jacks as they watch the final commercial flight of Concorde make its last approach to Heathrow Airport, London (October 24, 2003).

Where were you when?

The aircraft attained a speed of Mach 1.5 (1,125 mph) and flew supersonically for nine minutes. In general, pilots' reports on the progress of the two prototype aircraft were encouraging. Ground-handling characteristics were said to be very good, and there was praise for the ease and precision of control in flight. When the visor was raised, the absence of noise on the flight deck was said to be impressive and even, on first experience, rather startling.

—Arthur Gibson, Concorde Development Team, British Aircraft Corporation, 1976

THE LAST FLIGHT OF THE CONCORDE

The Concorde's attraction was as much about design as technology, and 27 years after it first went into regular service, people would still stop and stare as it flew overhead—albeit partly in awe that anything so graceful could possibly be that noisy. But the Concorde was destined not to make 28 years in service. Air France retired its fleet by the end of May 2003, and on October 24 that year, more than 1,000 people gathered at London's Heathrow Airport to watch the Concorde arrive from JFK Airport, New York, at the end of its last commercial flight, marking the end of an era.

"The Concorde is noisy as hell."

1976

TIMELINE

06/27/76 An Air France Airbus is hijacked shortly after takeoff from Athens. The hijackers force the pilot to fly to Libya, where they release all non-Jewish passengers before flying on to Entebbe in Uganda.

06/29/76 The hijackers demand the release of 53 Palestinian prisoners in return for the 98 Jewish/Israeli hostages, setting a deadline of July 3, after which they say they will begin killing the hostages.

07/03/76 Israeli prime minister Yitzhak Rabin makes the final decision to recover the hostages by force rather than capitulating to the hijackers' demands. Israeli commandos rescue 94 of the 98 hostages and return them to Israel.

Above Major Dan Shomron, commander of the Israeli raid on Entebbe, describes the operation at a press conference (July 3, 1976).

The Entebbe hostage crisis

When 98 Jewish and Israeli airline passengers were taken hostage, Israel took military action and rescued 94 of them.

On June 27, 1976, an Air France Airbus with 250 passengers on board took off from Athens Airport bound for Tel Aviv. Soon after takeoff, five Palestinians and two Germans hijacked the plane and forced the pilot to fly to Benghazi in Libya, where they separated the Jewish passengers from the rest, released all the non-Jews and then flew on to Uganda. There, with the assistance of Ugandan dictator Idi Amin and his armed forces, they held the 98 Jewish passengers hostage at Entebbe Airport, threatening to kill them unless 53 members of Al-Fatah (the Palestine National Liberation Movement) were released from prisons in Israel and four other countries.

International opinion, as well as public and government opinion in Israel, was that Israel must reluctantly capitulate to the hijackers, but minister of defense Shimon Peres felt differently. He had a plan, and on July 3 Prime Minister Yitzhak Rabin gave that plan the go-ahead.

RAID ON ENTEBBE

Later that day, four giant Hercules transport planes loaded with Israeli commandos took off from the southern tip of the Sinai Peninsula, traveling the 2,500 miles to Entebbe under radio silence. The Israeli troops took the hijackers and the Ugandans completely by surprise, and in a 35-minute gun battle, they succeeded in killing 20 Ugandan soldiers and all 7 hijackers, as well as destroying 11 MiG fighter planes—one quarter of the Ugandan air force. Three civilian hostages and one commando were killed in the crossfire, but the remaining hostages were taken aboard the transport planes and flown straight back to Israel after one of the most daring, spectacular and successful rescues of all time.

The Ugandan response to the rescue was to murder 75-year-old Briton Dora Bloch in the hospital bed where she had been taken after choking while being held hostage. Idi Amin was reported to be in a state of shock but later recovered sufficiently to publicly congratulate his troops on "repulsing the invaders."

JORDANIAN HIJACKING

On September 6, 1970, PLO (Palestine Liberation Organization) terrorists hijacked three airliners, forcing two of them to land in the Jordanian desert and taking a third to Cairo, where they released the passengers and crew and blew up the plane. A fourth attempted hijack failed, but the arrest of one of the terrorists, Leila Khaled, led to the hijack of a fifth plane that was also taken to Jordan. On September 12, after releasing 255 hostages, the hijackers blew up the three planes in the desert, but held another 56 passengers, who were eventually exchanged for Leila Khaled. The incident led to international concern about governments capitulating to hijackers' demands and to King Hussein's taking military action to eject the PLO from Jordan (see p. 147).

Where were you when?

The decision which was taken was in clear opposition to what had recently been the prevailing mood within the government. The balance of opinion seemed to be in favor of exchanging the hostages for Fatah terrorists. As minister of defense I had worked with my colleagues throughout that week to find another solution—a means of freeing the kidnap victims by an armed intervention of our own.

—Shimon Peres, then Israeli minister of defense, in his memoirs

Jubilant survivors of the Entebbe hostage crisis arrive home after their dramatic rescue by Israeli commandos (July 1976).

Box office takings:

- USA & Canada $461 million (IMDb)
- Australia $Aus 24.3 million
- UK £30.7 million

Opposite *Star Wars* film poster featuring the sinister presence of Darth Vader looming over the characters of (l-r) Princess Leia, Luke Skywalker, C-3PO, and R2-D2.

Below As Karen Lynn Gorney looks on, John Travolta strikes the immortal and oft-mimicked pose that epitomizes *Saturday Night Fever* (1977).

The release of *Star Wars*

***Star Wars* was the start of a subindustry that has produced six films, a new mythology and merchandising on an unprecedented scale.**

A long time ago, in a studio far, far away, film director George Lucas decided to make the greatest adventure movie ever: *The Story of Mace Windu*. Then the script mutated into a 500-page monster, so he split it into three parts and decided to make the greatest *series* of adventure movies ever. He secured a deal with Fox Studios to make the first of the series, now called *The Star Wars*, and began filming in 1976. And then, at 10:00 A.M. on May 25, 1977, the history of the film industry changed forever when *Star Wars* (as it was now called) was released in 32 American movie theaters, with long lines in New York and Los Angeles for more than two hours beforehand.

"THE YEAR'S BEST MOVIE"

In the days before meaningless hyperbole became the norm, *Variety* said, "*Star Wars* is a magnificent film": *Newsweek* enthused, "I loved *Star Wars* and so will you;" and *Time* magazine fronted six pages of coverage with a headline that proved to be a massive understatement: "*Star Wars*: The Year's Best Movie." *Time* went on to describe it as "a subliminal history of the movies, wrapped in a riveting tale of suspense and adventure, ornamented with some of the most ingenious special effects ever contrived for film."

The public response was phenomenal. In 1977 more than 5 percent of American filmgoers saw *Star Wars* more than once. Ten Oscar nominations convinced Fox to rerelease the film the following year, and by November 1978 it was America's highest-grossing film ever, with $273 million; by the end of the following year, with foreign sales included, it had grossed $430 million, prompting Hollywood to change its approach to the foreign market.

Star Wars revived a flagging Hollywood film industry, redefined special effects, reestablished symphonic soundtracks, vastly expanded the horizons of merchandizing, created a pop mythology ("May the Force be with you") and, according to *Time Out*, presented pulp space fiction for the first time as a truly viable movie genre: "Discounting *2001*, which isn't a genre movie, it's like watching the first western to use real exteriors."

SATURDAY NIGHT FEVER

Space was the fashionable theme for the films of 1977, with George Lucas and Steven Spielberg swapping shares in each other's releases—*Star Wars* and *Close Encounters of the Third Kind*—and composer John Williams having a busy year writing the scores for both films. But for those who preferred their fashion closer to home and their close encounters on the dance floor, John Travolta donned his white suit and set the disco world alight with his role in *Saturday Night Fever*—the story of an uneducated Brooklyn teenager whose prowess on the dance floor brings him romance and the opportunity to move on to greater things. The film earned Travolta an Oscar nomination for best actor and made him a star, a status that was confirmed the following year by the success of *Grease*.

Where were you when?

The most fascinating single scene, for me, was the one set in the bizarre saloon on the planet Tatooine. As that incredible collection of extraterrestrial alcoholics and bug-eyed martini drinkers lined up at the bar, and as Lucas so slyly let them exhibit characteristics that were universally human, I found myself feeling a combination of admiration and delight.

—Roger Ebert, film review in *Chicago Sun Times*, January 1977

It was great. The space-age gadgets and special effects were like nothing I had ever seen before. It made it respectable for us to enjoy what was, in reality, just a fairy story about a princess, a brave knight, and a wicked goblin. Great stuff.

—Tim Hill, Surrey, England

1977

ELVIS LIVES

Like most who die, Elvis lives on in the hearts and minds of those who knew him. And like all artists, he lives on in the work he left behind, even reaching the top of the UK charts again in 2005, 28 years after his death. But Elvis also lives on in two other ways. First, in the global industry that has been established to exploit his image, which includes the transformation of Graceland into a shrine to his memory, and in the emergence of an army of impersonators that has swelled from some 38 during his lifetime to an estimated 11,000 today. And second, he lives on in the sense that he is regularly sighted around the globe and (less regularly) on the moon. By 1981 Elvis sightings were such a universally recognized phenomenon that everyone knew what Kirsty McColl meant by the title of her song "There's a Guy Works Down the Chip Shop Swears He's Elvis."

Above Thai rock singers impersonating Elvis pose at a Bangkok nightclub during a memorial party organized by the Thai Elvis Presley fan club to commemorate the anniversary of their hero's death (August 15, 2000).

The death of Elvis

Elvis Presley, for more than 20 years the king of rock 'n' roll, died on August 16, 1977, after collapsing at Graceland, his Memphis home.

The death of Elvis Presley at the age of 42 shocked his millions of fans, many of whom refused to believe that "The King" was dead—that Elvis had definitively and finally "left the building." But those noting Presley's lifestyle, increasing weight and declining health would have known an early death was inevitable. In 1976 *Rolling Stone* magazine commented on his decline: "It seems to be a continuing battle...and Elvis is not winning... Like some aging politician, [he] is reduced to the ranks of grotesque."

DOA

Despite these warning signs, it still came as a shock to the world to hear the news that Presley had been found collapsed on a bathroom floor at Graceland and pronounced dead on arrival at the Baptist Memorial Hospital. According to the death certificate, Elvis died of heart failure, but the underlying causes of the heart failure are not specified, something that has led to conjecture ever since that the immediate cause of death was drug related. The Memphis telephone system was overwhelmed with calls from around the globe, thousands of fans gathered outside Graceland (which has remained a shrine to Elvis ever since), and radio stations suspended normal programming to discuss Elvis's life or play his music nonstop throughout the night. But while reactions were united in their grief, they were divided in their predictions for the future. One record company executive said simply, "This is the end of rock 'n' roll," but he was directly contradicted by former Beatle John Lennon, who said, "The King is dead, but rock 'n' roll will never die. Long live the King." (*See also: "Elvis on 'The Ed Sullivan Show,'" p. 80.*)

"The King is dead, but rock 'n' roll will never die. Long live the King."

Opposite Thousands of Elvis fans gather for the grand finale of the annual "Elvis Week"—a candlelight vigil at Graceland in Memphis, Tennessee, on the anniversary of his death (August 16, 2004).

Opposite below Police motorcycles escort a white hearse containing the body of Elvis through the streets of Memphis, Tennessee, en route to his funeral (August 18, 1977).

Where were you when?

*I remember this very clearly. I was fifteen, and high up in the mountains of Corsica on a school trip—my first experience of proper walking. We came down into a village to restock, and I saw the banner headlines of a newspaper (*Nice Matin*?) which read, "Le Roi est Mort." Well, my French wasn't brilliant, and remote though we were, I knew it wasn't about the guillotining of Louis XVI.*

—Mark Smalley, Bristol, England

I was visiting the Chicago Sun Times, *where I was trying to sell some freelance articles. I was standing in the newsroom when a guy ran in yelling "Elvis is dead!" Seconds later a voice boomed across the*

ELVIS AARON

Elvis Presley was born in T
on January 8, 1935, the so
Gladys Presley. He moved to
Soon after signing a contract
in 1954 he achieved tremendous
musical and acting career in
television, and concerts made
most successful and outs
in the world. He died on A
buried here at his Memp

newsroom: "Stop the presses." It was a moment I'd only seen in the movies. To this day, I still get chills when I think of that editor ordering the Sun Times's presses to stop.

—Unnamed freelance reporter, quoted in *Elvis the King of Rock 'n' Roll* by Rupert Matthews

Oh, God, what can I say? I just feel so lost, I feel shattered. I feel like I lost a very, very, close, very, dear friend, part of my own family.

—Beverly Hochstedt, Elvis fan, as quoted in the *Washington Post*

1978

STEPTOE AND EDWARDS

The scientists who made possible the birth of Louise and thousands of other IVF babies were obstetrician and gynecologist Patrick Steptoe and physiologist Robert Edwards. Steptoe, who was a pioneer of the procedure of laparoscopy, became director of the Oldham Hospitals in 1951 and began researching IVF in 1966. He met Edwards two years later, after which they worked together to perfect the technique, Steptoe providing the obstetric expertise and Edwards creating the right artificial environment for the eggs to survive, ripen and achieve fertilization outside the womb.

Patrick Steptoe (l) and Robert Edwards during a television interview in which they announced that they had successfully fertilized a human ovum in a test tube (February 14, 1969).

Birth of the first "test-tube baby"

Born on July 25, 1978, Louise Brown was the world's first "test-tube baby," conceived by a process now more commonly known as IVF.

The birth of any child is testament to the wonders of nature, but the birth of Louise Brown was more than that: It was also testament to the wonders of science. And along with inspiring joy in her parents, Lesley and John, Louise's birth also provided hope for millions of infertile couples in the developed nations of the world. The press immediately dubbed Louise a "test-tube baby," although eggs undergoing IVF (in vitro fertilization) are fertilized not in a test tube but in a receptacle known as a Petri dish. Petri dishes were originally made of glass (many are now made of plastic), hence the name of the fertilization process—"in vitro" means "in glass."

CONCEPTION AND BIRTH

Lesley Brown could not conceive naturally because her fallopian tubes were blocked, preventing her eggs from reaching her womb. In all other respects she was perfectly healthy, so doctors were able to remove some of her eggs and fertilize them in a Petri dish using her husband's sperm. Then, in November 1977, when Louise was a bundle of just eight cells, they transferred one fertilized egg back into the womb.

From there the pregnancy continued normally until July 1978, when Mrs. Brown suffered from toxemia. As a result, Louise was delivered a month early by caesarean section and arrived in the world close to midnight on July 25, 1978, at Oldham General Hospital, England, weighing 5 lb 12 oz/2.6 kg.

Where were you when?

All examinations showed that the baby is quite normal. The mother's condition after delivery was also excellent. [Mrs. Brown] is enjoying a well-earned sleep.

—Patrick Steptoe, IVF pioneer, announcing the birth to the press

We'd been trying for years to have a baby, and when we heard about the birth of little Louise, it gave us real hope that one day we might be able to have children of our own.

—Jane Williamson, New York

Louise Brown shortly after her sixth birthday (July 29, 1984).

1978

TIMELINE

1958   Willy Higinbotham produces the first video game, a form of two-dimensional table tennis.

1961–1962   Steve Russell devises *Spacewar*, the first computer video game.

1971   *Computer Space*, written by Nolan Bushnell and based on *Spacewar*, is launched as the first arcade computer video game.

1972   Bushnell founds Atari and produces a screen-tennis game called *Pong*, later producing an advanced version called *Breakout*.

1978   Taito Corporation launches *Space Invaders*, an imaginative variation on *Breakout*.

1980   Namco launches *Pac-Man*, globally one of the biggest computer games of the early 1980s and the first game to feature a central "character."

1981   Nintendo launches *Donkey Kong*, introducing Jumpman, the cartoon plumber who will later be christened Mario.

1985   Nintendo launches *Super Mario Brothers*, whose central character, Mario, is by 1990 reportedly more widely recognized by American schoolchildren than Mickey Mouse.

1996   Game Freak launches *Pokémon*. Core Design launches *Tomb Raider*, whose central character, Lara Croft, becomes one of the most widely recognized computer-game characters to date.

EARLY VIDEO GAME CHARACTERS

In early video games the player controlled some inanimate device such as a Ping-Pong bat, a gun or a spaceship, but *Pac-Man* introduced the idea of controlling a "character"—albeit a featureless one. *Pac-Man*'s Japanese designer, Toru Iwatani, said: "I designed *Pac-Man* to be the simplest character possible, without any features such as eyes and limbs. Rather than defining the image of *Pac-Man* for the player, I wanted to leave that to each player's imagination." It was not long before *Pac-Man*'s simplicity was superseded by a generation of cartoonlike characters such as Mario (*Super Mario Brothers*, et al.) and Sonic the Hedgehog (*Sonic*), and they in turn encouraged the sophisticated graphics of a new breed of heroes and heroines, such as Lara Croft.

The launch of Space Invaders

Space Invaders transformed computer video games from an amusement arcade novelty into a social phenomenon—and a global industry.

Today, in an age of ever more sophisticated computer graphics and ever more powerful home consoles, the era of players standing in amusement arcades at the *Space Invaders* "cabinet" seems as remote as the heyday of the pinball machine. *Space Invaders* became an international obsession in an age when players compared high scores the way golfers compare handicaps—an age when a player's greatest satisfaction was to enter his initials in the top 20 high scores and then keep returning to the same machine to see whether he had been knocked off the chart.

FROM *PONG* TO SPACE INVASION

Credit for launching the computer games industry usually goes to American computer-programmer and former amusement arcade worker Nolan Bushnell, the founder of Atari, with his games *Spacewar*, *Pong* and *Breakout*. In the mid-1970s the Japanese entered the market with a number of computer games that were essentially variations on *Breakout*, and then in autumn 1978 a company named Taito made the conceptual leap that was to revolutionize the entire industry. In *Space Invaders*, Taito transformed the abstract blocks through which the player had to "break out" into alien invaders that advanced threateningly down the screen.

This "characterization" of the abstract elements of video games was the precursor of player-controlled beings such as Pac-Man (see Early Video Game characters, page 172), which in turn developed into fully-fledged characters such as Mario the plumber, the "era-defining mustachioed hero" of *Super Mario Brothers* fame. But before the arrival of these descendants, *Space Invaders* held sway for two years as the most popular computer game on the market, particularly in Japan, where, according to one Japanese media studies lecturer, it created "a cultural sensation on a scale comparable with rock music...a social phenomenon on such a scale that will probably never be paralleled."

Where were you when?

Space Invaders *became a big hit in the autumn of 1978, and it seemed that not only the games arcades but nearly every coffee shop in Japan was equipped with a machine.... The game was so popular that it created a scare over the shortage of 100 yen coins.*

—Masuyama, video game producer and president of dabb inc., Japan

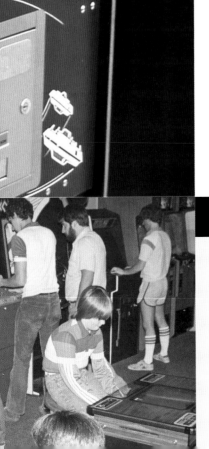

Left A busy video game arcade in California; during the 1980s the film and record industries saw computer games as a serious threat to their business (July 8, 1982).

Left top Taito's *Space Invaders*.

1979

Crisis at Three Mile Island

In spring 1979 disaster was thankfully averted after the partial meltdown of a nuclear reactor at Three Mile Island power station in Pennsylvania.

After the horrors of Hiroshima and Nagasaki (see p. 36), it seemed that some good could come of nuclear research in providing a supposedly cheap, efficient and clean source of energy. But while officials repeatedly insisted that nuclear power was safe, environmentalists were pointing out the difficulty of safely disposing of nuclear waste, the danger of containing nuclear reactions and the extreme consequences of leaks or accidents. The environmentalists were proved right in 1979, when a reactor came close to meltdown at the Three Mile Island nuclear power station on the Shenandoah River in Pennsylvania.

RADIATION LEAK

On March 29 that year, radiation was detected more than 20 miles away after a burst of radioactive steam escaped through the ventilation system at Three Mile Island. Valves in

WINDSCALE

The Three Mile Island crisis was not the first time that the safety of nuclear power had been called into question. In October 1957 a serious fire broke out at Windscale, a weapons plant on the same site as Britain's first nuclear power station, Calder Hall. The resulting radioactive leak led to the dumping of 500,000 gallons of contaminated milk from local cows and saw airborne fallout spreading as far as continental Europe. The following year, there was an explosion at a nuclear waste processing plant in the Urals, in what was then the USSR. And in 1976 Windscale was again the scene of controversy after radioactive water leaked from the power station, whose name has since been changed to Sellafield.

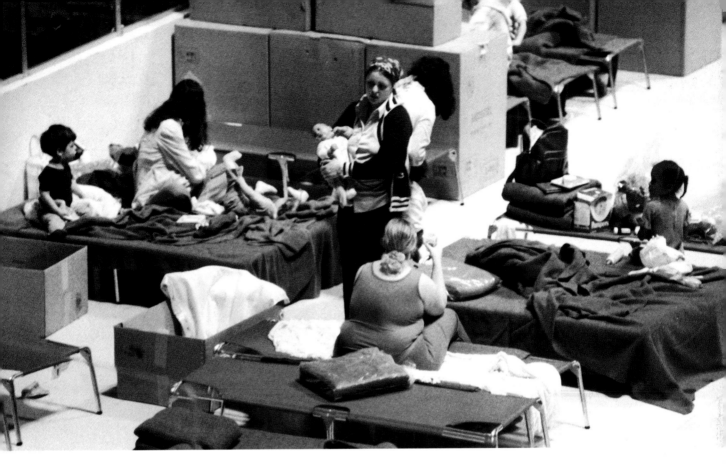

the cooling system had malfunctioned, and operators had exacerbated the fault by taking inappropriate action, leaving part of the reactor with no coolant and thereby melting part of the radioactive core. Children and pregnant women were advised to evacuate the area amid fears that a complete core meltdown could cause devastation in a five-mile radius and as many as 10,000 deaths—a hopelessly conservative estimate compared with the results of the explosion at Chernobyl seven years later (see p. 208).

Thankfully, the damage was isolated and brought under control before complete meltdown occurred. On April 9 officials declared that the crisis was over and insisted that once new safety measures were in place, nuclear power would once again be perfectly safe. In 1986, just weeks before the Chernobyl disaster, the *Economist* magazine even went so far as to declare that a nuclear power station was "as safe as a chocolate factory."

Above Evacuees in a civil defense shelter at a local sports arena after the nuclear accident at Three Mile Island.

Opposite top The advanced gas-cooled reactor at Sellafield nuclear power station (formerly Windscale) in Cumbria.

Opposite below Three Mile Island nuclear power station near Harrisburg, Pennsylvania (April 11, 1979).

Where were you when?

I was surprised at how bad it was, but I was younger then and thought nothing could happen to me.

—Richard Piers, Pennsylvania

No one wrote about all the dead birds that I found or how people would get a metallic taste in their mouths.

—Roger Gersky, Pennsylvania

"As safe as a chocolate factory."

1979

TIMELINE

1978 The USSR sends some 1,000 military "advisers" to Afghanistan to support a pro-Soviet, anti-Islamic regime that had seized power in April.

09/79 The Afghan regime is overthrown.

12/25/79 Soviet motorized divisions cross the border into Afghanistan and, simultaneously, Soviet Special Forces seize Kabul airport in Afghanistan, enabling the USSR to begin airlifting troops and equipment into the country.

12/28/79 U.S. president Jimmy Carter condemns the invasion as a "blatant violation" of international law and "a threat to peace."

01/29/80 The Islamic Conference of 36 Muslim nations condemns the invasion.

02/22/80 The USSR declares martial law in Afghanistan and Soviet president Brezhnev calls for "an end to outside interference."

03/80 The American Olympic Association agrees to boycott the Moscow Olympics in protest at the invasion.

11/09/82 Thousands of Soviet troops die in a fire in the Salang Pass road tunnel.

01/15/86 Soviet president Mikhail Gorbachev refers to the continuing war in Afghanistan as a "bleeding wound."

02/08/88 Gorbachev announces that Soviet forces will begin withdrawing from Afghanistan in May.

02/14/89 The last Soviet troops finally leave Afghanistan.

The USSR invades Afghanistan

The USSR invaded Afghanistan to prop up a Soviet-friendly regime but found itself fighting a 10-year war that it could not win.

Soviet intervention in Afghanistan—beginning with support for an unpopular regime and resulting in a decade of guerrilla warfare against an "invisible" enemy—was reminiscent of the American presence in Vietnam. During 1978 the USSR sent more than 1,000 military "advisers" to Afghanistan to support a pro-Soviet, anti-Islamic regime that had seized power in April that year. Despite Soviet support, the regime was overthrown in September 1979, but Afghanistan's new leader, Hafizullah Amin, failed to restore control, a failing that the USSR exploited by invading on December 25. The USSR claimed that it was responding to a request "to render urgent political, moral, military and economic assistance," but U.S. president Jimmy Carter denounced the invasion as a "blatant violation" of international law and "a threat to peace."

THE INVASION

Although the war was to drag on for nearly 10 years, the invasion itself was conducted with lightning speed and efficiency. On the night of December 24–25, 1979, Soviet Special Forces seized Kabul Airport as the prelude to a massive airlift of troops and equipment into the capital. At the same time, motorized divisions of the Red Army rolled across Afghanistan's northern border, covered by squadrons of Soviet fighter planes as they sped southward. Amin was killed two days later, and the pro-Soviet leader Babrak Karmal was then installed in his place.

In terms of political leadership, the USSR had achieved its goal, but in practical terms that meant nothing, because the real struggle for power was being fought in the mountains and deserts of Afghanistan by Muslim guerrillas known as the mujaheddin ("holy warriors"). Like the conflict in Vietnam, it was a war whose casualties shocked the world and a war that humiliated a superpower.

CARTER'S PHONE CALL

Outside Afghanistan, for those more interested in sport than in foreign affairs, the most obvious repercussion of the invasion was the U.S. boycott of the 1980 Moscow Olympics, urged by U.S. president Jimmy Carter, who was swift and firm in his condemnation of the Soviet invasion. On December 31, 1979, Carter told the American public that he had spoken to Soviet leader Leonid Brezhnev, who, Carter said, claimed that the USSR "had been invited by the Afghan government to come in and protect Afghanistan from some outside third-nation threat, [a claim that] was obviously false because the person he claimed invited him in, President Amin, was murdered or assassinated after the Soviets pulled their coup."

Where were you when?

For the first six months, as a member of a propaganda unit, I had close contact with Afghans, driving around mountain villages to hand out food and fuel and show films. We got on well, and whenever we were coming up to a village with mujaheddin in it, they would start to shoot over our heads and we would turn around and head off.

—Vladimir Grigoryev, Russian soldier interviewed for BBC News

Above Afghans gather outside Pulicharkhi prison in Kabul demanding the release of inmates. Although Babrak Karmal's regime released 126 prisoners, some 1,000 Afghans stormed the compound to free another 12 inmates (January 14, 1980).

Opposite Supporters of the Afghan Communist regime march through Kabul on the first anniversary of the Communist April Revolution (April 28, 1979).

1980–1989

1980

TIMELINE

10/22/79 U.S. president Jimmy Carter allows the former Shah of Iran to enter the United States for medical treatment.

11/04/79 Supporters of Ayatollah Khomeini storm the U.S. embassy in Teheran and take some 100 staff and marines hostage.

11/17/79 Khomeini orders the release of all black and female hostages but says that the remaining 53 will stand trial for espionage.

11/21/79 Khomeini warns that if the United States attacks Iran, all the hostages will be killed.

03/08/80 Carter refuses to apologize for U.S. actions in Iran in return for the release of the hostages.

04/07/80 Carter breaks off diplomatic relations with Iran, gives Iranian diplomats 48 hours to leave the United States, freezes Iranian assets, and imposes economic sanctions.

04/24/80– A U.S. military rescue attempt fails
04/25/80 due to helicopter malfunctions, a fiasco compounded by a collision between a helicopter and a tanker plane that kills eight Special Forces personnel.

01/21/81 Khomeini releases the hostages after they have spent 444 days in captivity.

Ayatollah Ruhollah Khomeini (l) is greeted in Teheran on his return to Iran after 15 years in exile in Iraq and France (February 2, 1979).

Failed attempt to rescue U.S. hostages in Iran

Military intervention to rescue U.S. diplomats and embassy staff held hostage in Iran ended in embarrassment for President Jimmy Carter.

On November 4 1979, militant supporters of Iranian leader Ayatollah Khomeini (see below) stormed the U.S. embassy in Teheran in response to U.S. president Jimmy Carter's decision to allow the former Shah of Iran to enter the U.S. for medical treatment. Nearly 100 embassy staff and U.S. Marines were taken hostage, almost half of whom Khomeini released two weeks later with a warning that if the U.S. attacked Iran, the remaining 53 would be killed. Five months later, with the situation still deadlocked, Carter imposed economic sanctions and froze Iran's US assets—and ten days after that, despite Khomeini's warning, Carter announced that military intervention to rescue the hostages was the only course of action left open to him.

OPERATION EAGLE CLAW

On April 24 1980, eight U.S. helicopters landed in the Iranian desert to pick up the 90 commandos who would carry out Operation Eagle Claw, but the secret mission had to be aborted after one helicopter was damaged on landing and two others suffered mechanical failure. Then, as the troops prepared to leave, one of the helicopters collided with a tanker aircraft, killing eight Americans and leaving Carter to explain to the American people: "It was my decision to attempt the rescue operation. It was my decision to cancel it when a problem developed in the placement of the rescue team. The responsibility is purely my own." Fortunately, Khomeini did not carry out his threat to kill the hostages, and after much negotiation they were eventually released in exchange for a ransom, the lifting of sanctions and the release of Iran's frozen assets. But Khomeini had one more humiliation for Carter, delaying the release until the day after Carter's successor, Ronald Reagan, was sworn in as President.

AYATOLLAH KHOMEINI

Ruhollah Musavi was born in Khomeyn (then Persia, now Iran) in 1900 and rose through the ranks of the Shiite Muslim hierarchy to become an ayatollah (an expert in the laws and religion of Islam), taking the title Ayatollah Khomeini. An outspoken opponent of the then Shah of Iran's pro-Western regime, Khomeini was exiled from Iran from 1964 to 1979. Following the overthrow of the Shah, Khomeini returned to Iran and became effectively head of state, leading the Islamic Revolution that returned the country to the strict observance of Islam. In addition to holding U.S. citizens hostage for 444 days, Khomeini is also infamous for declaring a fatwah (religious edict), ordering the death of the author Salman Rushdie for Rushdie's book *The Satanic Verses*.

An American hostage is paraded in front of the cameras by his Iranian captors.

CANADIAN AMBASSADOR AIDS ESCAPE

In the confusion that followed the initial raid on the embassy, six Americans managed to flee the compound and go into hiding. After four days on the run, they contacted the Canadian embassy and were given shelter for 79 days in the private residences of ambassador Ken Taylor and diplomat John Sheardown at great risk to both men and their families. Taylor was eventually able to organize the fugitives' escape by having his staff fly in and out of the country to establish a travel pattern and then issuing the Americans with false Canadian passports so that on January 28, 1980, they were able to simply go to the airport and fly home. Taylor was presented with a Congressional Gold Medal and the Order of Canada for his actions.

Where were you when?

They blindfolded me, and I didn't know what to do. I'd never experienced a blindfold before. I thought maybe they were going to take us out and shoot us. I just didn't know what to expect.

—Bill Belk, Communications Officer, U.S. embassy Teheran, quoted by James Edward Bancroft

Bloody cockup, no other word for it. I was talking to one of the Yank chopper pilots a few months later. He said their maps were wrong and that Intelligence had told them all sorts of things that turned out to be untrue. You've got to feel sorry for the poor buggers, but it was an almighty cockup.

—John Sturgent, Germany

1980

THE SAS

The Special Air Service (SAS) was conceived by Captain David Stirling during World War II while he was recuperating from a parachute accident. Stirling presented the idea to his commanding officer, and the SAS was duly created in 1941 as a desert raiding force known as the "Desert Rats," with the specific aim of undermining German Field Marshal Erwin Rommel's infrastructure in North Africa. The first successful SAS raid took place in North Africa in December 1941, and operations were later extended into Europe, where the SAS played a significant part in the Allied war effort. The regiment protected its anonymity and remained relatively unknown until the spectacular raid on the Iranian embassy was broadcast live around the world.

Above The SAS on the balcony of the Iranian embassy (May 5, 1980).

Opposite Armed and plainclothes police on the balcony during the SAS raid on the Iranian embassy in London (May 5, 1980).

The SAS storm the Iranian embassy in London

In a lightning raid lasting just 11 minutes, British Special Forces rescued 18 of 19 hostages from the Iranian embassy in London.

On April 30, 1980, five terrorists entered the Iranian embassy in Knightsbridge, London, and took 26 hostages, demanding the release of political prisoners being held in Iran by the Ayatollah Khomeini (see p. 180). While the government negotiated with the terrorists, securing the release of five hostages, British Special Forces were planning a rescue operation that was to catapult the Special Air Service (SAS, see left) from semimythical secrecy to international fame. The talking came to an end on May 5 when the terrorists, frustrated at the lack of response from Khomeini, shot one hostage and dumped his body on the steps of the embassy and threatened to murder another every 30 minutes until their demands were met. Now it was time for action.

COUNTER-REVOLUTIONARY WARFARE

Twenty minutes later, television broadcasts around the world were interrupted by pictures of the innocuous-looking white-fronted Georgian building in Knightsbridge, and viewers watched in awed amazement as the rescue unfolded live before them. At the front of the embassy black-uniformed members of the SAS Counter-Revolutionary Warfare team appeared on the first-floor balconies and blew in the window frames, while at the back of the building others abseiled down from the roof and crashed in through the picture windows.

Inside the embassy, policeman Trevor Lock, who had been on duty when the siege began, tackled the terrorist leader and prevented him from killing the first SAS serviceman to enter the building. (Lock was later awarded the George Cross for his action.) The terrorists opened fire on their hostages, killing one, wounding another, and almost killing a third, who was saved when the bullet was deflected by a coin in his pocket. But the SAS were moving quickly through the building and shot four of the five terrorists before they could kill anyone else, the fifth one surviving only because he was protected by hostages who pleaded for his life. It was all over in 11 minutes, with 18 of the remaining 19 hostages hustled to safety out of the now blazing building.

Where were you when?

The live action shots of the SAS bursting in through the windows were astonishing, particularly in such a posh part of London. Window cleaners with attitude, chasing up a nonpayment, perhaps? With hindsight, this was the birth of rolling news TV stations like BBC News 24 and CNN. As a London cyclist, I'd ride past the burned-out building every day and play the images back in my mind.

—Mark Smalley, Bristol, England

1980

BACK FROM THE DEAD

One of the most ludicrous *Dallas* story lines of all began in 1985 when Patrick Duffy decided to leave the series and his character, Bobby Ewing, was killed off in a hit-and-run car accident. Ratings dropped, Larry Hagman persuaded Duffy to return, and the following year the dead Bobby reappeared. His wife, Pam, had remarried and was on her honeymoon when, perhaps in a scriptwriting in-joke for the actor who had played the lead in *The Man from Atlantis*, Bobby stepped out of the shower and asked her for a towel. The explanation was simple: Pam had dreamed the entire intervening series.

Above Actor Patrick Duffy, as Bobby Ewing, returns from the dead in the *Dallas* episode "Blast from the Past" (May 1986).

Who shot J.R.?

In November 1980 more than 100 million people tuned in to the first episode of the new season of *Dallas* to discover who shot J.R.

Dallas **is, to date, the world's most successful** television soap opera. At its peak of popularity, during the 1980s, it was watched regularly by an estimated 83 million viewers in the United States, a then record 76 percent audience share, and it has since been broadcast in more than 90 other countries worldwide. The series ran for 13 years and related the increasingly improbable adventures of the oil-rich, power-crazed, sex-obsessed Ewing family, stretching even soap opera's flexible boundaries for believable story lines.

When *Dallas* first went on air, Patrick Duffy, as Bobby Ewing, was considered to be the star, but before long it was clear that the drama was being driven by Larry Hagman as the evil "J. R." Ewing: a characterization that has been described as "one of the most memorable villains in TV history."

CLIFF-HANGER

Because J.R. was so evil, there were plenty of characters with a motive to kill him, which meant that when he was shot by an unseen assailant at the end of the last episode of the 1979–80 season, there were plenty of possible answers to the question on everyone's lips: "Who shot J.R.?" Trying to guess the answer became an international obsession, with the question discussed in newspapers around the world and the shooting itself even replayed on broadcast news.

The cliff-hanger was not, in fact, a clever ploy for ratings, but the result of a contract dispute that meant the producers were uncertain whether Hagman would return for the next series. It was a long summer for addicts waiting to find out who had shot him and whether he had survived, and in November record numbers of viewers tuned in to discover that he had, of course, survived and that his assailant was his sister-in-law Kristin Shepard, who was pregnant with his baby.

It was a long summer for addicts waiting to find out who had shot him.

Where were you when?

I've never heard anything like it before. All the newspaper and magazine articles, all the media coverage, people gambling in Las Vegas and London... and we hear they actually showed the shooting on BBC News in Britain...I mean...it's incredible.

—Linda Gray, *Dallas* actress, July 1980

All of my life people have thought of me as Bing Crosby's daughter. Now they'll remember me as the person who shot J.R.

—Mary Crosby, who played Kristen, talking after the show

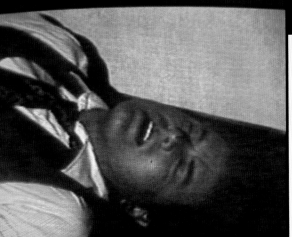

Left Who Shot J.R.?—actor Larry Hagman, as J. R. Ewing, immediately after the shooting.

Above The cast of *Dallas* poses at Southfork ranch: (standing l-r) Patrick Duffy (Bobby Ewing), Victoria Principal (Pamela Barnes Ewing), Barbara Bel Geddes (Eleanor Southworth Ewing, a.k.a. Miss Ellie), Larry Hagman (John Ross Ewing, Jr., a.k.a. J.R.); (front l-r) Charlene Tilton (Lucy Ewing), Jim Davis (John Ross Ewing, a.k.a. Jock), and Linda Gray (Sue Ellen Ewing) (1979).

1980

THE DAKOTA

The Dakota apartment building was designed by architect Henry J. Hardenbergh and completed in 1884, at a time when apartment living was such a novel idea that the buildings were known as "apartment-hotels" or "French flats." The location was considered so remote from downtown New York that the building was named after what was then known as the Dakota Territory (North and South Dakota did not become states of the Union until 1889), but it proved to be a pioneering move that led to the settlement of New York's Upper West Side. The Dakota was one of the buildings that made apartment living respectable, and it soon became one of the city's most prestigious addresses, attracting stars such as Lauren Bacall, Roberta Flack and, of course, the Lennons.

John Lennon is murdered

In December 1980 John Lennon was shot dead outside his New York apartment building by schizophrenic fan Mark David Chapman.

In the early 1970s, after the Beatles disbanded, John Lennon and his wife, Yoko Ono, moved to New York. Lennon's well-known and vociferous anti-establishment outlook meant that it took him four years to secure a green card to live and work in the United States. His application was not helped by the politics expressed on his 1972 album *Sometime in New York City*, but he was eventually accepted and settled at the architecturally renowned Dakota apartment building (see left). The Dakota was to be where he would enjoy some of his happiest moments, but it was also to be where he died.

In 1975 Lennon disappeared from the recording scene and took five years off to bring up his son, Sean, taking out a newspaper advertizement in 1979 to explain his absence. The following year, he recorded the No.1 album *Double Fantasy* with Yoko Ono, and both his personal and professional life seemed to have reached a new high. Then, on December 8, he was shot dead on the steps of the Dakota.

THE SHOOTING

Lennon and Ono were returning from a recording session when they were approached by Mark David Chapman, a so-called fan who had been stalking Lennon for three days and was later diagnosed as schizophrenic. Lennon had signed an autograph for Chapman earlier the same day, but this time Chapman, who claimed that Lennon was the anti-Christ, did not ask for an autograph: Instead he shot Lennon five times at point-blank range with a .38-caliber revolver. Lennon was rushed to Roosevelt Hospital but could not be saved, while Chapman sat around reading *The Catcher in the Rye* as he waited to be arrested.

Lennon fans gather annually at the Dakota, and in a nearby section of Central Park now known as Strawberry Fields, to remember the man who defined the music of one generation and had a lasting influence over the music of the next.

Where were you when?

I was walking south, near 72nd Street, when I heard four shots. I went around the corner and saw Lennon being put into the back of a police car. Some people...said John was hit twice and that the assailant had been crouching in the archway of the Dakota...Lennon arrived in the company of his wife, and the assailant fired.

—Stan Strub, quoted in the *Detroit Free Press,* December 9, 1980

I was five years old in 1980. My mother adored John Lennon. I can still picture her cross-legged on the carpet in front of my grandparent's big wooden stereo console, flipping through her Beatles albums, pointing out to me which one was Paul, Ringo, George and her favorite, John. I sat on my heels next to her and listened. The day John was shot, I had been playing in my bedroom and my mother came in. When I looked up, she had red, bleary eyes and told me, "Somebody shot John Lennon." She sat on the bed and sobbed. I am not sure for how long. I asked her if she thought Yoko would be sad.

—Cristina Ludden, New York

Above Among the crowd gathered in Central Park, New York, to mourn the death of John Lennon, one man holds a photograph of Lennon and Yoko Ono holding a "love-in" peace protest (December 1980).

Opposite A crowd gathers outside the Dakota after news breaks of Lennon's murder. A flag flies at half-mast over the building (December 1980).

1981

BLANKS FIRED AT THE QUEEN

On June 30, 1981, three months after Reagan was shot and just six weeks after the shooting of the pope (see p. 272), a gunman fired six blanks at Britain's queen Elizabeth II as she rode down the Mall for the famous ceremony of the Trooping of the Colour. A look of shock momentarily crossed her face before she leaned forward to reassure her horse and then rode on toward the Horse Guards Parade, looking outwardly as though nothing had happened. Meanwhile, police arrested Marcus Sargeant, who was charged later that afternoon under the Treason Act of 1842. Just as Reagan had been lucky that Hinckley used a .22 instead of a .45, so the queen was lucky that Sargeant had not acted with deadly intent and had fired blanks at her rather than live rounds.

Above Queen Elizabeth II, after blanks were fired at her in Horse Guards Parade, London (June 30, 1981).

Opposite Police and Secret Servicemen rush to surround John Hinckley after he fired six shots at President Reagan (March 30, 1981).

Assassination attempt on Ronald Reagan

On March 30, 1981, Ronald Reagan came within inches of being the fifth U.S. president to be assassinated in office.

Ronald Reagan had been in office for just two months and ten days when he was shot and wounded by a disenchanted disc jockey on the streets of Washington, D.C. Apart from the physical danger to Reagan, the shooting also revealed a jittery administration not yet prepared for such an emergency.

The 70-year-old president had been addressing a gathering of trade unionists at the Hilton Hotel. As he left the hotel, he raised his arm to wave to the crowd and then looked up in surprise as a man fired six shots from just 10 ft./3 m away, hitting Reagan's press secretary, a secret serviceman, and a Washington policeman, as well as Reagan himself. Seconds later the assailant had been pinned against a wall, surrounded by secret servicemen, and Reagan's bodyguards had shoved the president bodily into his car. Reagan was immediately rushed to George Washington Hospital, where he told the medical staff, "I hope you guys are Republicans."

"HONEY, I FORGOT TO DUCK"

Republicans or not, surgeons removed a .22-caliber bullet from Reagan's left lung, where it had lodged just 3 in./76 mm from his heart. One surgeon pointed out that if the gunman, later identified as John Hinckley III, had been using a .45, "he would have blown him away"—a comment that did not help to calm nerves in a government whose Secretary of State, Alexander Haig, was in such a panic that he erroneously informed the press that he was the next in line to the presidency after Reagan and Vice President George Bush.

Reagan himself seemed less ruffled than his underlings, and when his wife, Nancy, visited him at the hospital, he reminded the world of his Hollywood background by quoting from a 1930s film, telling her, "Honey, I forgot to duck."

Where were you when?

I was almost to the car when I heard what sounded like two or three firecrackers over to my left—just a small fluttering sound, pop, pop, pop. *Just then, Jerry Parr, the head of our Secret Service unit, grabbed me by the waist and literally hurled me into the back of the limousine.*

—Ronald Reagan, in his autobiography, published by Simon & Schuster

I remember Peter Jennings on ABC announcing the shooting, and the big "Welcome Home" banners hanging from White House balconies when Reagan returned.

—John Coulter, San Diego

1981

THE DRESS

The design of Diana's dress has been described as "the best-kept fashion secret of the century." The pundits promised that Diana would look like a fairy princess and tried to predict, based on the previous work of its designers, Elizabeth and David Emmanuel, what the dress might be like, but nothing prepared the world for Diana's splendor on the day. The ivory silk dress with its scooped neck and full skirt and sleeves was a romantic break with relatively austere royal tradition, and it sported a 25 ft./7.6 m train described by one newspaper as "a stream of mist." As soon as the dress appeared on television (as Diana left Clarence House), Ellis Bridals Ltd. began making a copy that, five hours later, was on sale for $830/£450 in Debenhams department store on Oxford Street.

The wedding of Charles and Diana

The marriage of Charles and Diana was the most-watched wedding in history, seen on television by 750 million people in 74 countries.

For most of the 1970s, Prince Charles was considered one of the world's most eligible bachelors, and Britain's tabloid press spent the decade linking him with nearly every woman who stood close to him. Then, on September 8, 1980, *The Sun* newspaper broke the news of the romance that was to lead to "the wedding of the century": Charles was courting kindergarten assistant Lady Diana Spencer. Less than five months later, on February 6, 1981, Charles proposed to Diana. Within days Diana had chosen a $53,000/£28,500 diamond-and-sapphire ring from Garrard's, the crown jewelers, and at 11:00 A.M. on February 24 Buckingham Palace officially announced the engagement.

THE WEDDING OF THE CENTURY

The wedding took place on July 29, 1981, at St. Paul's Cathedral, London. Celebrations began the night before when some half a million people gathered in Hyde Park to watch a firework display as Charles lit the first of more than 100 bonfires, a chain of beacons that stretched across the country. The next morning an estimated 750 million people around the globe watched on television as Diana left the Queen Mother's home, Clarence House, and traveled with her father in a horse-drawn carriage to St. Paul's. In keeping with tradition, she arrived a minute late at the cathedral before walking resplendently up the aisle in an ivory silk dress (see opposite) to join Charles at the altar, where nerves got the better of them—both made slight mistakes in their vows, which simply endeared them more to the public. After the ceremony the newlyweds returned to Buckingham Palace for the wedding breakfast and the obligatory appearance on the balcony, where their public kiss became one of the most famous wedding photographs in history.

Left "That Kiss" on the balcony of Buckingham Palace (July 29, 1981).

Far left A sketch of Diana's wedding dress, designed by David and Elizabeth Emmanuel.

Where were you when?

At the wedding rehearsal yesterday I got my heel stuck in some grating in the cathedral and everyone was saying, "Hurry up, Diana." I said, "I can't, I'm stuck."

—Diana, Princess of Wales

I definitely remember what I was doing while Charles and Diana were getting married! I came home to an empty flat and looked out of the kitchen window to see my "beloved" driving off with the dog looking out of the back window. Never to be seen again.

—Tony Edlin, Hertford, England

1982

03/19/82 Argentinian scrap merchants land and raise the Argentinian flag on the uninhabited British Crown colony of South Georgia.

04/01/82– Argentinian forces invade the
04/02/82 British Crown colony of the Falkland Islands.

04/04/82 The first warships leave Britain as part of a military task force being assembled to retake the islands.

04/22/82 The British naval task force arrives in Falklands waters.

04/25/82 Royal Marines retake South Georgia.

05/02/82 Argentinian cruiser *General Belgrano* is controversially sunk by British nuclear submarine HMS *Conqueror*.

05/04/82 British destroyer HMS *Sheffield* is sunk by an Exocet missile.

05/21/82 Some 5,000 British troops are landed on the Falklands at Port San Carlos.

05/28/82 British forces take Darwin and Goose Green.

06/06/82– A second large contingent of British
06/08/82 troops is landed at Bluff Cove.

06/14/82 The Argentinians surrender when British forces retake the capital, Port Stanley.

06/17/82 General Galtieri is deposed as president of Argentina.

07/11/82 The new Argentinian leadership formally acknowledges that hostilities are at an end.

The Falklands War

After claiming sovereignty of the Falklands, Argentina invaded the islands in April 1982. Two months later Britain took them back.

The Falklands War, or Falklands Conflict, as British government spin doctors insisted on calling it, was a short but bloody campaign in which Britain succeeded in regaining control of a Crown colony some 8,000 miles from home. The Falkland Islands had been under British control since 1833, but Argentina claimed *Las Malvinas*, as they called them, as part of Argentina's inheritance from the Spanish empire. Britain had discussed ways of transferring control of the islands to Argentina, but in 1980 the islanders, who wanted to remain British, rejected the proposals. Then, on the night of April 1–2, 1982, a large Argentinian force landed on the Falklands and within three hours overwhelmed the 70 Royal Marines who were garrisoned there.

TASK FORCE

British prime minister Margaret Thatcher was determined to retake the islands, a stance supported by the Opposition, which agreed that "it is our duty to defend the right of the Falkland islanders to stay British." A task force of more than 70 ships was immediately assembled, comprising 44 warships with auxiliary and air support, as well as a number of merchant ships requisitioned as troopships. As the task force steamed southward, the Argentinians refused, in Thatcher's words, to "reconsider its rejection of diplomacy"—this despite a UN directive to withdraw, diplomatic intervention from the United States and economic sanctions imposed by the European community. By the time the task force arrived in Falklands waters on April 22, it was clear that the Argentinian president, General Galtieri, was not going to give up *Las Malvinas* without a fight.

WAR

On May 1 the British began bombing the airfield at Port Stanley, the islands' capital, but the war did not begin in earnest until May 2, when the British submarine HMS *Conqueror* controversially sank the Argentinian cruiser *General Belgrano*, killing 368 Argentine sailors (see opposite). Two days later the Argentinians responded by sinking the British destroyer HMS *Sheffield* (the first major British warship to be sunk since World War II), killing

Where were you when?

The nation has been told that we are not at war, we are at conflict.

—Adrian Mole, fictional hero of Sue Townsend's *The Diary of Adrian Mole, aged 13½*

We (we!) drop leaflets on the Argentine troops based in Port Stanley, urging them to lay down their arms. Were such leaflets dropped on our troops, we would consider them contemptible and ludicrous; our leaflets are represented as a great humanitarian gesture.

—Alan Bennett, playwright, diary entry for June 4, 1982

20 British sailors, but despite such devastating attacks, the task force succeeded in moving into position to land troops and launch a ground assault.

After clandestine raids by Special Forces, the main British counterinvasion began on May 21 when some 5,000 troops went ashore at San Carlos Bay on East Falkland. During the next week, British forces recaptured key settlements including Darwin, Goose Green and Fitzroy before linking up with reinforcements who had been landed at Bluff Cove for the final assault on Port Stanley. This last battle lasted from June 11–14 and entailed breaking a ring of Argentine defenses surrounding the capital. Six separate engagements finally drove the Argentinians into Port Stanley itself, where, according to one newspaper, "white flags began to blossom like flowers." At a cost of 255 British and 652 Argentinian lives, the Falklands were back in British hands, reviving the waning popularity of Thatcher's government and leading to Galtieri's removal from power.

Above British frigate HMS *Antelope* takes a direct hit in San Carlos Bay, East Falkland.

Opposite Lance-Corporal Gary Hearn of the Royal Signals gives Sandra Kelly a farewell kiss before leaving for the South Atlantic as part of the British task force (May 12, 1982).

Below British Prime Minister Margaret Thatcher meets personnel aboard HMS *Antim* during her five-day visit to the Falkland Islands (8 January 1983)

THE SINKING OF THE *BELGRANO*

The most controversial act of the Falklands War was the sinking of the Argentinian cruiser *General Belgrano*, which at the time was some 30 miles outside a 200-mile exclusion zone declared by Britain around the islands. Justification for the attack rested on the disputed issue of whether or not the *Belgrano* was steaming toward or away from the exclusion zone and the British task force; the Argentinian government described the sinking as "a treacherous act of armed aggression," while British prime minister Margaret Thatcher defended it as the removal of "a very obvious threat to British forces." The *Belgrano*, originally named *Phoenix*, had been sold to Argentina by the United States after World War II, and was the last surviving warship of those attacked at Pearl Harbor (see p. 22).

1983

BLACK FRIDAY

The most extensive bushfires Australia has experienced in the 20th century raged across Victoria from December 1938 to January 1939, killing 71 people and destroying between 3.7 and 5 million acres (1.5 and 2 million hectares). The fires peaked on Friday, January 13, known thereafter as Black Friday, and ended on January 15 after statewide rainfall. A Royal Commission described the fires as being "the most disastrous forest calamity the State of Victoria has known," which remains true to this day. The commission led to increased fire awareness and better prevention measures, and for more than 60 years no fires spread on anything approaching the same scale until the Eastern Victorian Fires of January 2003. Started by lightning, they burned for 59 days, destroying more than 3 million acres (1.2 million hectares).

Ash Wednesday bushfires

On "Ash Wednesday," February 16, 1983, more than 100 bushfires raged across Victoria and South Australia, killing 75 people.

The natural environment of Victoria, in Australia's southeast, is one of the most fire-prone areas in the world. In summer, high temperatures and low rainfall produce conditions of very high fire danger in the state's large eucalypt forests. Added to this, sudden wind changes, which can quickly cause fires to rage out of control, are common. Victoria has suffered bushfires throughout its history, two of the most horrific being Black Friday in 1939 (see sidebar) and Ash Wednesday in 1983.

Toward the end of 1982, after a drought lasting for more than 10 months, Victoria's firefighters began preparing for the worst, organizing extra personnel and equipment. On November 24 a Total Fire Ban day was declared, the earliest ever. The first big bushfire broke out the next day, followed by four more big fires on December 3 and 13, January 8, and February 1.

ASH WEDNESDAY

February 1983 was one of the hottest and driest on record. On Wednesday, February 16, more than 100 fires broke out. (Some estimates put the number as high as 180.) Fanned by a hot, dry northerly wind, they developed into long, narrow fires running in a southerly direction. Strong winds lifted 200,000 tons of dried soil from the ground, forming a dust cloud so large and thick that it blocked out the sun in Melbourne. Spot fires broke out ahead of the main fire and joined up. Then came a catastrophic blow—the wind swung to the west, causing the main fire to change direction. The long sides became long raging fronts moving at devastating speed. The terrible hour that followed saw the greatest number of lives lost and properties destroyed.

Where Were You When?

I could not believe the speed at which the flames moved... there's no way you could have beaten it running.

—Unnamed resident of Warrnambool, western Victoria

The sky was brownish red and I knew it was a bushfire that had created a dust storm. It was 43 degrees Celsius that day. Some of the women...started to scream. They hadn't been in Australia very long and had never seen anything like this before. They thought the world was going to end.

—Craig Lapsley, Deputy Chief Officer, Country Fire Authority of Victoria (recalling the events 21 years later)

More than 17,500 firefighters, police, and defense force personnel helped to fight the Ash Wednesday fires, using some 400 vehicles, 11 helicopters, and 14 fixed-wing aircraft. In Victoria, the fires killed 47 people and destroyed some 519,000 acres (210,000 hectares) and over 2,000 homes, causing more than $200 million worth of damage. In neighboring South Australia 28 people were killed, 383 houses destroyed, and almost 570,000 acres (230,000 hectares) burned, at a similar financial cost.

AIDS

With the 1980s came the first recognition of a frightening medical syndrome that, by the turn of the millennium, would be affecting an estimated 36 million people worldwide. During 1980 and 1981 American doctors began to notice a pattern of illness among homosexual men that suggested they were being infected by a new type of sexually transmitted disease, and in December 1981 the first public announcement was made of an unnamed disease that the media reported as "a new type of lung infection and skin cancer [that] may be common in homosexuals. It appears to destroy the body's immune system so that after a period of weight loss the victim succumbs to infections."

In 1982 the mystery disease was named AIDS, an acronym for Acquired Immunodeficiency Syndrome, and the following year French scientists identified the virus responsible: the Human Immunodeficiency Virus, or HIV, which attacks the body's immune system. The basic media outline of the syndrome was correct: AIDS *is* characterized by wasting, and victims often suffer from the lung disease *Pneumocystis carinii* (a rare form of pneumonia) and the cancerous condition Kaposi's sarcoma, among other illnesses, once their immune systems have been destroyed. However, the assumption that it was a "gay plague" proved wholly inaccurate and tragically damaging, both for the gay and heterosexual communities—for gays because many people claimed that they had "brought it upon themselves," hindering a unified approach to containing AIDS, and for heterosexuals because complacency led to the

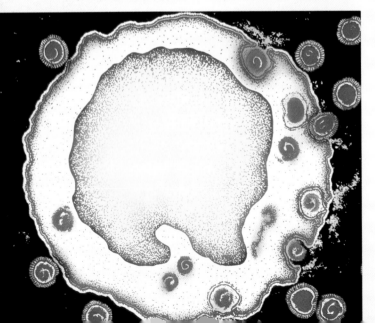

further spread of the disease beyond its initial high-risk group. By the end of 1984, it was clear that along with gays, AIDS was also rife among promiscuous heterosexuals of both genders, intravenous drug users and many other people, particularly hemophiliacs, who had received transfusions of infected blood.

CURBING THE SPREAD OF AIDS

By then it was known that HIV is spread by the exchange of infected blood or bodily fluids—knowledge that enabled steps

Artwork based on a transmission electron micrograph of AIDS virus particles, in red, erupting from and destroying a T-4 lymphocyte white blood cell.

Larry Kramer, author, gay activist and founder of ACT UP, comforts his friend, author Vito Russo, who is suffering from AIDS (June 1990).

to be taken to slow down the spread of AIDS. These steps included the screening of blood before transfusion, the advocacy of the use of condoms, and the provision of clean needles to prevent drug users from sharing them—the last two steps being roundly condemned in some quarters as encouraging sexual promiscuity and drug use.

In July 1985 public attitudes toward AIDS changed enormously when film star Rock Hudson became the first high-profile celebrity to announce that he was suffering from the disease. Confirmation of the open secret about Hudson's homosexuality did little to dispel the myth that AIDS was a gay plague, but his star profile did ensure that with his death on October 2 that year, AIDS was brought into the public eye—a

vital step toward encouraging public awareness, education and a greater understanding of the dangers of the disease.

No cure for HIV infection or AIDS has yet been discovered, but in 1987 the drug azidothymidine (AZT) was licensed in the United States as a means of inhibiting the action of the enzyme that HIV uses to reproduce, thus extending the period between the detection of HIV and the onset of AIDS. Further research has shown that certain combinations of AZT and other antiviral drugs can decrease HIV in the blood to minuscule levels for prolonged periods, raising hopes of an eventual cure.

1984

TIMELINE

1969 Intel develops the microprocessor, dubbed "the computer on a chip."

1970s The existence of microprocessors leads to the development of the "microcomputer" and the advent of computer hobbyists' groups such as the Homebrew Computer Club in Silicon Valley, California.

1975 The Altair 8800 computer, sold in kit form, becomes the first successful hobby computer.

1976 Steve Jobs and Steve Wozniak found Apple Computer.

04/77 Apple Computer launches the Apple II, the first "home/personal computer," which creates a revolution in home computing.

1979 Dan Bricklin and Bob Frankston write the first spreadsheet program, VisiCalc, for the Apple II, prompting the transition of home computers into corporate business.

1981 IBM launches the IBM PC, legitimizing the personal computer, setting the industry standard and ultimately leaving Apple with a small market share.

1983 Microsoft launches the first, unsuccessful, version of Windows (see p. 229).

01/84 Apple launches the Macintosh (Mac), with a mouse and graphical user interface (GUI), again revolutionizing the computer industry.

04/92 Microsoft launches the more successful Windows 3.1.

Apple launches the Mac

Apple pioneered both the personal computer and the graphical user interface, but it was IBM and Microsoft that cornered the market.

Fifty years ago there were only some 250 computers in the world. These valve-operated "mainframes" took up entire rooms, cost hundreds of thousands of dollars and took days to process calculations. Then in 1969 the advent of the microprocessor created a revolution that led to the development of so-called microcomputers, which were sold in kit form and were of little interest to anyone other than "hobbyists" with technical expertise. But that all changed in April 1977, when hobbyists Steve Jobs and Steve Wozniak launched the world's first "home/personal computer," the Apple II. Instead of users having to buy the components separately and build their computer themselves, everything arrived ready assembled, with a keyboard and a visual display unit (screen). The Apple II revolutionized the computer industry and led to the development of hundreds of other personal computers by other manufacturers. The company that eventually cornered the market was IBM, whose IBM PC, launched in 1981, set the standard that most manufacturers were to follow, until some 85 percent of PCs were IBM compatible, leaving Apple with only a small market share.

THE MAC

Then, in 1984, Apple did it again. Until that time most computer users had to type text commands via a keyboard in order to get their computer to do anything. In the early 1980s the Xerox Corporation developed the concept of a "graphical user interface" (GUI), which provided graphics on screen instead of rows of written commands and enabled users to operate the computer by using a mouse (see "The Applemouse," opposite) to point and click at the on-screen graphics. Steve Jobs acquired this technology, improved it and launched it in January 1984 as the defining feature of the Apple Macintosh. Apple had once again revolutionized the industry, this time with its GUI, but was once again squeezed out of the market when Microsoft was stung into improving the Windows GUI operating system it had developed for IBM PCs (see p. 229).

Where were you when?

Using a computer generally means using Microsoft's Windows 95, software so intuitive that you press a button marked "Start" to shut the computer down. Or so I'm told: I have always used Apple machines, having bought almost every model since the 1984 Macintosh.

...Not for the first time has the best technology failed to win out, and Microsoft's dreadful mockery of Apple's approach has come to dictate the way most people interact with their computer.

—James Dyson, design engineer, in his book *James Dyson's History of Great Inventions*

Steve Jobs with the revolutionary new Apple Macintosh computer, a.k.a. the Mac (January 30, 1984).

Steve Jobs acquired this technology, improved it and launched it in January 1984 as the defining feature of the Apple Macintosh.

THE APPLEMOUSE

Steve Jobs is sometimes credited with inventing the mouse, because the first time an "X-Y position indicator for a display system" was used commercially was with the Apple Lisa, a precursor of the Macintosh. The Applemouse was developed for Jobs by Dean Hovey and David Kelley, whose first prototype was made from a butter dish and a roll-on deodorant ball. Hovey later described the intricate design process behind this technological breakthrough: "Over the weekend I hacked together a simple spatial prototype of what this thing might be, with Teflon and a ball. The first mouse had a Ban Roll-On ball." The end product was eventually tested by logging hundreds of "mouse miles" on the spinning turntable of a record player.

1984

LORD MOUNTBATTEN KILLED

On August 27, 1979, the IRA murdered Queen Elizabeth II's cousin, 79-year-old Lord Louis Mountbatten, during the annual holiday that he habitually took in the fishing village of Mullaghmore in the Irish Republic. A bomb on board his boat *Shadow V* was detonated by remote control as Mountbatten and his family left Mullaghmore harbor, destroying the boat and killing Mountbatten, his 15-year-old grandson and a 15-year-old local boatman. Four other members of the party were injured, one of whom died later in the hospital. Since the IRA claimed responsibility for the "execution," U.S. president Jimmy Carter said he was "profoundly shocked and saddened," and the Irish Deputy prime minister said, "I know all Irish people will join me in condemning this cowardly and heartless outrage."

Right The wrecked façade of the Grand Hotel, Brighton, after it was bombed by the IRA (October 12, 1984).

Below Prime minister Margaret Thatcher addresses the Conservative Party conference in Brighton the day after the bombing (October 13, 1984).

GRAND

The Brighton bomb

On October 12, 1984, the IRA came close to killing several members of the British Cabinet with a bomb planted in a Brighton hotel.

During the 1970s and 1980s the IRA (Irish Republican Army) planted scores of bombs in the city centers of Northern Ireland and the British mainland, killing and maiming hundreds of innocent civilians. They also occasionally focused on high-profile individual targets, killing politicians and even one member of the royal family (see "Lord Mountbatten Killed," opposite) with car bombs and other devices. But in October 1984 they perpetrated the most audacious attack on the British government since the Gunpowder Plot was foiled on November 5, 1605. On that occasion Guy Fawkes was caught before the perpetrators could blow up the Houses of Parliament, but in 1984 the bomb exploded, killing five people and injuring more than 30 others, including Margaret Tebbit, the wife of the trade and industry secretary, who was left paralyzed from the neck down.

"LIFE MUST GO ON"

The bomb went off at 2:54 A.M. in a sixth-floor bathroom of the Grand Hotel in Brighton, where most of the senior members of the Conservative Party were staying for the party's annual conference. Several guests plunged through several stories as floors gave way and the central part of the hotel façade collapsed. Prime Minister Margaret Thatcher had reportedly just left a bathroom that was destroyed but escaped injury as she sat in the lounge of her suite working on her conference speech. Despite the trauma of the attack, which she described as an attempt "to cripple Her Majesty's democratically elected government," she arrived punctually at the conference later that morning, saying, "Life must go on."

The IRA immediately claimed responsibility for the attack and sent out a chilling warning to the government: "Today we were unlucky, but remember—we only have to be lucky once. You will have to be lucky always."

Where were you when?

This was shocking, and morally very challenging for me, because I hated Margaret Thatcher and everything that she stood for. Yet here was an attempt to kill an entire government, in their beds. I was also in bed when it happened, just a mile down the road, with my girlfriend. Even tho' we didn't hear the explosion, we heard it reported on the morning news bulletin, and I still recall the shock and the mixed emotions. And the bad jokes that followed for years afterward.

—Mark Smalley, Bristol, England

1984

TIMELINE
(INDUSTRIAL ACCIDENTS)

04/26/42 A mining disaster in Hinkeiko, China, kills 1,549 miners.

04/16/47 An explosion of ammonium nitrate stored on the freighter *Grandcamp* in the port of Texas City kills 752 people.

11/09/63 A mining disaster in Omuta, Japan, kills 447 miners.

11/19/84 An explosion at the PEMEX gas plant in Ecatepec, Mexico, kills 540 people.

12/03/84 A gas leak at the Union Carbide chemical plant in Bhopal, India, kills 2,500 people.

07/06/88 An explosion and fire on the Piper Alpha oil rig in the North Sea kills 173 people.

06/03/89 An explosion of liquid gas stored beside a railway in Chelyabinsk, USSR, kills up to 800 people.

04/22/92 Explosions after gas leaks into sewers in Guadalajara, Mexico, kill 230 people.

05/10/93 A fire in a doll factory in Bangkok, Thailand, kills 187 people.

Above A young victim of the Bhopal disaster (December 6, 1984).

Disaster at Bhopal

In the worst industrial accident of the century, a gas leak at a Union Carbide chemical plant in Bhopal, India, killed 2,500 people.

Most people had not heard of methyl isocyanate before 1984, but on December 4 that year, it hit the headlines in the worst possible way when large amounts of this deadly poisonous gas leaked from a chemical works and pesticide factory close to the densely populated city of Bhopal. At least 2,000 people were killed almost immediately by the gas, which is a derivative of cyanide, and another 500 died in the days that followed the leak, many of them suffering liver or kidney failure as their bodies tried to process the poison. The leak affected the health of another 200,000 people, with at least 20,000 people being blinded or disabled by the gas. It was the worst industrial accident in modern history and affected not only workers at the plant but also people living in the deprived areas of the city close by.

COMPENSATION

The immediate task was to treat those who were suffering, many of whom had to wait days to be treated for their painfully burning eyes and to find out whether they would see again. Meanwhile, the Indian government declared Bhopal an official disaster area and called in the army and the local militia to begin collecting the dead bodies of people and animals that lay in the streets where they had fallen. According to one report, "The skies over Bhopal glowed red from hundreds of funeral pyres."

After the grief came anger at the owner of the plant, American company Union Carbide—anger that was fanned when one newspaper reported that there had been four previous minor leaks from the factory. The safety standards of all foreign companies operating factories in India were questioned at the government level, and Union Carbide pledged to treat compensation claims as if the accident had occurred in America, eventually paying more than $470 million to the Indian government.

"The skies over Bhopal glowed red from hundreds of funeral pyres."

ECATEPEC

On November 19, 1984, less than a month before the disaster at Bhopal, 540 people were killed and more than 260 injured in an explosion at the PEMEX natural-gas processing plant in Ecatepec, a suburb of Mexico City, Mexico. A series of explosions began when a lorry carrying cooking gas cylinders caught fire, and before long the entire plant was ablaze, sending flames 300 ft./91 m into the air and igniting wooden shacks in the neighboring slums. Like Bhopal, the explosion did not only affect those in the plant—many of the dead were pulled from the rubble of a supermarket nearby. Ecatepec was one of the world's worst industrial accidents to that date, which gives some perspective on the scale of the Bhopal disaster, in which the death toll was five times higher.

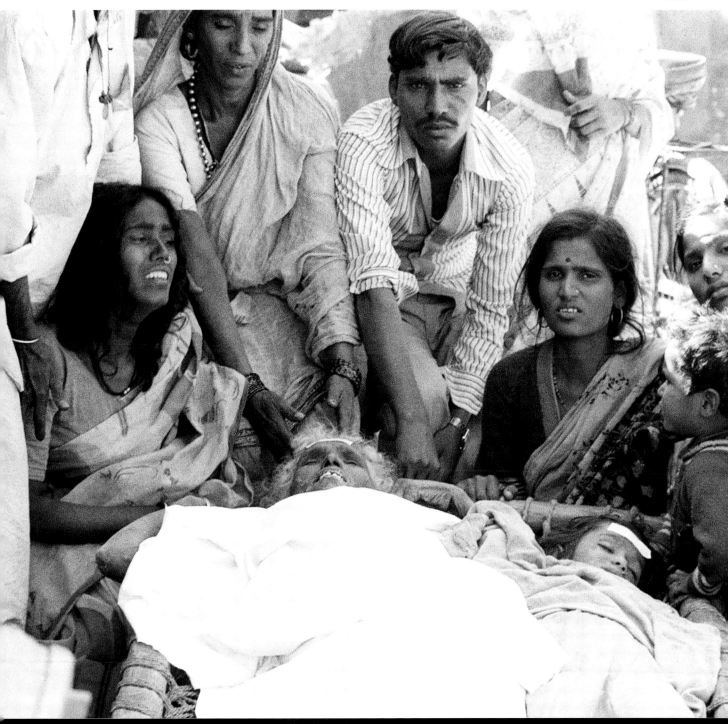

Relatives mourn victims of the Bhopal disaster (December 4, 1984).

Where were you when?

At about 12:30 A.M. I woke to the sound of Ruby coughing badly. The room was not dark but lighted by a streetlight, right outside. In the half-light I saw that the room was filled with a white cloud. I heard a lot of people shouting. They were shouting "Bhago, bhago" [Run, run]. Then Mohsin started coughing too and then I started coughing, with each breath seeming as if we were breathing in fire. Our eyes were burning too…. Meanwhile, other members of the family were also coughing and groaning. They closed all the doors and windows to stop more gas from coming in.

—Aziza Sultan, Sambhavna Trust statement 2004

1985

MICHAEL BUERK'S REPORT ON THE ETHIOPIAN FAMINE

In 1984 the Ethiopian rains failed for the sixth season running, and a humanitarian crisis became a catastrophe. Tens of thousands of people left their homes in search of aid, many of them dying at the side of the road or in the camps, where they congregated when they found they had nowhere else to go. On October 24 that year, BBC correspondent Michael Buerk filed a report on the famine that subsequently aired on 425 television stations around the world, and it was this report that prompted Bob Geldof to initiate the Christmas single. At first Buerk was skeptical about what good a record could do, but he said later, "I went back to Ethiopia a fortnight after Christmas and there were about eight Hercules on the ground [unloading aid].... It was impressive."

A man carrying a starving child during the famine in Ethiopia (October 25, 1984).

Live Aid

Live Aid brought together the world's biggest rock stars for two concerts that raised more than $90 million for starving Africans.

Like many others, Irish rock star Bob Geldof was deeply moved by television coverage of the 1984 famine in Ethiopia. Unlike many others, he decided to do something about it. That year, he established the Band Aid charitable trust and then persuaded 40 of Britain's biggest rock and pop stars to record the single "Do They Know It's Christmas?," which became Britain's biggest-selling single of all time and raised $15 million for the cause. But this was not enough for Geldof, and the following summer, on July 13, he galvanized not just Britain's but the world's biggest stars into performing for free in two simultaneous concerts. Officially known as Live Aid, the concerts were

Where were you when?

It was only when I walked on stage with the band that the romance of it and the hugeness of it got to me .... Time became elastic, like I stood there for hours and my hand just stayed in midair.

—Bob Geldof, rock musician, organizer of Live Aid, interviewed by Carl Wilkinson for The Observer Music Monthly magazine

I was supposed to do a live broadcast from the Concorde. The captain obviously knew about it and said I could do it, but I wasn't supposed to tell anybody.... Here he was telling me not to tell anybody, and the broadcast's going out to 1.5 billion people.

—Phil Collins, rock musician, interviewed by Carl Wilkinson for The Observer Music Monthly magazine broadcast live to 1.5 billion people, or one quarter of the world's population, in 160 different countries and were soon dubbed the "global jukebox."

17 MINUTES EACH

Egos were left at home as performers were given just 17 minutes each to strut their stuff, with a "traffic light" system to warn them to get off stage in time for the next act. Proceedings began at midday at Wembley Stadium in London with rock perennials Status Quo performing "Rockin' All Over the World" and continued for 16 hours, overlapping with a second concert on the other side of the Atlantic at JFK Stadium in Philadelphia. Phil Collins, singer-drummer of supergroup Genesis, managed to appear at both concerts thanks to the Concorde, but even this feat was eclipsed by Queen's performance toward the end of the evening (with Freddie Mercury at his strutting, pouting, audience-rousing best) and by the return of all the stars to the stage to sing the anthem whose title said it all: "Feed the World."

Freddie [Mercury] *was our secret weapon. He was able to reach out to everyone in that stadium effortlessly, and I think it was really his night.*

—Brian May, guitarist with Queen, interviewed by Carl Wilkinson for *The Observer Music Monthly* magazine

The only thing I remember of the day is stabbing Mick [Jagger] *in the foot with my high heels. Then they put us on the cover of* Life *magazine.*

—Tina Turner, rock goddess, interviewed by Carl Wilkinson for *The Observer Music Monthly* magazine

Above The *Live Aid* concert, Wembley Stadium, London (July 13, 1985).

Top Organizers Midge Ure (l) and Bob Geldof onstage at the *Live Aid* concert.

1986

COLUMBIA DISASTER

On February 1, 2003, the space shuttle *Columbia* exploded on re-entering Earth's atmosphere, just 16 minutes from home at the end of a 16-day mission. As *Columbia* crossed the skies some 40 miles above New Mexico at 18 times the speed of sound, heat sensors failed and the shuttle began experiencing excessive drag. A minute later mission control lost contact with *Columbia*, which was now over Texas, and witnesses on the ground heard a huge bang and saw several white smoke trails in the clear sky. The day before, one of the seven astronauts had sent an e-mail to her family and friends that ended, "This was definitely one [adventure] to beat all. I hope you could feel the positive energy that beamed to the whole planet as we glided over our shared planet."

Above Crew members of the space shuttle *Columbia* pose weightlessly during their mission. Top row (l-r) David M. Brown, William C. McCool, Michael P. Anderson; bottom row (l-r) Kalpana Chawla, Rick D. Husband, Laurel B. Clark, Ilan Ramon. This picture was on a roll of unprocessed film later recovered from the wreckage (January 2003).

The *Challenger* disaster

NASA's space shuttle program had a perfect safety record until January 28, 1986, when *Challenger* exploded 74 seconds after liftoff.

Shuttle flights were becoming routine by 1986, but *Challenger*'s flight on January 28 was special because, under NASA's Space Flight Participation scheme, it was the first time that an ordinary citizen had been able to join the highly trained astronauts on the mission. Thousands of civilians watched on television with a tinge of envy, thinking, "That could have been me," as 37-year-old Christa McAuliffe, who had been chosen from 11,000 schoolteachers applying for the place, made her way to the shuttle with the six other crew members. At Cape Kennedy, McAuliffe's husband and two children watched with the families of the other astronauts as *Challenger* lifted off, accelerated to twice the speed of sound, and climbed to a height of about 10 miles before suddenly exploding in a massive ball of flame and smoke.

ASTEROIDS

The voice recorders indicate that the crew was unaware of any problem until just one second before the explosion. As the shuttle reached maximum acceleration after 60 seconds, with flames already trailing from one of the booster rockets, pilot Michael Smith exclaimed, "Feel that mother go!" Twelve seconds later the booster rocket broke away from the fuel tank, and a second after that Smith said, "Uh-oh," probably in response to the instruments indicating falling fuel pressure. A second after that the shuttle exploded.

Subsequent investigations showed the cause of the disaster to be a faulty rubber "O-ring seal" on the booster rocket, creating a flame that quickly spread and ignited the shuttle's liquid oxygen and hydrogen fuel, causing the explosion. On March 26, 1986, Soviet astronomers named seven asteroids in honor of the seven crew members who died in the accident: mission commander Francis R. (Dick) Scobee, Gregory B. Jarvis, Ronald E. McNair, Ellison S. Onizuka, Judith A. Resnik, Michael J. Smith and Christa McAuliffe.

Where were you when?

Pilot: There's Mach one.
Commander: Going through 19,000.
Commander: OK, we're throttling down.
Commander: Throttling up.
Pilot: Throttle up.
Commander: Roger.
Pilot: Feel that mother go. Woooohoooo.
Pilot: 35,000 going through one point five.

Commander: Reading four eighty six on mine.
Pilot: Yep, that's what I've got, too.
Commander: Roger, go at throttle up.
Pilot: Uh-oh.

—Transcript of voice-box recording conversation in the cockpit of *Challenger*, NASA website

Above *Challenger* explodes (January 28, 1986).

Left President Ronald Reagan (3rd from r) and White House aides watch a television replay of the *Challenger* disaster in the president's private study.

1986

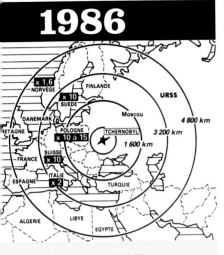

TIMELINE

04/26/86 The top blows off the No. 4 reactor at Chernobyl nuclear power station in the Ukraine.

04/30/86 After high radiation levels are recorded in Scandinavia, the USSR finally acknowledges that an "accident" has occurred, giving no hint of its seriousness.

05/86 Winds carry the radioactive cloud over Soviet and European states including Austria, Belarus, Britain, Czechoslovakia, Denmark, Finland, Germany, Greece, Ireland, Italy, Norway, Poland, Portugal, Romania, Russia, Sicily, Spain, Sweden, Switzerland, Turkey and Ukraine.

03/96 A European Union inquiry into the disaster concludes that up to 30 million Ukrainians might be at risk from radioactivity, mainly from contaminated water washed into rivers. The report states that fish in Lake Kozhanov, 156 miles from Chernobyl, have 60 times the permitted level of radiation.

04/10/96 At a conference in Vienna, a minute's silence is held for the "past, present and future" victims of Chernobyl.

Above French map showing the areas affected by the radioactive fallout from Chernobyl.

Opposite Computer-enhanced satellite picture of Chernobyl after the accident, taken from an altitude of more than 400 miles: The red areas are radioactive.

Chernobyl

In the world's worst nuclear accident, an explosion at the Chernobyl power station scattered radiation over much of the USSR and Europe.

Opponents of nuclear power had long predicted such a disaster, while its supporters had claimed it could never happen. In the early hours of April 26, 1986, the top blew off one of the four reactors at Chernobyl nuclear power station in the Ukraine, releasing a radioactive cloud that was to contaminate more than 20 countries and would eventually be detected as far away as North America. On April 25 unusually warm weather prompted a decision to shut down the No. 4 reactor in the expectation of a low demand for power. A combination of poor communication and bad decision-making meant that at about 11:00 P.M., with the cooling system already shutting down, the deputy chief engineer demanded more power in order to test a turbine. The reactor overheated, and at 1:23 A.M. a series of explosions rocked the building, killing thousands of people, buckling concrete walls 3 ft./1 m thick, blowing off the roof of the reactor and disabling the very emergency systems that were designed to prevent a complete meltdown and an even greater catastrophe.

THE FALLOUT

The first the outside world knew of the incident was three days later, when scientists in Sweden detected high levels of airborne radiation. The following day, the Soviet authorities admitted that "an accident" had taken place, but it was not until the Soviets appealed for Western assistance that the true extent of the catastrophe was revealed. Firefighters and the military battled for more than two weeks to contain the blaze, which was eventually put out when helicopters dropped some 5,000 tons of lead, limestone, sand, and boron into the reactor. But the real damage was invisible. An international commission estimated that the accident produced 200 times more radioactive fallout than the bombs on Hiroshima and Nagasaki combined (see p. 36). Scientists predicted that over the next 70 years the disaster would result in up to 50,000 deaths from cancer, as well as an inestimable number of genetic abnormalities. The true cost will never be known, and an international conference in Vienna in 1996 provided a chilling reminder that the disaster is not yet over when delegates held a minute's silence for the "past, present and future" victims of Chernobyl.

VENIAMIN PRIANICHNIKOV

As firefighters battled to put out the blaze, one vital piece of information was whether the reactor core was melting through its concrete foundations. Physicist Veniamin Prianichnikov volunteered to go underneath the reactor to find out: "When I pulled open the cover, I felt something pouring onto my head. I was wearing just a thin protective cap. I immediately knew I was in a dire situation, and I was probably finished. I shouted to the people who were with me to hand me the meter so I could measure the radiation intensity.... The meter showed about 200 units. It was then I realized I was all right—I was alive." Thankfully, the reactor did not melt down, and is now encased in concrete, with plans to bury it over half a mile belowground.

Where were you when?

In my mind's eye I saw all the people of Pripyat, including my wife and my seven-year-old daughter, as living corpses.

—Veniamin Prianichnikov, physicist, who witnessed the explosion from his apartment

Over the reactor hall I saw the glow, which was very rich in color. You could see a shining column of white-blue light. You couldn't take your eyes away from it. You felt spellbound.

—Leonid Teliatnikov, one of the first firefighters to arrive at Chernobyl

Never trust a government. I was living in rural West Wales at the time. We were assured the milk was safe to drink—there were fears of radioactive fallout contaminating the grass the Welsh dairy cows fed on—so therefore I switched to dried milk for a few months. Disgusting stuff. In other words, minimal impact on me, but just think of Sebastian Salgado's haunting photos of Chernobyl today—a ghost city. Remind me, why are we continuing with nuclear power?

—Mark Smalley, Bristol, England

1988

TIMELINE
(DECEMBER 21)

8:15 A.M. Passengers begin checking in for Air Malta flight KM180 from Luqa Airport in Malta, to Frankfurt, Germany. Investigators later conclude that a brown Samsonite suitcase is loaded at Luqa.

1:00 P.M. Investigators later conclude that the brown suitcase is transferred from flight KM180 to Pan Am flight 103A for London Heathrow and then New York.

5:00 P.M At Heathrow airport, baggage is loaded onto Pan Am flight PA103 for New York. Investigators later conclude that the brown suitcase passes through the baggage-in-transit system and is loaded onto the Pan Am Boeing 747 *Maid of the Seas*.

6:25 P.M Flight PA103 takes off 25 minutes late, heading north toward Scotland before it is scheduled to head out over the North Atlantic.

7:03 P.M A Semtex bomb goes off in the brown suitcase and the plane breaks up over the village of Lockerbie, killing all 259 passengers and 11 people on the ground.

During a ceremony commemorating the 15th anniversary of the shooting down of an Iranian airliner by U.S.S. *Vincennes*, relatives stand in front of a painting depicting the scene (July 3, 2003).

Lockerbie

The Scottish town of Lockerbie became the focus of world attention when a transatlantic flight was blown up overhead.

On December 21, 1988, a Pan American World Airways jumbo jet named *Maid of the Seas* took off from Heathrow Airport for New York with 259 people on board, mostly Americans flying home for Christmas. The plane had been in the air for nearly 40 minutes when it suddenly disappeared from air-traffic-control radar screens. It transpired that a Semtex bomb had exploded in a suitcase loaded in the left-side front cargo bay, ripping the plane apart so quickly that the pilot was unable to even send a distress message and everyone on board was killed. Debris was spread over 850 square miles of the Scottish countryside, and burning wreckage fell onto the town of Lockerbie, destroying several houses and killing another 11 people on the ground.

LIBYAN CONSPIRACY

Maid of the Seas had taken off from London 25 minutes late, and investigators assumed that the timer, subsequently discovered to have been hidden inside a Toshiba radio-cassette player, was intended to detonate the bomb when the plane was flying over the sea. However, determining the cause was much simpler than bringing the perpetrators to justice. Eleven years later two Libyans were charged with the atrocity, and in 2000 they were extradited to face trial in Scotland. In 2001 Abdel Baset Ali Mohamed Al-Megrahi was found guilty and sentenced to 20 years' imprisonment; the other defendant was acquitted. In August 2003 Libyan president Muammar Gaddafi finally agreed to pay $2.7 billion to compensate the families of the victims in return for the lifting of UN sanctions against his country.

The plane had been in the air for nearly 40 minutes when it suddenly disappeared from air-traffic-control radar screens.

UNITED STATES SHOOTS DOWN AIRLINER

When it was established that a terrorist bomb had brought down the *Maid of the Seas*, the initial theory was that it was a revenge attack for an Iranian A300 Airbus shot down over the Persian Gulf on July 3 that year by the cruiser U.S.S. *Vincennes*, killing all 290 people on board. *Vincennes* had been involved in a skirmish with Iranian gunboats and had launched a missile at what the ship's missile guidance system mistook for an F-14 Tomcat fighter plane. U.S. president Ronald Reagan said that he was "saddened by this terrible tragedy" and apologized for the loss of life, but said that it was "a justified act of self-defense."

Where were you when?

The whole sky lit up and it was virtually raining fire. The plane was trailing flames when it went over, and there was a terrible explosion.

—Mike Carnahan, Lockerbie resident

I just heard this thin screaming sound. The ground shook. It was like an earthquake.

—Anonymous Lockerbie resident

Part of the wreckage of the *Maid of the Seas* lies where it hit the ground near Lockerbie, Scotland (December 22, 1988).

1989

TIMELINE
(OIL SPILLS)

03/18/67 The tanker *Torrey Canyon* runs aground off the southeast coast of England, spilling 120,000 tons of oil and polluting much of the Cornish coastline.

01/24/76 The Tanker *Olympic Bravery* spills 250,000 tons of oil off the coast of Brittany, France.

03/16/78 The tanker *Amoco Cadiz* runs aground off the coast of Brittany, France, spilling 220,000 tons of oil.

1978 In the nine months after the *Amoco Cadiz* disaster, six more spillages prompt the Inter-Governmental Maritime Consultative Organization to introduce stricter safety measures for oil tankers.

07/19/79 The tankers *Atlantic Empress* and *Aegean Captain* collide off Trinidad, spilling 300,000 tons of oil in the world's heaviest-ever oil spill.

08/06/83 The tanker *Castillio de Bellver* spills 255,000 tons of oil off Cape Town, South Africa.

11/10/88 The tanker *Odyssey* spills 140,000 tons of oil off the coast of Canada.

03/24/89 The tanker *Exxon Valdez* runs aground in Alaska, spilling 35,000 tons of oil.

12/03/92 The tanker *Aegean Sea* runs aground near La Coruna, Spain, creating an oil slick 12.5 miles long.

Above A week after the disaster, three tugboats push another tanker toward the holed *Exxon Valdez* prior to offloading the remaining oil (March 30, 1989).

Exxon Valdez oil spill

The disaster caused when the tanker *Exxon Valdez* ran aground spurred environmentalists to action on a scale never before seen.

In terms of tonnage of oil spilled, the *Exxon Valdez* disaster does not even rank in the world's worst 10 oil spills, but because of where it took place, in the unspoiled wilderness of Alaska, it was unprecedented in terms of its ecological impact. On March 24, 1989, the 987 ft./300 m supertanker, belonging to the Exxon oil company, ran aground on a reef in Prince William Sound soon after leaving the oil terminal at Valdez. A hole was torn in the hull, resulting in more than 11 million gallons, or 35,000 tons, of crude oil spilling into the sea and creating a slick some 100 square miles in area.

Fish, seabirds, marine mammals, coastal flora and the local fishing industry were all devastated, and although Exxon promised to pay for the clean up operation, the company was strongly criticized by the Alaskan authorities for its allegedly slow response to what happened for apparently not having a contingency plan for a spillage and for attempting to understate the scale of the disaster.

ALCOHOL

A week after the accident, Exxon fired the ship's captain, Joseph Hazelwood, when it was revealed that he had at least twice the legal level of alcohol in his bloodstream at the time the tanker had run aground. Investigators were told that Hazelwood had gone to his cabin after the ship left port, putting an unqualified member of the crew in charge for the difficult task of navigating through Prince William Sound to the open sea. Although Hazelwood was not tested for alcohol until 10 hours later, his blood alcohol level was still between 0.6 percent and 0.9 percent: The legal limit was 0.4 percent.

The ship's captain had at least twice the legal level of alcohol in his bloodstream.

THE VALDEZ PRINCIPLES

The scale of the disaster prompted environmentalists around the world to unite in establishing the "Valdez Principles" as part of a campaign for an international agreement on stricter safety procedures, better contingency plans for ecological disasters, and the elimination of pollutants. The Valdez Principles also pressed for legislation to force companies producing environmentally damaging products to change those products, to take steps to restore the environments damaged by those products, and to pay compensation where those products create injury or illness. Opinion polls showed that after the disaster, for the first time, a majority of Americans considered the environment to be the most important issue facing the governments of the world.

Where were you when?

Finally, realizing the ship was in serious trouble, Cousins phoned Hazelwood again to report the danger—and, at the end of the conversation, felt an initial shock to the vessel. The grounding, described by helmsman Robert Kagan as "a bumpy ride" and by Cousins as six "very sharp jolts," occurred at 12:04 A.M.

—Alaska Oil Spill Commission, Final Report, published February 1990 by the State of Alaska

The enormity of the clean-up operation becomes apparent as a worker rubs the oil off a rock face on Naked Island, Alaska, after the *Exxon Valdez* oil spill (1989)

1989

TIMELINE

04/15/89 Liberal reformer Hu Yaobang dies of a heart attack, triggering mourning and then protest.

04/17/89 Chinese students begin demonstrating in Tiananmen Square. A fluctuating crowd of several thousand maintains a continuous presence there until the night of June 3–4.

04/18/89 Students from Peking University and the People's University stage a sit-in in the Great Hall of the People and announce seven demands of the government.

04/22/89 Yaobang's funeral passes peacefully, but afterward students intensify their protest.

04/26/89 The government publicly denounces the protests in the "April 26 Editorial."

05/89 Many students die in hunger strikes in protest at the "April 26 Editorial."

05/18/89 The government declares martial law.

06/03/89– 06/04/89 The government sends in the People's Liberation Army to forcibly clear the Tiananmen Square, resulting in some 500 deaths.

The Tiananmen Square massacre

The massacre on the night of June 3–4, 1989, was the culmination of six weeks of pro-democracy demonstrations and protest marches.

Tiananmen means "heavenly peace," but Tiananmen Square in Beijing, China, belied its name in June 1989 when the Chinese People's Liberation Army (PLA) forcibly dispersed thousands of students and workers demonstrating there for democracy and greater freedom. In doing so, the PLA killed an estimated 500 people in a massacre that marked the end of what one participant described as "the biggest, broadest, longest-lasting, and most influential pro-democracy demonstrations anywhere in the world in the twentieth century."

The protests were triggered by the death, in April, of liberal reformer Hu Yaobang (see below), a politician who had become a powerful symbol of political reform and open government. Across China, thousands of students took part in formal mourning ceremonies, and on the afternoon of April 17 some 600 students marched into Tiananmen Square with banners and wreaths. Overnight the crowd swelled to some 3,000 students, and the following morning hundreds of them staged a sit-in, making pro-democracy demands of the government that irrevocably changed the gathering from the mourning of a popular leader into a platform to push for political reform.

THE PROTEST INTENSIFIES

China's Politburo ignored the students' demands, assuming that they would disperse after Yaobang's funeral on April 22. Instead, the students intensified their demonstrations, maintaining a large and continuous presence in Tiananmen Square, demanding a dialogue with the government, and urging workers to strike—an action that if successful, could have toppled the Communist Party of China. But rather than trying to appease or reach a compromise with the students, the government publicly denounced the protest, prompting many students to go on hunger strike, further increasing public support for their cause.

Demonstrations increased with the visit of Soviet president Mikhail Gorbachev in May for a Sino-Soviet summit, by which time hundreds of thousands of students and workers a

HU YAOBANG

Hu Yaobang (sometimes given as Hu Yao-pang) was a veteran of the Long March made by Chinese Communists in 1934–35 to escape nationalist troops, after which he held a number of political posts under Deng Xiaoping, the leader who would later be responsible for the Tiananmen Square massacre. Yaobang was always something of a rebel, being rusticated as a capitalist during the Cultural Revolution and later being rehabilitated before rising to Communist Party Leader, a post from which he was dismissed in 1987 for his lenient handling of a wave of student unrest. It was this leniency that made Yaobang such a powerful figurehead for the students mourning his death two years later, leading to his posthumous role in the pro-democracy protests.

day were in the square demanding reform—a level of protest that led to the declaration of martial law on May 18. Knowing that the repercussions would now be so great that they had to continue in the desperate hope of forcing democratic reform, the protesters continued their demonstrations until the government sent in tanks, troops and armed police on June 3, bringing the pro-democracy uprising to its bloody and unsuccessful conclusion the following day.

Opposite Students place flowers and wreaths beneath a portrait of Hu Yaobang, as thousands more students gather in Tiananmen Square to mourn the death of the liberal reformer.

Where were you when?

As I was moving with the students in the streets of Tiananmen Square, I got myself a little bit tear-gassed. Now, obviously, since the minute that things hotted up, I had felt scared silly. I would be lying if I said anything different.... We were getting shot at, we were getting tear-gassed. But because there were dead [bodies] all around us, and because of the anger that we felt, all of us, even myself, would have done anything.

—Steve Jolly, *Eyewitness in China*, published by Committee for Workers International

Student protesters sit face-to-face with police outside the Great Hall of the People in Tiananmen Square (April 22, 1989).

1989

Fall of the Berlin Wall

The Berlin Wall was both a symbol and an instrument of division, and its removal was an equally powerful symbol of freedom.

In the 28 years of its existence, at least 75 East Germans were killed while trying to escape to the West over the Berlin Wall, the last of them in March 1989 when it still seemed that the Wall would never be brought down. But just eight months later, after the greatest political upheavals in Europe since World War II, the Wall was no more. The possibility of change came with an announcement from the USSR that it would no longer intervene in the affairs of its Eastern European satellites, and possibility became probability when Soviet president Mikhail Gorbachev visited East Germany in October 1989 to urge the government to introduce widespread and fundamental reforms.

HUMAN TIDE

In the four weeks after Gorbachev's visit, millions of East Germans attended pro-democracy rallies, the Communist government fell, and the new government announced that from midnight on November 9, 1989, East Germans would be granted freedom of movement across the country's borders—including through checkpoints in the Wall. That night the world watched on television as crowds gathered on both sides of the Wall. At midnight the checkpoints were opened, as promised, and a flood of human beings began crossing over and through the Wall; the barrier of oppression had become a gateway to freedom, and over the next days and weeks it was demolished by official industrial contractors and unofficial enthusiastic individuals, with a few sections left standing as reminders of what had been.

The demolition of the Wall was followed by free East German elections, leading in turn to the economic reunification of Germany in July 1990 and full political reunification on October 3 that year. However, reunification, while politically desirable, proved economically difficult, with many East Germans complaining of being treated as second-class citizens and West Germans complaining of falling standards of living as a result of shouldering the financial burden of reunification.

TIMELINE

10/07/89 Soviet president Mikhail Gorbachev urges the East German government to introduce reforms.

11/04/89 Pro-democracy rallies sparked by Gorbachev's October visit culminate in a million-strong protest in East Berlin.

11/07/89 The entire East German government resigns, to be replaced the following day with Hans Modrow as premier.

11/09/89 At midnight all border points are opened, including checkpoints in the hated Berlin Wall.

11/10/89 Bulldozers begin demolishing the Wall.

03/90 Free elections take place in East Germany.

09/90 The reunification document "Treaty on the Final Settlement with Respect to Germany" is concluded.

10/03/90 The treaty concluded in September comes into force, and Germany is formally reunified as a sovereign state.

12/02/90 The first all-German elections take place, and the new German government takes power from January 1, 1991.

THE COLLAPSE OF COMMUNISM ACROSS EUROPE

Germans refer to reunification as *die Wende* ("the change"). East Germany was not the only country formerly controlled by the USSR to experience political change in 1989 following Gorbachev's encouragement of reform. In January, Hungary legalized opposition parties (a new center-right coalition government was elected the following year); in August, Poland established its first non-Communist government since 1948; in September, Hungary opened its borders, effectively raising the "Iron Curtain"; in November the Communist regimes collapsed in Bulgaria and Czechoslovakia, as well as in Germany; and in December the Communist regime in Romania was overthrown. The dissolution of the USSR itself followed in 1991 (see p. 224).

Where were you when?

The Germans are the happiest people in the world today.

—Walter Momper, mayor of West Berlin

Yes. It was right here. They tore it down as soon as they could to get rid of the nightmare, but now I think they should have left it standing. All you foreign tourists keep stopping to ask where the Wall has gone. If it was still there, you could see it for yourselves.

—Berlin shopkeeper, Berlin, Germany, 1993

Above East German border guards are overwhelmed by the crowd of people waiting to pass through the newly breached Berlin Wall.

Opposite A German man is hauled up onto the Berlin Wall by those already standing on the top (1989).

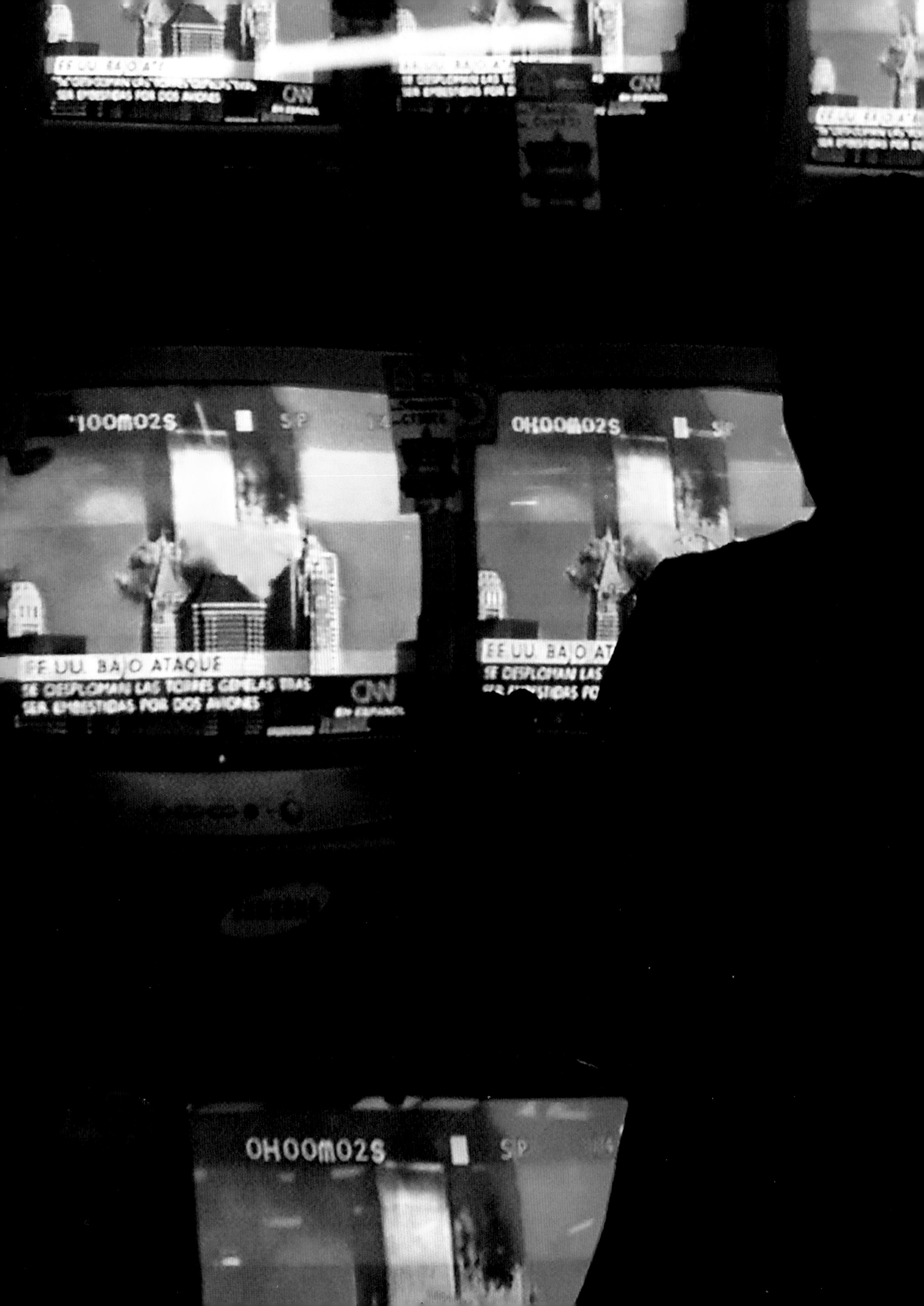
EE.UU. BAJO ATAQUE
CNN

1990-200

1990

MANDELA'S BIRTHDAY BASH

On June 11, 1988, more than 80,000 people packed into Wembley Stadium, London, England, for a daylong tribute concert to mark Nelson Mandela's 70th birthday. (His birthday actually fell just over five weeks later, on July 18.) The concert, broadcast to a television audience estimated at 1 billion viewers in 60 countries, boasted a star-studded line up including Stevie Wonder, Whitney Houston, George Michael, UB40, the Eurythmics, Youssou N'dour and South Africa's Mahotella Queens. Naively, broadcasters and sponsors attempted to keep politics out of a concert that, by its very existence, was overtly political.

Above Supporters of Nelson Mandela pack the stands of Orlando Stadium, Soweto Township, South Africa, at an ANC rally to celebrate his release (February 20, 1990).

The release of Nelson Mandela

Anti-apartheid activists campaigned for years to free ANC leader Nelson Mandela and finally achieved their goal on February 11, 1990.

In the early 1940s a young lawyer named Nelson Mandela established South Africa's first black legal practice. In 1944 he joined the African National Congress (ANC) and for 20 years led a campaign of defiance against the South African government's policy of racial segregation known as apartheid; then, after organizing a three-day national strike in 1961, Mandela was charged with offenses including sabotage and treason.

On April 20, 1964, facing the possibility of the death penalty, he told the court, "During my lifetime I have dedicated my life to this struggle of the African people.... I have cherished the ideals of a democratic and free society in which all persons live together in harmony with equal opportunities. It is an ideal which I hope to live for, and to see realized. But My Lord, if needs be, it is an ideal for which I am prepared to die."

IMPRISONMENT AND RELEASE

Mandela did not receive the death penalty but was instead sentenced to life imprisonment. As a political prisoner, he became an ever more potent symbol of black resistance to apartheid, particularly in the light of his refusal to be party to any deal with the South African government. As the years passed, calls from around the world for his release became more insistent, reaching a crescendo in the year of his 70th birthday with a tribute concert that was broadcast in 60 countries (see Mandela's Birthday Bash, left).

Political change came with the election of F. W. de Klerk as South African prime minister in 1989, and the greatest symbol of de Klerk's intention to end apartheid was the freeing of Nelson Mandela. On the afternoon of February 11, 1990, some 2,000 jubilant supporters—the maximum number allowed by the authorities—gathered outside Victor Verster prison to greet their hero. The crowd became frustrated and angry as the appointed hour of release came and went, but the atmosphere changed to one of jubilation two hours later when, after 27 years in jail, Mandela finally walked free. In Cape Town 50,000 more supporters had congregated outside the city hall, which was decorated with flags and a

Where were you when?

My memory is of a particularly quiet and hot day. TV news covered the release live, and I watched it with my family. I was 16 and impatient. The forecast time of release came and went and it was after 4 P.M. when he finally emerged.

Pietersburg was a conservative town in those days. The kids at my high school believed that once Mandela walked free, there would be a revolution. It was another 12 years, however, before Pietersburg was renamed Polokwane and its conservative legacy was erased. It happened peacefully and without unrest, but I know that without Mandela it would not have been possible.

—Lili van Levwan, Pietersburg resident

banner reading "Nelson Mandela—the nation welcomes you home," a sentiment echoed in celebrations around the world.

THE AFTERMATH

Mandela was dignified in release but remained defiant, saying, "I greet you in the name of peace, democracy and freedom for all" and calling for a peaceful and definitive end to "the dark hell of apartheid." He thanked all the people who had campaigned for his release and praised De Klerk, with whom he was to share the Nobel Peace Prize the following year, as a man of integrity. Two days later Mandela was fêted at the Soweto Soccer City stadium by a crowd of 100,000, whom he told that the pleasure of release was marred by the fact that people "are still suffering under an inhuman system." But reform came quickly—the apartheid constitution was dissolved in December 1993, and free multiracial elections were held the following year, as a result of which de Klerk became vice president, and on May 10, 1994, Nelson Mandela was inaugurated as South Africa's first black president.

> "I greet you in the name of peace, democracy and freedom for all."

Nelson Mandela and wife, Winnie, raise their fists in joy and triumph as he leaves Victor Verster prison (February 11, 1990).

1991

TIMELINE

08/02/90 Iraqi forces invade Kuwait. The United Nations, and a majority of Arab nations, immediately condemn the invasion and call for a withdrawal.

08/06/90 The UN imposes sanctions and invokes Article 51, the right to "individual or collective self-defense," paving the way for military action.

08/08/90 Iraq annexes Kuwait.

08/09/90 U.S. forces begin arriving in Saudi Arabia as U.S. president H. W. George Bush begins assembling a coalition of UN countries against Iraq.

08/28/90 Iraqi dictator Saddam Hussein declares that Kuwait is now the 19th province of Iraq.

11/29/90 The UN sets a deadline of January 15 for Iraqi withdrawal and authorizes the use of "all necessary means" to enforce its ruling.

01/16/91 Coalition forces begin an air offensive against Iraq. Iraq responds by attacking Israel (which had taken no military action against Iraq).

02/24/91 Coalition forces launch a ground-based attack, code-named Desert Storm.

02/27/91 Coalition forces successfully drive Iraqi forces out of Kuwait, and Bush calls a cease-fire, which he announces publicly the following day.

04/11/91 The cease-fire is made permanent.

Where were you when?

They came from every continent and from diverse religious, political and social cultures, including Marxist and Muslim as well as Christian and agnostic, Arab and Slav as well as Latin and Anglo-Saxon. The presence of strangers with entirely foreign customs—such as women wearing visible trousers and driving motor vehicles—was upsetting to Saudi Arabian society, but the upset was overridden by the urgency of the war's aim, to get the invader out of Kuwait.

—M.R.D. Foot, historian as quoted in Martin Gilbert's history of the 20th century

I saw a direct analogy between what was occurring in Kuwait and what the Nazis had done, especially in Poland. This in no way diminished the evil crimes the Nazis inflicted upon helpless millions or the suffering into which they plunged all of Europe.... I caught hell on this comparison of Saddam to Hitler, with critics accusing me of personalizing the crisis, but I still feel it was an appropriate one.

—H. W. George Bush, former president of the United States, in his memoirs

The First Gulf War

In August 1990 Iraq invaded Kuwait. Six months later, after the expiration of a UN deadline, a U.S.-led coalition drove out the invaders.

By the 1980s military historians were predicting that World War III, if it happened, would start not because of the Cold War, but as a result of tensions in the Middle East. And in 1990, as the Cold War came to an end, the Iraqi dictator Saddam Hussein invaded and annexed Kuwait. U.S. president H. W. George Bush likened Saddam to Hitler and, with the backing of the United Nations, immediately began assembling a coalition of UN countries to drive out the invaders and restore Kuwait's independence. On the night of January 16, 1991, after economic sanctions had failed and the Iraqis had ignored a UN deadline to withdraw, coalition forces began the nightly bombing of Iraqi military targets in both Iraq and Kuwait. Iraq responded by launching missile attacks against Israel, hoping to draw Israel into the conflict and so unite the Arab nations, which had hitherto condemned Iraq's action, against a common enemy. Fortunately for coalition solidarity and world peace, Israel agreed to a policy of nonretaliation.

DESERT STORM

After more than a month of aerial bombardment, Iraq began calling for a cease-fire, although Saddam refused to end his occupation of Kuwait and declared, "The mother of all battles will be our victory." But the mother of all battles did not go as Saddam had planned when, on February 24, coalition forces led by U.S. general Norman Schwarzkopf launched a ground attack code-named Operation Desert Storm. By the end of the first day, the coalition had advanced more than 200 miles into Kuwait and taken more than 20,000 prisoners. The Iraqi army, made up mainly of unwilling conscripts, offered only token resistance, and four days later Bush appeared on television to announce the end of the war: "Kuwait is liberated. Iraq's army is defeated; our military objectives are met."

Left The bow of the aircraft carrier U.S.S. *America* looms above the sand dunes as it passes through the Suez Canal en route to the Red Sea during the buildup to the Gulf War (January 15, 1991).

Below Kurdish families fleeing their homes en route to the Zakho refugee camp, on the Iraqi side of the Iraqi–Turkish border (May 2, 1991).

THE AFTERMATH

U.S. president H. W. George Bush was both praised and criticized for his decision to end the war after liberating Kuwait rather than continuing to Baghdad and deposing Saddam Hussein: praised for not overstepping his UN remit but criticized because the dictator who had caused the war remained in power. In the long term, Saddam's continued dictatorship was to lead to the Iraq War (see p. 256), and in the short term it led to a humanitarian disaster as Saddam turned his attention to the suppression of two ethnic groups in Iraq: the Kurds and the Shiites. Coalition forces were able to provide safe havens and humanitarian aid for the refugees until their final withdrawal in April, after which Saddam re-established his reign of tyranny within Iraq.

1991

The collapse of Communism

After nearly 70 years of oppression in the USSR and over 40 years in Eastern Europe, Communist rule finally collapsed between 1989 and 1991.

TIMELINE

03/11/85 Mikhail Gorbachev is appointed Communist Party leader.

10/01/88 Gorbachev is elected president of the USSR.

08/24/89 Poland becomes the first Soviet bloc country to elect a non-Communist prime minister.

10/89 The Hungarian National Assembly approves an amended constitution describing Hungary as an independent democratic state. The first free multiparty elections take place in 1990.

11/89 Communist rule ends peacefully in Bulgaria, Czechoslovakia, and East Germany. The Berlin Wall is breached (see p. 216).

12/89 The Communist regime in Romania is violently overthrown.

1990 Multiparty elections across the USSR bring nationalist and anti-Communist candidates to power. Gorbachev is awarded the Nobel Peace Prize for improving East–West relations, leading to the end of the Cold War.

1991 Following the previous year's free elections, many Soviet republics declare independence.

12/21/91 Eleven former Soviet states found the Confederation of Independent States, effectively dissolving the USSR.

12/25/91 Gorbachev resigns.

12/26/91 The Supreme Soviet meets in Moscow and officially dissolves itself.

The beginning of the end for Communism came with the election in 1985 of Mikhail Gorbachev as leader of the Communist Party. A committed reformer, Gorbachev introduced sweeping constitutional changes to the USSR and encouraged Eastern European communist leaders to do the same. His aim was to create a "revolution within the revolution"—in other words, reform under the control of the Communist Party. But after years of oppression, people wanted total, not partial, reform, and the increased freedom given them by Gorbachev allowed them to make their feelings known.

In August 1989 Poland became the first Soviet bloc country since 1945 to elect a non-Communist leader (Tadeusz Mazowiecki, a member of the once outlawed opposition movement Solidarity). Over the next four months other countries followed suit, either peacefully or with violence, bringing Communist rule to an end in Bulgaria, Czechoslovakia, East Germany, Hungary, and Romania.

DISSOLUTION OF THE USSR

The following year open multiparty elections across the USSR brought a number of nationalist and anti-Communist parties to power in the constituent republics, and in 1991 most Soviet republics carried out referenda endorsing independence. Soon after these republics declared their independence in August, hardliners within the Communist Party tried to depose Gorbachev and restore Soviet control. The attempted coup was defeated by reformists led by Boris Yeltsin, who thought that Gorbachev was not being radical enough in his reforms. They reinstated Gorbachev but seized the opportunity to take things a step further by founding the Commonwealth of Independent States (CIS), effectively dissolving the USSR and bringing an end to Communist rule in the former Soviet bloc.

Left Russian president Yeltsin (r) insists that Soviet president Gorbachev does things his way after saving Gorbachev from a coup.

PERESTROIKA AND GLASNOST

The cornerstones of Gorbachev's reforms in the USSR were his policies of *perestroika* (restructuring) and *glasnost* (openness). *Perestroika* was intended to revitalize the economy by relaxing government controls and to democratize the Communist Party by reducing the power and corruption of the bureaucracy. The openness associated with *glasnost* involved greater civil liberties, increased freedom of speech, more honest dissemination of information, and greater public participation in government. However, these policies revealed more government failings than they corrected, and Gorbachev, who found himself attacked by conservatives for going too far with his reforms and by radicals for not going far enough, found himself overseeing the collapse of the Soviet Union rather than its rebirth.

Where were you when?

After we considered everything in the evening of December 7 in Belavezha, Yeltsin ordered his team to draft a document—a statement or declaration. We had not yet decided on a name for the document. Yeltsin's aides wrote that document and left it for a woman to type it up in the morning. Since her office was already locked, they slid the document into the office through a slit under the door. But in the morning the typist said, "I haven't found anything." There was no document! It turned out that a cleaning woman, who came to the office earlier, saw some papers on the floor and swept them away.

—Leonid Kravchuk, Ukrainian president, writing in *Fakty* magazine, 1992

Muscovites holding a huge Russian flag flash victory signs in Red Square, Moscow, as they celebrate the failure of a hardline Communist-led coup that nearly toppled Soviet president Mikhail Gorbachev (August 22, 1991).

1993

TIMELINE

01/20/93–
01/23/93 Representatives of Israel and the Palestine Liberation Organization (PLO) hold the first of several secret meetings in Oslo, Norway.

02/11/93–
02/13/93 Israel and the PLO hold a second round of talks in Oslo, at which they produce a draft Declaration of Principles.

08/20/93 Israel and the PLO sign the Oslo Accords, outlining a peace agreement between them. Israeli foreign minister Shimon Peres later writes, "Here was a small group of Israelis, Palestinians and Norwegians—partners to one of the best-guarded secrets ever, a secret whose imminent revelation would mark a watershed in the history of the Middle East"

08/30/93 The Israeli government approves the grant of self-rule to Palestinians living in the Gaza Strip and Jericho; the PLO signs this plan on September 9.

09/13/93 In Washington, D.C., PLO leader Yasser Arafat agrees to renounce terrorism. He and Israeli prime minister Yitzhak Rabin sign the Declaration of Principles. Arafat and Rabin shake hands on the White House lawn.

10/14/94 Arafat, Rabin and Peres are awarded the Nobel Peace Prize.

Above Palestinians in Nablus, West Bank, celebrate self-government, as agreed in the Declaration of Principles signed at the White House the previous day (September 14, 1993).

Rabin and Arafat shake hands at the White House

After 45 years of bitter dispute and bloodshed, the leaders of Israel and the PLO gave peace a chance with a symbolic handshake.

For more than 40 years the Palestine Liberation Organization (PLO) refused to recognize the existence of the State of Israel (see p. 48)—and for more than 40 years successive Israeli governments refused to negotiate with the PLO, which they denounced as a terrorist organization, or with its leader, Yasser Arafat, whom they called a "man of blood." But in 1993, as Israelis and Palestinians continued killing one another in an ongoing *intifada* ("uprising"), the first steps toward peace were taken at a series of secret meetings in Oslo, Norway, between representatives of Israel and the PLO.

THE OSLO ACCORDS

Under the principles agreed in Oslo, known as the Oslo Accords, Israel's main concession was self-government for Palestinians in Gaza and Jericho, and in return its main demand was that the PLO renounce terrorism. The principle of self-government was approved in late August, and all that remained was to sign the Declaration of Principles embodying the Oslo Accords. Arafat and Israeli prime minister Yitzhak Rabin traveled to Washington, where on September 13, U.S. president Bill Clinton was to witness the signing of the historic document. But Arafat had still not renounced the use of terror. Then, at the last minute, he signed a letter agreeing to issue the statement that "in the light of the new era marked by the signing of the Declaration of Principles, the PLO encourages and calls upon the Palestinian people in the West Bank and the Gaza Strip to take part in steps leading to the normalization of life, rejecting violence and terrorism [and] contributing to peace and stability."

Immediately afterward, millions watched on television as the two bitter enemies met on the White House lawn, signed the Declaration of Principles and uneasily shook hands with

PEACE WITH JORDAN

The year after his historic handshake, and 12 days after being jointly awarded the Nobel Peace Prize with Arafat and Israeli Foreign Minister Shimon Peres, Rabin agreed a peace treaty with King Hussein of Jordan. Rabin said that it was time "to make the desert bloom," while Hussein promised a "warm peace" (in contrast with the "cold peace" that had existed since 1978 between Israel and Egypt). Three days later King Hassan of Morocco reinforced the mood when he announced, "We must prove that the Mediterranean can become a region of solidarity and equilibrium, a true Sea of Galilee, around which the three religions and the sons of Abraham, united by historical bonds, will be able to build a magnificent bridge for the century to come."

each other. Rabin told Palestinians, "We, like you, are people who want to build a home, plant a tree, love, live side by side with you—in dignity, in empathy, as human beings, as free men. We are today giving peace a chance and saying to you, 'Enough.' Let us pray that a day will come when we all say, 'Farewell to arms'." The previously unimaginable handshake between the two leaders was a symbol of progress toward Rabin's dream, but the peace that it brought was as uneasy as the gesture itself and, for many people, hardly distinguishable from the hostilities that preceded it.

> "Let us pray that a day will come when we all say, 'Farewell to arms'."

Where were you when?

I knew that the hand outstretched to me from the far side of the podium was the hand that held the knife, that held the gun, the hand that gave the order to shoot, to kill. Of all the hands in the world, it was not the hand that I dreamed of touching. But it was not Yitzhak Rabin on that podium, the private citizen who lives on Rav Ashi Street.... I stood as the representative of a nation, as the emissary of a state that wants peace with the most bitter and odious of its foes, a state that is willing to give peace a chance.

As I have said, one does not make peace with one's friends. One makes peace with one's enemy.

—Yitzhak Rabin, in a new edition of his memoirs published shortly after the historic handshake

U.S. president Bill Clinton (c) smiles as Israeli prime minister Yitzhak Rabin (l) and PLO chairman Yasser Arafat shake hands after the signing of the Israel-PLO peace accord at the White House (September 13, 1993).

1995

TIMELINE

1970s The development of microprocessors leads to the development of the "microcomputer" (see p. 198).

1975 Bill Gates and Paul Allen form Micro-Soft (later Microsoft).

1980 Microsoft wins the contract to write the operating system for IBM PCs; the result is MS-DOS.

1983 Microsoft launches the first version of Windows, a graphical extension of MS-DOS that has limited success because it is heavily restricted by the DOS memory limit.

1987 Microsoft launches Windows 2, still restricted by the DOS memory limit.

1990 Microsoft launches Windows 3, which proves more successful despite many severe bugs.

04/92 Microsoft launches Windows 3.1, with most of the bugs eradicated.

10/92 Microsoft launches Windows for Workgroups 3.1, enabling groups of users to network their computers.

08/24/95 Microsoft launches Windows 95, Windows NT for office networks and Windows CE for handheld computers.

Right As Windows 95 goes on sale at midnight in Sydney, Australia, a delighted Mikol Furneaux becomes one of the first people in the country to buy the new software (August 24, 1995).

Below Microsoft chairman Bill Gates holds up a CD-ROM of *Bookshelf*, which holds all the information contained in the books pictured.

MICROSOFT

Microsoft was born in 1975, when "microcomputers," so-named in comparison with the giant "mainframe" computers that preceded them, still came in kit form and required technical expertise to assemble them. The first commercially successful microcomputer was the Altair 8800, which was launched in 1975. Two young entrepreneurs and computer hobbyists named Bill Gates (19) and Paul Allen (20) decided to write software that would enable users to interact with their microcomputers more easily, starting with an interpreter that enabled users to write programs for their Altair 8800 using the programming language BASIC. Gates and Allen called their partnership Micro-Soft, a company that, after they dropped the hyphen, was to become one of the biggest in the world.

Microsoft launches Windows 95

With Windows 95, Microsoft, for better or worse, dictated the way that more than 80 percent of users interacted with their computers.

"Where do you want to go today?" was the question posed on millions of billboards, television screens, cinema screens and magazine pages in the summer of 1995. It was part of a $200 million advertising campaign by Microsoft (see opposite) to launch its latest software package, Windows 95, a system that was set to revolutionize the way most people would use their computers at home and at work.

Fifteen years earlier the future of Microsoft had been assured when the company won the contract to write the operating system for all IBM PCs. That system, known as MS-DOS, was a "command-line interface": in other words, like all other interfaces at the time, users had to communicate with the computer by typing instructions into a keyboard.

WINDOWS

Then, in 1983, Microsoft launched a graphical extension to MS-DOS known as Windows, which enabled users to interact with on-screen graphics using a mouse rather than having to type instructions (a "graphical user interface," or GUI). It was not a huge success, partly because it was confined to the limited memory of MS-DOS, and the following year Apple launched a far superior system with the Apple Macintosh (see p. 198).

However, Microsoft was to have the last laugh. During the 1980s and early 1990s Microsoft launched several improved versions of Windows and then, on August 24, 1995, came the big one: Windows 95, which completely overshadowed the Apple's GUI. Because Windows 95 (or its variation Windows NT) came already installed on all IBM PCs, Windows soon became, by default, the operating system of more than 80 percent of computer users—although not to everyone's delight if the software help book *Windows Annoyances* is anything to go by: The first chapter is entitled "So You're Stuck with Windows."

"It's as confusing as a new car's dashboard."

Where were you when?

My first impression of Windows 95 was how much of an improvement it was over Windows 3.x. I was using a pre-release (beta version) of the software on my machine, and within a few hours after installation, the extent by which the previous version of Windows had stunted *my* machine became apparent. However, there were several "features" in the new product that were irritating rather than helpful.

—David Karp, in his book *Windows Annoyances*

Windows 95 is an exciting, modern way to use the computer. That means it's as confusing as a new car's dashboard....

Never used a computer before, but bought Windows 95 because it's "easy to use"? Well, Windows 95 may be intuitive, but that doesn't mean it's as easy to figure out as a steak knife.

—Andy Rathbone, in the introduction to his *Windows 95 For Dummies*

1995

TIMELINE

06/13/94 Nicole Brown Simpson and Ronald Goldman are found stabbed to death outside Nicole's condominium in Brentwood, Los Angeles.

06/17/94 After a televised car chase, O. J. Simpson is arrested and charged with the double murder of his ex-wife and Goldman. Simpson is found to have been carrying a gun, a passport, thousands of dollars in cash and a fake beard in the car.

06/94 After appearing before the Los Angeles Municipal Court and pleading not guilty, Simpson is held without bail in a Los Angeles prison.

01/95 The trial begins.

06/15/95 In court Simpson puts on the bloodstained gloves of the murderer and announces, "See? Too small! Too small!"

07/06/95 The prosecution rests its case.

10/03/95 Simpson is acquitted of all charges.

02/97 In a civil suit brought by relatives of the victims, Simpson is found guilty of causing unlawful death and ordered to pay $8.5 million in damages.

Above Traffic comes to a standstill as drivers stop to watch police pursuing O. J. Simpson's white Ford Bronco along Los Angeles Highway 405 (June 17, 1994).

O. J. Simpson is acquitted

The O. J. Simpson trial was the ultimate courtroom drama and played like a soap opera for 16 months before reaching its tense finale.

It could only have happened in California—national sporting hero turned film star (see "O. J. Simpson," below) leads police on a bizarre 60-mile low-speed car chase before being arrested in his own driveway and charged with the double murder of his ex-wife and her male friend. And that was just the pre-title sequence. For the next 16 months Simpson's trial became an international obsession involving as much show business as legal business, with Simpson's defense lawyers nicknamed "The Dream Team," the proceedings dubbed "The Trial of the Century," the murders reenacted in a rap video, and *Vanity Fair* reporting, "Hollywood is obsessed with the O. J. Simpson circus. Every player in town has his own news and clues, sources, and theories."

All of which showed little respect for the memory of Nicole Brown Simpson and Ronald Goldman, the victims of the double murder.

THE VERDICT

As the trial was played out on television, media polls showed that an increasing number of Americans thought that Simpson was guilty, and pundits noted that many defendants had been sent to death row on far less evidence than the prosecution presented in this case. But this was the trial of O. J. Simpson, and factors other than mere evidence came into play. One commentator noted that the trial "exposed all the frailties and absurdities of American paranoia, prejudice and political correctness," and in the end the racial bigotry displayed by Detective Mark Fuhrman did more to convince jurors of Simpson's innocence than the seemingly overwhelming forensic evidence did of his guilt. On October 3, 1995, the jury took less than four hours to reach the unanimous verdict that stunned the world: Not Guilty.

Opposite Flanked by his attorneys F. Lee Bailey (l) and Johnnie Cochran Jr, O. J. Simpson reacts to the verdict (October 3, 1995).

Opposite below Kim Goldman, sister of murder victim Ron Goldman, reacts to the verdict (October 3, 1995).

O. J. SIMPSON

In his sporting prime Orenthal James Simpson, a.k.a. "the Juice," was an American institution. Born in San Francisco in 1947, he played football for the University of Southern California, winning the 1968 Heisman Trophy for the most outstanding player of the major college conferences. The following year he turned professional with the Buffalo Bills, with whom he played from 1969 to 1977 and made his name as a football legend to rank alongside the all-time greats. In the twilight of his playing career he returned to his hometown, playing for the San Francisco 49ers from 1978 to 1979, before launching a new career as a football commentator. O. J. also appeared in three feature films: *The Towering Inferno* (1974), *Naked Gun* (1988), and *Naked Gun 2½: The Smell of Fear* (1991).

Where were you when?

[David] Bowie called from a distant American hotel room to relay the O. J. verdict to me as it was delivered, describing the scene in court, etc. Then it was on our TV too, so we were watching it together. I don't know what city he was in—Detroit, I think. Incredible tension, with [Judge] Ito slowly going over the rules. Then the verdict—and the beautiful sad face of [prosecutor] Marcia Clark, outwitted by shysters. I am now even more convinced (by his reaction at the news) that Simpson was guilty and that he knew he was going to be acquitted. Somehow it was a fix. As David said, "It's all down to investigative journalism now."

—Brian Eno, musician and composer, diary entry for October 3, 1995

1995

REPATRIATION OF THE CONSTITUTION

After the Confederation of Canada in 1867 (see p. 120), the most important date in Canada's constitutional history is April 17, 1982, when the Constitution Act came into force, giving Canada full political independence from Britain. The ratification of the Act by all provinces except Quebec included the introduction of the Canadian Charter of Rights and Freedoms, which forms the first part of the Act and is effectively a bill of rights that guarantees the collective and individual rights of the Canadian people. In a Canadian Press millennium survey, the repatriation of the constitution was voted the second most important Canadian news story of the 20th century after D-Day.

Quebec referendum

Quebec's 1995 motion for independence from Canada was defeated by the tiniest of margins, 50.58 percent voting "Non" and 49.42 percent "Oui."

On October 30, 1995, the people of Quebec voted on a question that could have torn Canada apart—whether to secede from the Confederation as an independent sovereign state. Organized by the separatist provincial government—the Parti Québécois (PQ)—the referendum was the culmination of some 30 years of agitation for independence since the Quiet Revolution of the 1960s. Francophones had become increasingly marginalized since France ceded the colony of Quebec to Britain in 1760, but the Quiet Revolution ushered in economic, social, and political changes, providing impetus for a separatist cause that was given international attention during Expo '67 (see p. 120) when French president Charles de Gaulle controversially proclaimed: "Vive le Québec libre!" ("Long Live Free Quebec!").

RECORD TURNOUT

De Gaulle's proclamation proved to be a strong catalyst for those who believed in independence. The PQ was formed the following year with the stated aim of achieving independence for Quebec, while the Front de la Libération du Québec (FLQ) took more violent action in pursuit of independence (see p. 142). Popular support for political action brought the PQ to power in 1976, and four years later a referendum on independence was defeated by 60 percent "Non" to 40 percent "Oui."

Despite the no vote, Quebec still demanded the right to be treated as a distinct society, refusing to ratify the Constitution Act (see sidebar). The failure of two accords to find a way of accommodating Quebec's unique place within the Confederation led popular support for separatism to rise to 60 percent in public opinion poles, and the PQ was voted back into power in 1994 on the promise of a second referendum—this attracted a record turnout of 94 percent of Quebec's 5,087,009 eligible voters and was defeated by a much narrower margin than in 1980. The PQ has promised a third referendum should it be returned to power in the next provincial election (which must be held no later than 2008), but many Canadians feel that it would be undemocratic to continue holding referenda on an issue that has already been rejected twice.

Where were you when?

For the first time in my mandate as Prime Minister, I have asked to speak directly to Canadians tonight. I do so because we are in an exceptional situation. Tonight, in particular, I want to speak to my fellow Quebecers. Because, at this moment, the future of our whole country is in their hands. But I also want to speak to all Canadians. Because this issue concerns them—deeply. It is not only the future of Quebec that will be decided on Monday. It is the future of all of Canada. The decision that will be made is serious and irreversible. With deep, deep consequences... .

—The opening lines of Prime Minister Jean Chretien's address to the nation, October 25, 1995

Above A rally in Montreal to dissuade Quebecers from voting for secession (October 27, 1995).

Left A separatist supporter yells at police following the defeat of the "yes" vote (October 30, 1995).

Opposite A "yes" supporter with a portrait of Bloc Québécois leader, Lucien Bouchard, in Longueuil, Quebec (October 29, 1995).

1997

POLLY

Whatever the objections to cloning human beings, animal cloning is already proving to be of benefit to humans. The first commercial use of the cloning technology pioneered by the Roslin Institute was to produce a second sheep, named Polly, which had been genetically modified to include a human gene so that her milk contained human Factor IX, a blood-clotting agent that was then used to treat men suffering from hemophilia B.

Below The Roslin Institute initially offered to present Dolly to Britain's Science Museum, but when this proved impracticable, the institute instead donated a sweater knitted from Dolly's first fleece. The sweater is modeled here by its designer, 12-year-old Holly Wharton from Hertfordshire, England. Looking over her shoulder is the actress Jenny Agutter, who presented the sweater to the museum.

Opposite Dolly, the world's first cloned sheep, at the Roslin Institute in Scotland, where she was created as part of a long-term research project.

Dolly the sheep is born as the first cloned animal

The birth of Dolly the sheep was the first time that an offspring had been cloned from the cell of an adult animal.

During the 1990s cloning moved from the realms of science fiction to science fact—and all the previously hypothetical moral issues suddenly inflamed public opinion across the world. In 1993 two American scientists caused a furor by proving that clones could potentially be created by "splitting" human embryo cells to artificially create identical twins (although they did not create a human clone). Then, in 1995, British scientists at the Roslin Institute in Edinburgh, Scotland, produced two cloned ewes by a technique known as "nuclear transfer": They took the DNA from one embryo cell and "reprogrammed" eggs that had been emptied of their genetic material and thus created genetically identical lambs. The following year the Roslin Institute used the same principle to create something that had previously been thought impossible: the first cloned animal to have originated from an adult cell. In this case it was a cell from the udder of a long-dead ewe. Lamb 6LL3 was born on July 5, 1996, and because of the origin of the cell from which it was created, it was named after Dolly Parton.

IMPLICATIONS

When Dolly's birth was announced in February 1997, U.S. president Bill Clinton immediately launched an inquiry into the implications for human beings, adding momentum to a debate that has continued ever since. Supporters of cloning say that there are many potential benefits, such as the creation of specialized tissues to repair organs or treat currently untreatable diseases and the creation of organs suitable for transplant, either from human cells or from "humanized" animals. The potential pitfalls cited by the opponents of cloning include: ethical problems such as the question of "designer babies," the farming of clones for "spare parts," and the possibility that people involved in cloning might have to pay royalties on their own offspring.

Where were you when?

The new nuclear transfer technology will allow transgenic animals to be produced more cheaply. Genetic modification of the donor cells in culture before they are used in nuclear transfer will also allow us to introduce very precise changes in their DNA and open up the possibilities for a range of new products for the treatment of, for example, cancer and inflammation.

—Dr. Ian Wilmut, leader of the research team at Roslin Institute, 1997

1997

MARS SHUTTLE

In January 2004 NASA successfully landed two more rover vehicles on Mars, and on January 15 that year, U.S. president George W. Bush announced that he had given NASA the go-ahead to begin developing a new generation of space shuttles capable of carrying human beings to Mars. Mr. Bush projected that the imaginatively named Crew Exploration Vehicle (CEV) will be in service by 2014 and will ferry astronauts to the moon, where they will build a space station that will be used as the base for a manned mission to Mars planned for 2030. Bush said, "We don't know where this journey will end, yet we know this: Human beings are headed into the cosmos."

Above Photographers capture the launch of *Pathfinder* from Cape Canaveral, Florida (December 4, 1996).

Pathfinder sends back pictures from Mars

After a seven-month journey through space, *Pathfinder*'s robot explorer sent back pictures of Mars from 310 million miles away.

On July 4, 1997, NASA scientists celebrated the successful landing of the *Pathfinder* mission on the surface of Mars, and the following morning the world looked in awe at photographs sent back across the void of space from the dusty plains of Ares Vallis on the red planet.

Pathfinder was launched on December 4, 1996, and traveled through space for seven months before entering the Martian atmosphere. A 40 ft./12.5 m parachute slowed its descent, and about 10 seconds before landing, four air bags were inflated to create a protective ball around the lander in order to cushion the delicate equipment against the impact. Four seconds later, three rockets fired to slow the descent still further, and about 2 seconds after that, at a height of 70 ft./21.5 m, the air-bag–encased lander separated from the other, heavier parts of the spacecraft and dropped to the ground, landing at 4:56 p.m. GMT. It bounced about 40 ft./12 m into the air and then bounced some 15 more times before coming to rest about half a mile from the initial point of impact.

SOJOURNER

About 90 minutes later, *Pathfinder* opened its three solar panels, known as "petals," and soon afterward the on board cameras began sending panoramic views of the landing area back to Earth. The following day was spent clearing an air bag out of the way so that the robot explorer *Sojourner* could move slowly down a ramp from the lander onto the Martian surface to begin conducting experiments and analyzing soil and rock samples. For the next two months Pathfinder sent back data, and pictures of *Sojourner* going about its slow and deliberate business on the red planet, until communications were lost on September 27, 1997.

Where were you when?

The Mars Pathfinder *imaging team tonight unveiled the first photograph of Ares Vallis, an ancient water channel that at one time in Mars's early history carried more than 1,000 times the amount of flowing water carried by the Amazon River today.*

—Mission Status Report, Nasa, July 4, 1997

I want to thank the many talented men and women at NASA for making the mission such a phenomenal success. It embodies the spirit of NASA and serves as a model for future missions that are faster, better and cheaper.

—Daniel S. Goldin, NASA Administrator

Left *Pathfinder* team members celebrate the successful deployment of *Pathfinder*'s Martian rover *Sojourner* onto the surface of Mars (July 5, 1997).

Above *Sojourner* encounters a rock named Yogi on the Martian surface.

"We don't know where this journey will end, yet we know this: Human beings are headed into the cosmos."

1997

The death of Diana, Princess of Wales

The death of "the people's Princess" prompted unprecedented public grief and nauseating hypocrisy from the tabloid newspapers.

The details are still disputed, but the basic facts are: on August 30, 1997, Diana and her lover Dodi Fayed arrived at the Ritz-Carlton Hotel in Paris at the end of a 10-day trip around Europe; they dined in private in the hotel's Imperial Suite and then decided to go to Fayed's apartment on the Champs-Elysées. In order to avoid the paparazzi, they left from the back of the hotel, but when the photographers realized what had happened, they followed the lovers' Mercedes on motorbikes "like pursuing wasps."

What happened next will never be known for certain, but during the ensuing chase the Mercedes hit an underpass pillar at high speed, killing Diana, Fayed, and driver Henri Paul, none of whom were wearing seatbelts, and seriously injuring Diana's bodyguard, Trevor Rees-Jones.

PUBLIC GRIEF

The shock at hearing the news reverberated around the globe, with tributes being paid by world leaders, European royalty, international charities and show-business celebrities. Britain had never seen such an outpouring of public grief, fueled by the very newspapers and magazines whose thirst for photographs had led to the fatal car chase. The Mall and Kensington Gardens became a sea of flowers, cards, and toys left by mourners whose feelings had been summed up by Prime Minister Tony Blair on the morning the news broke: "I feel like everyone else in this country today, utterly devastated…. We are today a nation in Britain in a state of shock, in mourning, in grief that is so deeply painful for us…. She was the people's Princess and that's how she will stay, how she will remain in our hearts and in our memories forever." [*sic*]

The funeral on television

- UK 32.1 million viewers
- USA 33 million viewers
- Australia >6 million viewers
- worldwide 2.5 billion viewers (unofficial estimate)

TIMELINE

AUGUST 30

11:45 P.M. Diana and Dodi Fayed arrive at the Ritz-Carlton Hotel in Paris.

AUGUST 31

12:05 A.M. Diana, Dodi and bodyguard Trevor Rees-Jones leave the Ritz-Carlton by the back door in a Mercedes 600 driven by the hotel's acting head of security, Henri Paul.

12:25 A.M. The car is pursued by paparazzi into an underpass off the Place de l'Alma and collides with a concrete pillar. Dodi and Henri Paul are killed instantly, but Diana is still alive.

2:00 A.M. Emergency services finally manage to cut Diana free of the wreck.

4:00 A.M. Diana is pronounced dead by doctors at Salpetrière Hospital.

Above In the Alma tunnel in Paris, France, police lift the wrecked Mercedes onto a tow truck (August 31, 1997).

Opposite A sea of floral tributes outside Diana's home at Kensington Palace, London, on the day before her funeral (September 5, 1997).

THE DEATH OF MOTHER TERESA

On September 5, 1997, less than a week after the death of the woman the press dubbed Saint Diana when referring to her charity work, another saintly charity worker died quietly in Calcutta: Mother Teresa. In 1948 Mother Teresa left her convent in Calcutta to work alone as a nurse in the slums of the city, founding the Order of the Missionaries of Charity in 1950 and opening her House for the Dying in 1952. Five years later she began working with lepers and established a colony in West Bengal known as Shanti Nagar ("Town of Peace"). She was awarded the Pope John XXIII Peace Prize in 1971 and the Nobel Peace Prize in 1979. For all the illness she had witnessed, she felt moved to say in 1971: "The biggest disease today is not leprosy or tuberculosis, but rather the feeling of being unwanted."

Where were you when?

I was traveling in Australia at the time and was in Byron Bay, on the east coast. We heard about the accident on the television news in the hostel. Suddenly every headline was shouting it, with huge text and images. It was very surreal for the hysteria to reach us in this tiny town by the sea so far away from home.

—Sophie Persson, London

The day Diana died was the day of my daughter Emily's christening. We were all up early preparing for the party, when my mother came rushing into the kitchen to say Diana was dead. My first thought was, "Oh God, what has she done now?" We were so engrossed in watching the news that we were late at the church and nearly missed the beginning of the service. The flag at the church was at half-mast, and everyone was rather subdued at what was supposed to be a day of celebration.

—Marie Clayton, London

GLOBALIZATION

As long ago as 1962, in his book *The Gutenberg Galaxy*, Canadian writer Marshall McLuhan wrote, "The new electronic interdependence re-creates the world in the image of a global village." McLuhan's ideas were considered controversial at the time, but the two central ideas of this quotation have both proved prophetic: "Electronic interdependence" is a very apt description of the Internet and makes far more sense now than it would have done in the 1960s—and the global village, already nascent in 1962, became unavoidable during the 1990s even at the most everyday level, with a core of the same shop fronts, goods and services taking over the high streets of every developed nation.

"Globalization" is a concept loved by the rich and hated by the poor—or, at least, loved by the leaders and corporate directors of the world's richest nations and hated on behalf of the poorest by anticapitalist protesters. Globalization began with the first international explorers in the days of sail and accelerated with the Industrial Revolution, but corporate globalization really began to fulfill its modern definition after World War II, with the rise of multinational corporations (MNCs, or transnationals), many of which now have annual turnovers greater than the gross national product of a large proportion of the world's countries.

INTERNATIONAL TRADE ORGANIZATIONS

In the same period, a global economy emerged through nation states joining with each other in international trade organizations, and through trade discussions between the world's richest nations. In the wake of World War II, the International Monetary Fund (IMF) and the United Nations Organization (UN) were established in 1945, and the General Agreement on Tariffs and Trade (GATT) in 1947. As the global economy grew, the heads of government of the world's richest nations began in 1975 to meet annually, first as a group of six (France, West Germany, Italy, Japan, the United Kingdom and the United States) and then, with the addition of Canada the following year, as "the group of seven," or G7. Two indicators of how much the global economy had grown by the 1990s were that GATT was superseded by the World Trade Organization (WTO) in 1995 and G7 became G8 in 1998 with the formal inclusion of Russia, which had participated as a guest in G7 meetings from the early 1990s.

OPPOSITION AND PROTEST

Although the rise of MNCs and the increase in international trade agreements both come under the general heading of "globalization," there are often clashes between corporate interest and the interest of a corporation's home nation. For instance, the main advantages of being an MNC are control over the supply of resources, including the ability to site operations and to source labor and materials in the cheapest nations; the avoidance of import tariffs; and the avoidance of high production costs, including certain taxes, in the most expensive nations. None of these practices is advantageous to the rich nations, which, inevitably, are the ones from where the MNCs originate. Political opposition to these aspects of MNCs is twofold: first, that they create unemployment in and undermine the economies of the richer nations, and second, that they exploit the poorer ones.

As globalization gained momentum throughout the 1990s, so did popular protest against both MNCs and international trade agreements between rich nations. The idea of the global village as a cooperative, peaceful, and mutually beneficial, seemed naive as opponents vociferously argued that globalization really meant powerful nations exploiting poorer ones and MNCs having undemocratic power and influence over the government of both large nations and small.

Antiglobalization protests first hit the headlines in December 1999, when an initially peaceful mass protest at a WTO summit in Seattle, Washington, turned violent with attacks on police and on businesses displaying the branding that has gradually taken over the developed world: most infamously, Starbucks Coffee.

This set the tone for future WTO and G8 summits, and a similar outbreak of violence at the G8 summit in Genoa, Italy, on July 20, 2001, resulted in the death of antiglobalization's first martyr, Carlo Giuliani. Inevitably, the details of Giuliani's death are disputed, but it seems that he was shot while attacking a police vehicle and that his body was then run over as the police drove away from the scene—to the protesters, what happened to Giuliani was a metaphor for what globalization is doing to the poorer nations of the world.

Opposite West meets East: McDonald's in Canton, China (1996).

1999

MIRACULOUS ECLIPSE

The fact that the science behind an eclipse is easily explained does not diminish its grandeur or the realization it brings that Earth is part of a much bigger system: In some ways, understanding the science provokes even greater wonderment. Normally the workings of the solar system are remote from everyday life, but people watching an eclipse experience those workings directly, as the shadow of the moon rushes across the surface of Earth, and at the moment of totality, the watcher is in direct alignment with the sun and the moon. The fact that nowhere else in the solar system will the sun and a planet's moon appear the same size prompted one BBC reporter to note, "For that event to happen where there is life to appreciate it seems truly miraculous."

Above Despite cloud cover over the Scottish capital, actors taking part in the Edinburgh Festival watch the solar eclipse from the Royal Mile in Edinburgh (August 11, 1999).

Opposite The moment of totality as seen from a village in Styria, Austria (August 11, 1999).

Total eclipse of the sun

On August 11, 1999, the second millennium's last total solar eclipse was visible across Europe, the Middle East, and southern Asia.

Partial solar eclipses are relatively common, but a total eclipse always causes great excitement, particularly when it can be seen from the more heavily populated parts of the world. The total eclipse of August 1999 came as a millennial gift from the skies, rushing across the Atlantic at 1,500 mph and then crossing southwest England (Cornwall and Devon), northern France, southern Germany, Austria, Hungary, Romania, Turkey, Iran, southern Pakistan, and India, before ending in the Bay of Bengal.

Most observers in Europe were disappointed by poor weather and massive traffic jams into and out of the path of the eclipse, but some were luckier, including RAF personnel who photographed the eclipse from above the clouds, enjoying a view shared by passengers on Concorde. Many Europeans opted to watch on television, and in Britain 13.4 million people tuned in—a record for a daytime event during the work week, involving such large numbers that there was also a record electricity surge on the national grid when people returned to work.

PRAYERS AND RITUALS

Many European enthusiasts traveled to Isfahan in central Iran after NASA announced that the town would be one of the best places to watch the eclipse. One French tourist in Isfahan said, "It's total frenzy; it's jam-packed everywhere, on the main square and the two banks of the Zayandah Rud River."

But while the eclipse provoked frenzied excitement in Westerners, for millions of Muslims and Hindus it was a more solemn spiritual experience—across the Middle East, Muslim clerics called the faithful to *namaz-e ayat* (special prayers offered at times of natural phenomena), while in India devout Hindus took ritual baths in the river Ganges or the sacred lakes in the holy city of Kurukshetra. And in Jordan, shopkeeper Samir Qalaji voiced the fears of the ancients, "We are scared that the sun will never rise again."

Where were you when?

As a radio producer, I was working at BBC World Service, and am very proud of a program I made tracking the transit of the eclipse across the face of the earth—squinting up at the sun high above the Thames through those tacky plastic glasses that came free with magazines. The captain of Concorde was on the program (Because of its speed, passengers experienced the eclipse longer than anyone else on Earth).

The eclipse finished as it set over the Bay of Bengal. I remember a reporter live on his rooftop in Bangladesh describing the spectacle of dozens of kites (feathered not fabric) rising up into the air from the surrounding trees with indignant cries, freaked by this sudden, untimely sunset.

—Mark Smalley, Bristol, England

2000

MILLENNIUM GAMES

The Sydney Olympics were a showcase for Australian talent, from the spectacular opening ceremony (watched by a worldwide television audience of 2.5 billion, including a record 10 million Australians) to the moving closing ceremony at which the International Olympic Committee president declared the Sydney Games to have been the best ever. And in between came a host of home sporting triumphs, the greatest among them being a second consecutive gold for the "Hockeyroos," the swimmers' greatest medal haul since 1972, and an unforgettable 400 meters from Cathy Freeman, who was described by *Time Europe*, after lighting the flame at the opening ceremony, as embodying "the image Australians wanted to show the world: young, beautiful, unpretentious—and on the verge of greatness."

The arrival of the new millennium

Dire occurrences were predicted for the arrival of Y2K, but the most common ill effect was a hangover from the world's biggest party.

The arrival of the new millennium both united and divided the planet. During the buildup the doom-mongers said that the world would end in biblical catastrophe or that the "Y2K computer bug" would wreak havoc with modern life; meanwhile, the optimists talked of the dawn of a new era bringing the hope of peace and understanding. The reality was that little changed on either score.

Some 6 billion people around the world came together in what was dubbed "the world's biggest party," but opinions were divided on almost every aspect of the celebration. First, Christians complained that Christ's 2000th birthday had been hijacked by secular society, while non-Christians pointed out that just as Christians had imposed their calendar on the rest of the world, everyone else had a right to join the party. Then there was the date: Most people wanted to see the nines roll over into zeroes and claimed that the old millennium ended on December 31, 1999; others pointed out that because the Roman calendar ran from 1B.C. to 1A.D. with no year zero, 2,000 years had not elapsed until the end, rather than the beginning, of the year 2000. And third, there was the time: Officially, according to Article V of the International Meridian Conference of 1884, the new millennium arrived everywhere in the world at midnight GMT; unofficially, it arrived at midnight local time—or sunrise, depending on custom.

PARTY TIME

By the night of December 31, 1999, the arguments were irrelevant—the world was going to party, and anyone who disagreed would simply be left out. Celebrations began at midnight local time on the recently renamed Millennium Island in the Republic of Kiribati, 14 hours ahead of GMT, and continued for 26 hours until midnight on the Ebon Atoll in the Republic of the Marshall Islands, 12 hours behind GMT. Some people partied twice—once at midnight local time and once at midnight GMT—while many partied all day just to make sure. And what a party it was—as journalist Euan Ferguson pointed out the next

Where were you when?

Some people collect things; I like to collect experiences. This is the equivalent of buying the Mona Lisa.

—Steve Beinar, of Massachusetts, in Times Square, New York

We close the century with most people still languishing in poverty, subjected to hunger, preventable disease, illiteracy and insufficient shelter.

—Nelson Mandela, at a ceremony in his former prison cell on Robben Island, South Africa

morning under the headline "Six Billion Unite in Peace: Just for a moment, it was possible to believe. With all the best parties there comes that one sublime moment, stranded in time, when all things seem possible…. And so it was with the biggest party on the planet, when most of its six billion souls stopped, if for one second, to remember that they were alive together on Earth, the beautiful accident."

Below Fireworks explode behind the Washington Monument at midnight in Washington, D.C. (December 31, 1999/ January 1, 2000).

Noon in damp and chilly Norwich, midnight in my Fijian village. I speak briefly and expensively by telephone to a cousin as their 2000 begins. This is for me, a Pacific village girl, a moment of religious significance as I believe in Jesus—while my typically English husband doesn't. But we certainly believe in one another and definitely drink to that.

—Akanisi Douse, Norwich, as quoted in *The Observer* newspaper

The light may be fading on the twentieth century, but the sun is still rising on America.

—Bill Clinton, U.S. president

Y2K makes no difference in Nigeria. We do not normally have light and water, so if we do now, then it must be a bonus.

—Ayodele Adewale, Lagos, Nigeria

2000

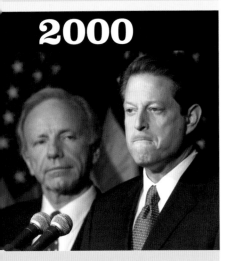

DIVIDED VOTE

The oft-ignored minority candidates played a significant role in the U.S. presidential election of 2000. As an example of just how confusing the Florida ballot paper was, critics pointed out that 3,400 votes were recorded in the predominantly Jewish area of Palm Beach for right-wing candidate Pat Buchanan, who had reportedly expressed "a qualified admiration for Hitler." And in New Hampshire disgruntled Democrats complained that Green Party candidate Ralph Nader had divided the anti-Bush vote—particularly galling to Democrats was that Gore lost the state, and with it four electoral votes that would have given him victory, by less than the 20,000 votes cast for Nader.

Above Al Gore (r), the Democratic presidential candidate in 2000, stands next to his vice-presidential running mate, Joe Lieberman, during a press conference in Nashville, Tennesse, on election day (November 7, 2000).

Opposite Judge Robert Rosenberg of Broward County Canvassing Board examines a dimpled chad on a punch-hole ballot card during a recount in Fort Lauderdale, Florida (November 24, 2000).

The controversial election of George W. Bush

The presidential election of 2000 was so close that it became the first in U.S. history to be decided by the Supreme Court.

Polling in the presidential election of 2000 ceased on November 7, but the election was not decided until December 12, after legal wrangles over a recount in Florida and the validity of certain votes there. Under America's Electoral College system each state carries a differing number of electoral votes, and a candidate requires 270 such votes to win. After the close of polling, it was quickly established that not counting the disputed state of Florida, Democratic candidate Al Gore had won 267 electoral votes and Republican George W. Bush 246. Florida carried 25 Electoral College votes, which meant that whoever won Florida would win the presidency.

COURT RULING

The first count in Florida gave Bush 2,887,426 popular votes and Gore 2,876,620, a difference of just 10,806 votes of more than 6 million cast. Initially Gore conceded defeat in a phone call to Bush but later retracted his concession and pledged to contest the result. Thousands of voters in Florida complained that the state's ballot paper was confusing, with the space for indicating a voter's preference not directly alongside each candidate's name.

There was further controversy over absentee ballots and military ballots, and over the validity of several thousand "dimpled" or "hanging chads" (partially punched holes in paper ballots where preference is indicated by a punched hole). Some of these (not all) were ruled eligible, following allegations that not to do so would discriminate against the frail and elderly. Had all these disputed ballots been counted, Gore would have been the winner.

The state ordered a recount, which determined that Bush had won Florida by a mere 537 votes. Democrats pressed for another recount, and after legal challenges, they were upheld by the Florida Supreme Court, which ordered it. But when Republicans then appealed to the U.S. Supreme Court, they were rewarded with a finding that Bush's apparent victory should stand.

Where were you when?

Gore calls Bush. "Let me make sure I understand," the Texas governor said, according to a report in Time *magazine. "You're calling me back to retract your concession." Bush tells Gore that Bush's brother, Florida gov. Jeb Bush, has assured the Texas governor that he has won Florida. "Your younger brother is not the ultimate authority on this," Gore replies.*

—CNN report, December 13, 2000

2001

1993 WTC BOMBING

The attacks of September 11, 2001, were not the first time that Islamic fundamentalists had tried to destroy the World Trade Center. On February 26, 1993, intending to shock the United States into withdrawing its support for Israel, Ramzi Yousef parked a van loaded with 1,210 lbs./ 550 kg of explosives in the underground garage beneath the WTC complex. When it exploded in the early afternoon, the truck bomb killed six people and injured more than 1,000, as well as starting an intense fire that sent acrid smoke billowing up to the 96th floor. The explosion, reportedly the most destructive terrorist attack perpetrated on U.S. soil to that date, left a 200 ft./60 m crater beneath the WTC but, fortunately, failed in its objective of bringing down the towers.

Above A shocked woman is given oxygen after Ramzi Yousef's bomb attack on the World Trade Center (February 26, 1993).

9/11

On Tuesday, September 11, 2001, normality was suspended as the world watched the apocalyptic scenes taking place in New York.

For those not directly involved in the horror of September 11, 2001, there was a strange sense of displacement while watching events relentlessly unfold that morning—a sense of numbed awe at watching two hijacked airliners being deliberately flown into the twin towers of the World Trade Center, and a third into the Pentagon. Under normal circumstances the news is carefully packaged and then presented with some measure of explanation or interpretation, but here was raw footage of an unimaginable happening broadcast with no such filter, with no explanation or reassurance, with no artificial distancing from reality as the horror reached a biblical scale with the collapse of first the south and then the north towers within a half hour of each other.

Newsmen and politicians knew no more than the viewers and were just as shocked. People spoke of a sense of unreality, but in fact, this was heightened reality: the need to make sense of something that was beyond comprehension or the control of the world's most powerful leaders. Here was news that was happening as people watched, not being reported after the event; news that was having an immediate and urgent effect on people not just at the epicenter but around the world. American airspace was shut down, and tall buildings in cities across the globe were evacuated in the fear that the same atrocity might be repeated elsewhere.

DISBELIEF

At first there was disbelief and a desperate need for more information. People gathered in crowds around televisions endlessly replaying what little news footage was available. They contacted loved ones to share the news and for comfort. They entered a displaced, dreamlike state of mourning for those they had never met, wanting and yet fearing to bridge the emotional gap between the visible destruction so reminiscent of countless Hollywood disaster movies and the human terror that could only be imagined—airline passengers knowing they were about to die, office workers making the decision to leap to certain death.

(continued on next page)

Where were you when?

When we emerged from the [subway] station, people were running frantically in the street area, and there was debris of all sorts everywhere. People were pointing, "It's over there, it's over there." And as we ran up the road toward the World Trade Center, I saw a plane sticking out of the building and I could not believe my eyes.

—Carol Paukner, police officer, NYPD

It was the most beautiful, crisp, sunny morning in New York. I had friends staying from abroad, and we were having a cup of morning coffee together. It was about nine o'clock when we first heard the noise of a plane flying over us. It sounded so low and distressed. My friend looked surprised and asked me if the planes normally fly so low. Then we heard the bang. It was not nearly as earth-shattering as you might think, considering what had actually happened. It sounded a bit like a car crash. I rushed out to our terrace, and I couldn't see what was wrong, as I was looking at the roads. Then I looked up and saw the big smoldering hole in the side of the World Trade Center.

—Katie Lydon, New York

Above During a presidential visit to a school in Sarasota, Florida, White House chief of staff Andrew Card (l) informs U.S. president George W. Bush of the attacks on the World Trade Center in New York (September 11, 2001).

The south tower of the World Trade Center collapses (September 11, 2001).

"THERE IS ONLY LOVE, AND THEN OBLIVION"

There was a collective sense of bereavement as people sought comfort in the company of others, talking endlessly about what had happened—face-to-face, by e-mail, on the telephone—as if to confirm their grip on reality. Novelists displaced politicians on the front pages of newspapers as nations turned to their authors and poets for some sort of perspective, some insight into what had happened.

In America, Jay McInerney wrote, "I want to hug strangers. I want to hurt other strangers.... It's not just me. Everyone I have spoken to is feeling indiscriminately compassionate. And furiously vengeful."

And in Britain, Ian McEwan described his stupefaction at seeing "the first plane disappearing into the side of the tower as cleanly as a posted letter; the couple jumping into the void, hand in hand," and at hearing the messages of love spoken into cell phones

by those trapped in the hijacked planes and the burning towers: "There is only love, and then oblivion. Love was all they had to set against the hatred of their murderers."

DEFIANCE

In the days and months that followed, the facts emerged along with the stories of individual anguish, suffering, and the heroism of the rescuers. As the cleanup operation and the search for the missing began, disbelief turned quickly to grief and then anger. The perpetrators were identified as Osama bin Laden's terrorist network Al-Qaeda, whom the United States vowed to hunt down and eradicate, but in the meantime those last phone calls continued to resonate. To quote McEwan again, "those snatched and anguished messages of love were their defiance."

"I want to hug strangers. I want to hurt other strangers.... It's not just me. Everyone I have spoken to is feeling indiscriminately compassionate. And furiously vengeful."

Above Rescue workers pause for a minute's silence during the harrowing process of sifting through the wreckage of the World Trade Center (September 13, 2001).

Top Dust chokes the streets of lower Manhattan (September 13, 2001).

2002

THE MADRID BOMBS

On March 11, 2004, a coordinated terrorist attack involving ten bombs placed in three Madrid stations during the morning rush hour killed 191 people. In the immediate aftermath, the Spanish authorities suspected the Basque separatist group Eta, but it now seems that the attacks were coordinated, as in Bali, by an Islamic fundamentalist group with possible links to Al-Qaeda. The Madrid attacks began at 7:39 A.M. with four explosions on a train entering Atocha station, near the city center, closely followed by three blasts on a train already inside the station. At 7:41 A.M. two bombs went off at the commuter station of El Pozo, and a minute after that, there was another explosion at the commuter station of Santa Eugenia, both in southeast Madrid.

The Bali bombs

The bombings of a bar and a nightclub by Islamic fundamentalists turned the island of Bali from holiday paradise to living hell.

Just 13 months after 9/11 people were very aware of the specter of terrorism, and throughout the world, security was tight in airports, public buildings, transport networks and government offices. What no one expected was that an Indonesian tourist paradise would be the victim of a terrorist attack, but on the evening of Saturday, October 12, 2002, two bombs wrought havoc in the popular Balinese resort of Kuta, killing more than 200 young vacationers and injuring several hundred more. Those killed and injured were mainly Australian but also included were British, Canadian, French, Swedish and Swiss tourists, as well as Indonesians working in the bars and clubs.

WAR ZONE

First a car bomb exploded on the crowded street outside the packed Paddy's bar, and then, a few minutes later, an even bigger explosion destroyed the Sari nightclub and the buildings around it. The second explosion could be heard more than 10 miles away, and eyewitnesses described seeing flames shooting 50 ft./15 m into the air above the club. Dazed and bloodied survivors wandered around the streets, which were littered with bodies, and one survivor described the resort as looking like a war zone. The Australian air force flew the most severely burned and badly injured to hospitals in Perth and Darwin, while the less badly injured and those who could not be moved were treated in Balinese hospitals.

The immediate assumption was that the bombings had been carried out by Al-Qaeda, but it now seems that they were perpetrated by an Indonesian-based Islamic fundamentalist organization known as Jemaah Islamiah.

"Outside it was awful, like something you'd see out of Vietnam."

Left The wreckage of a train bombed near Atocha station in Madrid, Spain (March 11, 2004).

Opposite Five days after the Bali bombings, a group of Australian survivors return to the site to grieve for the victims (October 17, 2002).

Where were you when?

I was sitting in Paddy's bar talking to a couple of guys I'd met about 10 minutes earlier.... There was just complete panic in the bar, loads of people diving for the door, trying to scramble over each other. Then outside it was awful, like something you'd see out of Vietnam. There were bodies everywhere. It was pretty dark, but you could tell some people were really badly injured. Lots of blood everywhere, people with burns. Some people with limbs that just, well, just terrible, terrible injuries.

—Matt Noyce, British tourist, talking to the BBC

2003

BUSH'S STATE VISIT TO LONDON

On November 18, 2003, President George W. Bush arrived in Britain on a state visit that had been arranged before the Iraq war. He brought with him an entourage of hundreds, including an unprecedented number of armed security guards. Wherever he went, he faced high-profile protests against the war in Iraq, many demonstrators brandishing posters, stating "WANTED: BUSH & BLAIR FOR WAR CRIMES." Protesters in London's Trafalgar Square toppled a papier-mâché statue of Bush as a satire on the U.S. forces' toppling of a statue of Saddam Hussein in Baghdad, which was itself a homage to the toppling of a statue of Stalin in Hungary in 1956 (see p. 82). Despite the furor, Blair announced that it was "precisely the right time for President Bush to be visiting this country."

Above "STOP BUSH": in Trafalgar Square, London, protesters topple an effigy of U.S. president Bush (November 20, 2003).

Opposite "NO WAR": a Greenpeace balloon leads antiwar protesters from the Brandenburg Gate to the Victory Column during an antiwar protest in Berlin, Germany (March 29, 2003).

Global protest against war in Iraq

On the weekend of February 15–16, 2003, more than 6 million people in 60 countries marched to protest against the threat of war in Iraq.

In the biggest antiwar demonstrations since the Vietnam War (see p. 112), between 6 and 10 million people took to the streets of cities across the world to protest against U.S. president George W. Bush's threat to take military action against Iraq (see p. 256).

London saw the biggest mass protest in the British capital's history, with reports of the numbers involved varying from a police estimate of 750,000 to the march organizers' estimate of nearly 2 million. London mayor Ken Livingstone reportedly told the crowd, "This war is solely about oil. George Bush has never given a damn about human rights."

In Australia, the only other country to have sent troops to the Gulf in preparation for war, more than half a million protesters turned out in the six state capitals, including more than 200,000 who took part in one of the biggest protests ever seen in Sydney. Like British prime minister Tony Blair, Australian Prime Minister John Howard ignored the protesters, saying, "In the end, my charge as prime minister is to take whatever decision I think is in the best interests of the country."

Rome, like London, recorded one of the biggest protests in the city's history, with reports as to the exact number varying even more than in London—from a police estimate of 650,000 to an organizers' figure of 3 million. Spanish police estimated that some 1.3 million people marched in Barcelona, with some 200,000 in Seville and more than 600,000 in Madrid.

U.S. PROTESTS

Although demonstrations took place all around the globe, the main focus was on New York, victim of the 9/11 attacks and yet visibly opposed to war against Iraq. Some 100,000 people, including relatives of the WTC victims, gathered near the UN headquarters to protest, and actress Susan Sarandon voiced their feelings when she announced, "There are alternatives to war. Nothing has been proved so far that warrants an invasion of Iraq."

Where were you when?

It was a wonderful feeling to be with over 150,000 people all opposed to our government's stance on the war.

—Ann de Hugard, Melbourne, Australia

My back is killing me, and I don't feel like marching on Saturday. I feel like sitting in a pub and drowning my pain in good booze and good company, but I'll be there. Now more than ever it is important for the peace movement to go forward and to confront the lies of this war.

—John Wilkinson, London

2003

09/11/01 The World Trade Center is destroyed and the Pentagon badly damaged in terrorist attacks by Al-Qaeda (see p. 248).

10/07/01 The United States and Britain attack Afghanistan in the first military action of the war on terror (see "War in Afghanistan," opposite).

10/01– The United States and Britain
11/01 destroy Al-Qaeda training camps and assist the Northern Alliance in deposing the Taliban. The United States controversially takes hundreds of alleged members of Al-Qaeda prisoner, to be interrogated and held without trial at Guantanamo Bay in Cuba.

01/29/02 U.S. president Bush denounces what he calls "the axis of evil"— the states of Iraq, Iran and North Korea.

11/02 The United States persuades the UN Security Council to pass Resolution 1441, requiring Iraq to prove that it has no weapons of mass destruction (WMDs). UN weapons inspectors find no evidence of WMDs.

02/05/03 Directly contradicting UN weapons inspectors, U.S. secretary of state Colin Powell claims to have evidence of illegal weapons and weapons research facilities in Iraq. The United States and Britain subsequently pressurize the UN to authorize military action against Iraq, but the UN refuses.

02/15/03– Between 6 and 10 million people
02/16/03 in some 60 countries march to protest against the expected invasion of Iraq (see p. 248).

03/20/03 The United States and Britain invade Iraq without UN authorization.

04/03 U.S. forces occupy the Iraqi capital Baghdad, British forces take the southern city of Basra, and the United States declares that "major combat operations" are over.

U.S.–British invasion of Iraq

After a UN refusal to sanction military action, the United States and Britain invaded Iraq in the most controversial military action since World War II.

In the aftermath of the 9/11 attacks (see p. 248), U.S. president George W. Bush declared a worldwide "war on terror," leading political observers to predict that the attacks on America would be used as a reason to wage war on Iraq whether or not a direct link with terrorist network Al-Qaeda could be proved. After the failure of U.S. and British forces to capture the leaders of Al-Qaeda during the war in Afghanistan (see opposite), Bush used his 2002 State of the Nation address to denounce what he called the "axis of evil," made up of the states of Iraq, Iran and North Korea, saying, "The United States will not permit the world's most dangerous regimes to threaten us with the world's most dangerous weapons." War on Iraq was now inevitable. In August 2002 Bush announced that he favored "regime change" in Iraq, and in November the United States managed to persuade the UN Security Council to pass Resolution 1441, requiring Iraq to prove that it had decommissioned its weapons of mass destruction (WMDs). UN weapons inspectors found no evidence of WMDs, but in February, U.S. secretary of state Colin Powell told the United Nations that he had evidence of illegal weapons and weapons research facilities in Iraq. The United States and Britain began pressurizing the United Nations to authorize military action, claiming that Iraq had not complied with Resolution 1441, but the United Nations refused on the basis that if such weapons existed, then the inspectors would find them.

But the United States and Britain were not prepared to wait—and in Britain, Prime Minister Tony Blair bolstered his case for war with the highly controversial claim that Iraq could deploy WMDs at 45 minutes' notice. When this was subsequently proved not to be the case, many antiwar protesters dubbed the prime minister "Tony Bliar."

OPERATION SHOCK AND AWE
Having failed to persuade the United Nations to authorize military action, the United States and Britain ("the coalition") went ahead anyway, launching Operation Shock and Awe on March 20, 2003, with an aerial bombardment of the Iraqi capital Baghdad and a

Where were you when?

On April 6 conditions were right for full entry into Basrah and the removal of the regime there. Some resistance was quickly overcome by superior firepower, the excellent protection offered by Challenger tanks and Warrior armored infantry fighting vehicles and UK troops' resourceful determination. By April 7 Basrah was liberated, the local regime removed and reconstruction under way.

—British Ministry of Defense report, Operations in Iraq, Lessons for the Future, December 2003

ground invasion from the south. Initially, coalition forces were hindered by sandstorms, but as the weather improved, the troops soon proved too strong for the Iraqi forces. Within a month Baghdad had fallen, Iraq was under coalition control, and the United States announced that "major combat operations" were over.

However, overcoming the Iraqi military proved to be far easier than restoring law and order and installing a new government in Iraq. And the political fallout was immense, the invasion sparking off an unprecedented level of worldwide protest at a bilateral act of aggression carried out against the express wishes of the United Nations and in contravention of international law.

Below Fires burn in and around Saddam Hussein's Council of Ministers in Baghdad, Iraq, during the first wave of attacks in the "Shock and Awe" phase of "Operation Iraqi Freedom" (March 21, 2003).

Bottom During the war in Afghanistan, two girls in the Nawabad refugee camp put their U.S. food aid packages to good use as school bookbags (October 25, 2001).

WAR IN AFGHANISTAN

On October 7, 2001, the United States and Britain launched a major attack on Afghanistan, the first military action of Bush's "war on terror." Although attacking Afghanistan was a military risk, particularly in the light of the Soviet invasion of 1979 (see p. 176), it was politically sound: Terrorist leader Osama bin Laden was known to be in hiding there, and some 50 Al-Qaeda training camps were known to exist there. The war was successful in enabling the native Northern Alliance to overthrow the oppressive regime of the Taliban, but it failed in its goal of capturing bin Laden and raised worldwide concern over the treatment and detention without trial of suspected Al-Qaeda members at a U.S. base in Guatanamo Bay, Cuba—another direct breach of international law.

2003

TIMELINE

Above J. K Rowling waves good-bye to fans as she leaves King's Cross Station, London, for a promotional tour of northern England (July 8, 2000).

Opposite A Finnish boy reads a copy of *Harry Potter and the Order of the Phoenix* while he lines up to pay for the novel in a bookshop in Helsinki, Finland (June 22, 2003).

Harry Potter and the Order of the Phoenix

Going on sale simultaneously in countries across the globe, the fifth volume of the Harry Potter series broke all publishing records.

In 1997 author J. K. Rowling burst onto the literary scene with *Harry Potter and the Philosopher's Stone*, the first of a series of books about the adventures of the eponymous young wizard. This first adventure was published in paperback as a children's book, but the publisher, Bloomsbury, soon realized that it had been somewhat modest in its expectations. It seemed that the book appealed to children, parents and grandparents alike, creating a social phenomenon known as Pottermania—a revolution that was credited with reestablishing reading as a major pastime after years of erosion by film, television and computer games.

THREE-YEAR GAP

After four Harry Potter books in four years, fans had a long wait for number five, but at least they had two feature films to tide them over. Such a long gap between novels can be disastrous in the publishing industry, but Bloomsbury used the time to create more hype than for any novel in history, so that by June 2003 fans were desperate to buy the new book. Thousands lined up for hours to be among the first to own a copy of *Harry Potter and the Order of the Phoenix*, and at one minute past midnight GMT on the night of Saturday/Sunday June 21–22, midsummer's night, the new volume went on sale simultaneously across the globe and the cash registers started ringing. In Britain more than 1.8 million copies were sold on the first day, and many bookshops had to ration their customers, some of whom wanted to buy several copies so that family members would not have to wait for one another to finish reading it. Similar scenes around the world made *Harry Potter and the Order of the Phoenix* the fastest-selling book ever and took J. K. Rowling from being one of the richest women in Britain to being one of the richest in the world.

J. K. ROWLING AND THE GENESIS OF HARRY POTTER

Legend has it that the reason Joanne Kathleen Rowling used her initials rather than her full name as author of the first Harry Potter adventure was because publishers Bloomsbury were aiming the book at boys, who might be put off if they knew it was written by a female author. J. K. wrote her first story at the age of six (about a rabbit called Rabbit) and kept on writing fiction in the hopes of becoming a published author until, on a train journey from Manchester to London, Harry Potter "just strolled into my head fully formed." She then spent five years developing the other characters and outlining the plots before starting to write *Harry Potter and the Philosopher's Stone*. And the rest, as they say, is history, mystery, magic and suspense.

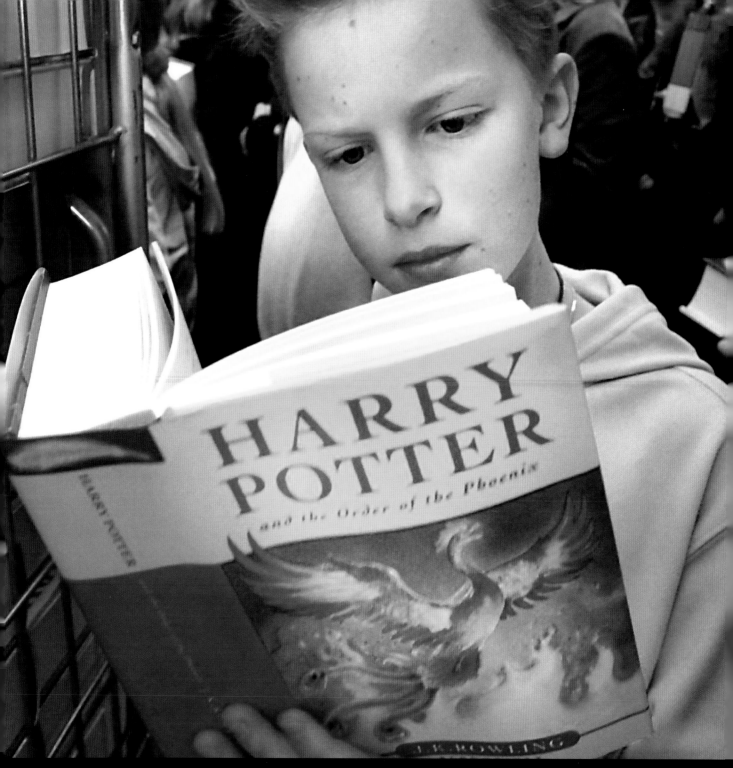

Where were you when?

This is a book about magic, but there's plenty of reality. Settling into a new school, making friends, learning who to trust and who not to trust and when to obey school rules and when to overlook them. There's a great deal of humor in the book. You might find the magic funny—visit Diagon Alley to purchase all your Hogwart's kit—but there is strong evil magic too, and you won't doubt the courage that Harry has to show in the final chapter.

—Book review, 1997, on www.readingmatters.co.uk

I love Harry Potter. Once I started reading the first book, I was hooked. And now all of my friends are reading these books, too, and we're all adults. I'm sure I'll be reading every book in the series.

—Kara Plikaitis, Chestnut Hill, Pennsylvania

2003

SADDAM'S QUEST FOR POWER

Saddam Hussein was born into a peasant family in Tikrit and joined the Arab Ba'ath Socialist Party in 1957 at the age of 20. Two years later he fled the country after being sentenced to death for the attempted assassination of head of state General Qassim, who had himself come to power by overthrowing the monarchy in a bloody coup the previous year. Saddam returned to Iraq in 1963, after the death of Qassim in a coup led by Colonel Salem Aref, but he was imprisoned in 1964 for attempting to overthrow Aref. In 1968 he played a central role in a successful coup that replaced the civilian government with the Revolutionary Command Council (RCC), and in 1979 he began his dictatorship when he became chairman of the RCC and president of Iraq.

Above In the course of an official visit to Baghdad, Iraq, during the Iran-Iraq War, U.S. envoy (now U.S. secretary of defense) Donald Rumsfeld (l) shakes hands with Iraqi dictator Saddam Hussein (December 20, 1983).

The capture of Saddam Hussein

Having failed to capture Osama bin Laden or to find weapons of mass destruction in Iraq, the Allies were jubilant when U.S. forces captured Saddam Hussein.

The arguments about the legality and the morality of the war in Iraq (see p. 256) will continue long into the future, but one thing is certain: Iraq is better off without Saddam Hussein in power. Early in the war, the United States announced its 55 "most wanted" and issued decks of playing cards depicting Iraqi officials and members of Saddam's family, with the No.1 most wanted, Saddam himself, as the Ace of Spades. After the fall of Baghdad in April 2003, Saddam successfully evaded capture for eight months until early in December, when, according to a U.S. military spokesman, U.S. forces extracted information about his exact whereabouts from one of his clan: "We brought in about five to ten members of these families and finally got the ultimate information from one of these individuals."

OPERATION RED DAWN

U.S. Special Forces immediately launched Operation Red Dawn, and on December 13 the former dictator was in custody after being discovered hiding in a tiny "spider hole," or cellar, dug into the earth beneath a hut in the grounds of a rural farmhouse close to his hometown of Tikrit. The narrow hole was 7 ft./2–2.5 m deep and wide enough to lie down in, equipped with a breathing hole in case of an elongated period in hiding and concealed with a rug, bricks, and dirt. U.S. military spokesman Major General Ray Odierno said, "He was caught like a rat. It was ironic that he was in a hole in the ground across the river from the great palaces he built using all the money he robbed from the Iraqi people."

After Saddam's identity had been verified by DNA tests, U.S. administrator Paul Bremer called a press conference and announced, "Ladies and gentlemen, we got him. The tyrant is a prisoner."

Opposite Two days after the event, American soldiers reenact the moment that Saddam Hussein was discovered in his "spider hole" in Ad Dawr, Iraq (December 15, 2003).

Where were you when?

We are celebrating like it's a wedding. We are finally rid of that criminal.

—Mustapha Sheriff, resident of Kirkuk, Iraq

This is the joy of a lifetime. I am speaking on behalf of all the people that suffered under his rule.

—Ali Al-Bashiri, resident of Kirkuk, Iraq

2004

OTHER 2004 FAREWELLS

The year 2004 also saw the last new episodes of two other popular U.S. sitcoms, *Sex and the City* (above), on February 22, and *Frasier* (below) on May 13, the week after the last episode of *Friends*. After six seasons *Sex and the City* bowed out with episode 94, the longest ever at just over 45 minutes, which featured central character Carrie wearing "the dress of a thousand layers"—a Versace creation with a retail price of $79,000. Three months later *Frasier* (a spin off of 1980s hit sitcom *Cheers*) ended, after 11 seasons and a record 31 Grammy Awards, with an hour long special (episode 264) that drew 25 million viewers in the United States.

The last episode of *Friends*

After 10 years and 234 episodes, U.S. sitcom *Friends* finally bowed out with an hour-long finale that drew record advertising fees.

One American TV critic complained that the finale of *Friends* featured "about a thousand good-byes (in fact, several hundred too many)," but it was what friends of *Friends* wanted. Some 52.5 million fans in the United States, 5.2 million in Canada, 2.54 million in Australia and a record 8.6 million in the UK (fully one-third of UK viewers) watched at home, while thousands of others decided that they were not going to say their farewells in private. Special drive-in television theaters were set up in many states, and outdoor screens were set up in London's Trafalgar Square, New York's Times Square and at the Universal Citywalk in Los Angeles, which hosted a special *Friends* Finale Party.

"SWEET AND DUMB AND SATISFYING"

American television network NBC devoted three hours of its schedule to the finale, broadcasting an hour-long retrospective before the final episode and afterward showing a special edition of *The Tonight Show with Jay Leno*, featuring all six co-stars on the set of the sitcom. Advertising rates for the show itself sold for an average of $2 million per 30-second slot—the sort of figure usually paid for events such as the Super Bowl and a record for a sitcom.

Before filming the final episode earlier in the year, Jennifer Aniston said on behalf of the cast, "This is gutting us. We're like delicate china, and we're speeding toward an inevitable brick wall." Fans were equally distraught, but some critics were glad to see the back of the show, *USA Today* saying that over 10 years it had "tarnished more than it tanned." Others claimed that the show had "left its signature on American TV history" and that the last episode marked "the end of TV sitcom as we know it." But *Newsday* was probably most in tune with the popular mood, with a summation that could have applied to the entire 10-year run: "Sweet and dumb and satisfying."

Where were you when?

Friends has left its signature on American TV history. People are really going to miss it. To have lasted more than 10 years with a show that has maintained such strength and popularity is an achievement few entertainers in U.S. history have been able to accomplish. What this group of six reflected was a microcosm of what people their age encountered in their daily lives. Viewers related to them.

—Steve Beverly, Professor of Communication Arts, Union University, Tennessee

Anyone new to Friends *who succumbed to the hype to tune in Thursday would have been surprised at how laughless the affair could be. Nearly every strained gag depends on the sheer stupidity of its characters.*

—Roger Catlin's review in *Hartford Courant*

Friends *was getting creaky even as it remained popular…After 10 years of pretty good TV, the show tarnished more than it tanned; its winks have turned to wrinkles…Time does indeed matter even among the best of Friends.*

—Editorial in *USA Today*

Above Fans watch the final episode of *Friends* during the 2004 Tribeca Film Festival in New York (May 6, 2004).

Opposite top *Sex and the City*'s Sarah Jessica Parker collects an Emmy for Outstanding Lead Actress in a Comedy Series (September 19, 2004).

Opposite below *Frasier* cast members, with Kelsey Grammer (front c) as Dr. Frasier Crane.

2004

TIMELINE

09/01/04 Masked Chechen separatist terrorists burst into Middle School No.1 in Beslan, Russia, and force more than 1,000 hostages into the school gym. That afternoon the terrorists demand the release of Chechen freedom fighters held by the Russians.

09/02/04 Negotiations between the Russian authorities and the terrorists fail, but the authorities nevertheless rule out the use of force to end the siege. In the late afternoon the terrorists release 26 women and children.

09/03/04 At 6:30 A.M. the terrorists fire two rocket-propelled grenades at Russian troops deploying around the school. At 9:30 A.M. the terrorists allow emergency workers into the building to remove hostages killed on the first day of the siege. Later, two large explosions destroy part of the school. Russian Special Forces move in, and by 3:55 P.M. Russian officials say they have the situation under control, although the media report that a "heavy gun battle" is still taking place.

Above Russian troops in front of the burning school buildings at Beslan (September 3, 2004).

Opposite A man carries an injured schoolboy out of the school during the rescue operation in Beslan (September 3, 2004).

Siege at Beslan

Over 300 children were killed in Beslan, Russia, after Chechen terrorists stormed a school and took more than 1,000 hostages.

However deep the (rightful) grievances of the Chechen people against Russian oppression, absolutely nothing can justify the action that Chechen separatists took on September 1, 2004. At 9:30 A.M., as a ceremony marking the first day of the new school year came to an end, masked terrorists burst into Middle School No.1 in Beslan and opened fire with machine guns, killing several people. They then herded hundreds of hostages into the school gym, which they proceeded to wire up with mines and bombs, and threatened to blow up the building if Russian Special Forces should attack—and, to prove that they were serious, they placed children in the windows to act as human shields against such an attack.

The terrorists demanded the release of Chechen freedom fighters held by the Russians, and for two days the Russian authorities negotiated with the terrorists to no avail. The separatists refused to exchange their child hostages for senior Russian officials, and they refused to accept food or water for those being held in the stifling heat of the gym.

EXPLOSIONS

Early on September 3 the terrorists fired two rocket-propelled grenades at Russian troops who were deployed around the school. Later that day, while the world questioned the wisdom of sending troops into such a volatile situation versus the consequences of not doing so, two explosions rocked the school. It is unclear whether the detonations were accidental or a deliberate response to the presence of the Russian troops, but the effect was immediate. Children began to flee through the resulting holes in the wall, the terrorists fired at the escaping children, and the Russian Special Forces fired back.

Mayhem ensued as troops and armed relatives stormed the school. Eventually the Russians took control, and only then was the full horror revealed—more than 300 charred bodies were found in the gym, most of them children. For all the media analysis of the siege, one image recorded by *The Guardian* newspaper told of the real human tragedy: "A curtain fluttered in the wind. Children's drawings from their art classes could still be seen taped across windows. But there was no one left to walk out of the ruins."

DUNBLANE AND COLUMBINE

Sadly, Beslan is not the only school whose name has been become associated throughout the world with violence. On March 13, 1996, aggrieved misfit Thomas Hamilton entered Dunblane primary school in Scotland with four guns and 743 rounds of ammunition. He then walked into the gym, where he killed 3 adults and 16 children, and injured 11 other children before shooting himself in the head.

On April 20, 1999, U.S. teenagers Eric Harris and Dylan Klebold took two Tec-9 submachine guns into their school, Columbine High School in Colorado, and carried out an attack they had planned for Adolf Hitler's birthday, in which they killed 15 students and injured many others before turning their guns on themselves.

It was like a sauna in there. No water or food, and we were all burning up with fear. They had put mines all around the room.... But when they tried to detonate them, only two of the mines worked. Both blasts missed me, although one was very close.... I ran to grab my child, and we hid in the small hall near the gym. There we stood for 20 minutes, dealing with the wounded and hiding until the spetznaz [Special Forces troops] found us and led us out.

—Ifa Gagiyeva, who was trapped in the school with her daughter Diana, 7

There are no words strong enough to express the disgust and horror all decent people feel toward such actions. Their campaigns are the very opposite of brave and heroic and bring the deepest and most profound shame upon the causes they pretend to represent.

—Editorial in *Arab News*

2004

THE ASSASSINATION OF PIM FORTUYN

Another Dutchman to be murdered for his controversial views was the subject of a film in progress by Theo van Gogh: politican Pim Fortuyn, who was vehemently against immigration into the Netherlands and was particularly opposed to Muslims due to Islam's intolerance of homosexuality. On May 6, 2002, as he was walking to his chauffeur-driven car after giving a radio interview, Fortuyn was shot five times at point-blank range. Perhaps surprisingly, his assassin was neither an immigrant nor a Muslim, but Dutch animal-rights activist Volkert van der Graaf, who was sentenced to 18 years' imprisonment but remained unrepentant, saying that he had eliminated "a danger to society."

The murder of Theo van Gogh

After making a controversial film about Islam, Dutch filmmaker Theo van Gogh was brutally murdered on the streets of Amsterdam.

Theo van Gogh was well known in the Dutch media as a talented and extremely provocative filmmaker, columnist and television interviewer, and in November 2004 he became famous around the world as the victim of what has been described as "peacetime Europe's most extreme act of intolerance." Sacked from several newspapers for offending the readership, van Gogh was a passionate believer in free speech and used that right to openly criticize Judaism and Christianity, as well as Islam, earning himself the epithet "equal-opportunity controversialist."

He received several death threats after the screening of his film *Submission*, which suggested that Islam encourages misogyny and that the Koran sanctions domestic violence, but he did not take the threats seriously and refused police protection, saying, "No one can seriously want to shoot the village idiot." But his faith in the tolerance of others was fatally flawed, and on November 2, 2004, he was gunned down as he cycled to work.

BUTCHER

According to eyewitnesses, van Gogh was shot several times but managed to stagger more than 100 ft./30 m before being shot again. He then begged on his knees for mercy, but his killer fired yet again and then, "with the detachment of a butcher," took out two knives from beneath his jellaba and slit Van Gogh's throat before pushing both blades into his chest, using one of them to pin a five-page letter to the body. The letter reportedly threatened Ayaan Hirsi Ali, a Somali-born Dutch MP who had collaborated with van Gogh on *Submission*, as well as threatening a holy war against infidels. Eight men were arrested for involvement in the killing, and the Dutch justice minister announced that the alleged killer, a Dutch-Moroccan named Mohammed Bouyeri, had "acted out of radical Islamic fundamentalist convictions."

"a danger to society."

Supporters of Pim Fortuyn hold up posters of the slain politician as they wait to pay their respects in Rotterdam, Netherlands, where thousands of people lined up to bid him farewell (May 9, 2002).

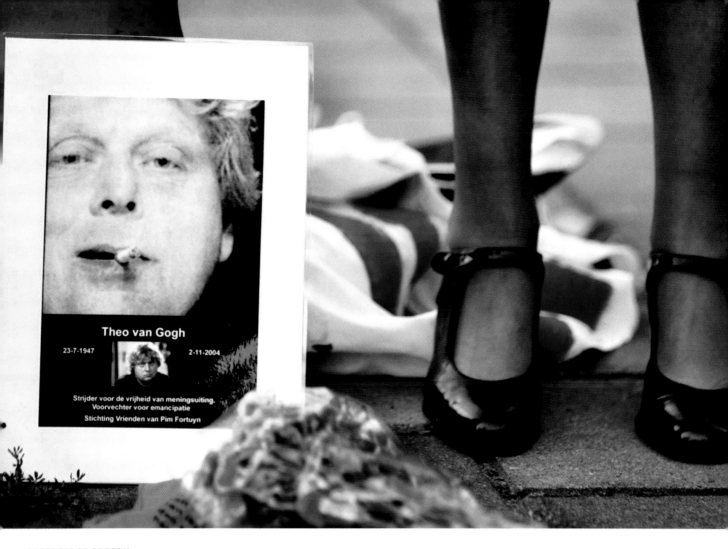

FREEDOM OF SPEECH

The night after the killing, several thousand people gathered in Amsterdam's central square banging improvized drums and blowing whistles and horns after van Gogh's friends and family had asked people to make as much noise as possible in support of free speech. It is an important issue for a country famed for its tolerance of the views of others, but also for the right to criticize and question those views—a point stressed by the mayor of Amsterdam, Job Cohen, who announced, "The freedom of speech is a foundation of our society and that foundation was tampered with today. Theo van Gogh picked fights with many people, myself included, but that is a right in this country."

During Theo van Gogh's funeral in Amsterdam, Netherlands, a woman stands next to a mourning card depicting the controversial filmmaker (November 9, 2004).

"No one can seriously want to shoot the village idiot."

Where were you when?

Bullets will never have the last word in the Netherlands. The world knows the Netherlands as a country where free speech is sacrosanct. We teach our children how important it is that we all accept each other's point of view. We will not allow violence to decide who dares say what.

—Jan Peter Balkenende, prime minister of Netherlands, November 2, 2004, quoted in *The Daily Telegraph*

I deeply, deeply regret this death of a man who just stood out because of his opinion, wasn't a racist of any kind, but just criticized the Muslim community and its repression of women.

—Jeroen de Rooij, Amsterdam, Netherlands

2004

OTHER TSUNAMIS

Tsunamis are not uncommon, but thankfully they rarely occur on the scale of the 2004 disaster, whose death toll makes it the worst ever, having surpassed the estimated 215,000 people killed in the Bay of Bengal, India, in 1876. The highest wave ever recorded (although not always defined as a tsunami, because it was caused by land sliding into the water rather than by an underwater landslide or earthquake) occurred in Lituya Bay, Alaska, on July 9, 1958. The wave traveled at 100 mph, and it swamped the hills on the other side of the fjordlike inlet to a height of 1,719 ft./ 524 m—considerably higher than the world's tallest building, which is 1,482 ft./452 m high—and the energy was then dissipated as the wave rolled back into the bay and harmlessly out to sea.

The awesome power of the tsunami pushes a torrent of seawater through the streets of Maddampegama, about 38 miles/60 kilometers south of Colombo, Sri Lanka (December 26, 2004).

Tsunami

On December 26, a strange word became grotesquely familiar as thousands of people were killed by a tsunami and its aftereffects.

At 7:59 a.m. on December 26, 2004, many tourists in Indonesia and Thailand were recovering from their Christmas celebrations, while the locals were going about their Sunday business. At that moment, the seabed 93 miles off the coast of the Indonesian island of Sumatra was shaken by the world's most powerful earthquake in 40 years, buckling parts of the seafloor by up to 32 ft./10 m and pushing millions of cubic feet of seawater away from the epicenter at immense speeds.

Within 15 minutes the Pacific Tsunami Warning Center in Hawaii had sent an alert to 26 countries, but for the most part the warnings simply did not reach the right people in time. Over the next one to three hours a series of giant waves slammed into the coastlines surrounding the Indian Ocean, wreaking havoc in Indonesia, Malaysia, Thailand, Burma, the Andaman Islands, India, Sri Lanka, the Maldives, and even Somalia, which lies 2,800 miles from the quake's epicenter.

UTTER DESTRUCTION

Satellite photographs presented a terrifying objective view of the destruction that occurred as the sea swept out and back in again. Survivors' accounts gave an equally terrifying subjective view: "The sea had gone out so quickly that the fish had been left stranded," said Swedish policewoman Karin Svard, who was with her children on a beach Thailand. "It was strange, but I thought maybe it was just the tide going out. I didn't understand its importance—until I looked at the horizon." Miraculously, her entire family survived after being swept inland and washed up onto high ground.

(continued on next page)

> "It was strange, but I thought maybe it was just the tide going out. I didn't understand its importance—until I looked at the horizon."

Where were you when?

The horror of this place reminds me of something from a biblical disaster story or the sketches of Hieronymus Bosch [a painter of monstrous scenes of hell]. *Everywhere I go I have to be careful I don't step on a corpse. The magnitude of this thing is that this goes on for hundreds of miles in both directions. In one area some 10 square miles of the city was completely flattened. It is feared that something like 30,000 bodies are still in there.*

—Chris Rainier, *National Geographic* magazine, January 11, 2005

My family and I remained riveted to the TV screen as we watched the almost unbelievable horror of the waves sweeping people to their deaths.

—Cheryl Lundeen, Manchester, Connecticut

2004 Tsunami cont.

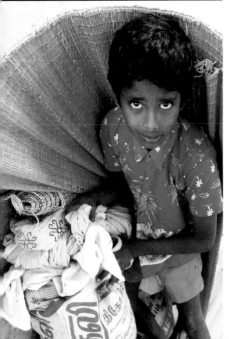

After flying over Sumatra to survey the damage, UN secretary-general Kofi Annan told reporters, "I have never seen such utter destruction mile after mile. You wonder, Where are the people? What has happened to them?" The answer was that almost 300,000 people on the various coastlines of the Indian Ocean had been killed by the awesome power of the very sea that had, in many cases, been their livelihood.

Around the world, religious leaders strove to explain what secular insurance companies refer to as "an act of God" and many believers call a natural disaster. The Bishop of Durham chose words with which atheists and believers alike could agree: that the earth "lives and moves. It is not inert, it is alive—that is why we can live. Last week's events were a stark reminder that what gives life also takes it away." He also told his congregation, "Words seem cheap when the cost of lives has been so expensive."

Left An Indian boy, with all that is left of his belongings, arrives at a shelter in Periyakuppam, India, for those made homeless by the tsunami disaster (December 31, 2004).

Below Volunteers from the Indonesian Red Cross recover bodies from the town of Banda Aceh, close to the epicenter of the earthquake that caused the tsunami (January 2005).

Opposite Carina Askerwall (r) embraces her son Ludvig on his arrival at Arlanda Airport in Stockholm, Sweden. Ludvig was on holiday with his father, John, in Kao Lak, Thailand, when the tsunami struck, but thankfully neither was injured (December 28, 2004).

Where were you when?

By 10:30 the tsunamis hit our island of Olhuveli, Maldives. We had seconds to react—the wave was so powerful. Whizzing past me was bedroom furniture, TVs, fridges. We had to fight for our lives. The experience was terrifying. I never thought we were going to get off the island alive. The whole island was destroyed.

—Rita Davie, quoted on BBC website

"I have never seen such utter destruction mile after mile. You wonder, Where are the people? What has happened to them?"

2005

ATTEMPTED ASSASSINATION

On May 13, 1981, just three years into his tenure as pope, John Paul II was being driven through St. Peter's Square in the open-topped "popemobile" to perform his weekly blessing when a man fired several shots at him from the crowd. The pope was immediately rushed to the hospital, where he underwent a five-hour operation to remove four bullets from his body, after which he made a full recovery. The would-be assassin was later identified as a 23-year-old Turk named Mehmet Ali Ağca, who had arrived in Rome under a false identity after escaping from a Turkish jail, where he was being held for the murder of a newspaper editor. On December 27, 1983, during a Christmas visit to Rebibbia Prison in Rome, the pope met Ağca in his cell and granted him forgiveness for his crime.

The coffin containing the body of Pope John Paul II is carried to its position before an altar set up on the esplanade in front of St. Peter's Basilica, Vatican City (April 8, 2005).

The death of Pope John Paul II

On the pope's death at 9:37 P.M. on April 2, 2005, the Vatican announced, "Our Holy Father John Paul has returned to the House of the Father."

After more than 26 years in office, John Paul II died as the third-longest serving pope in history. He was crowned pontiff in 1978 after succeeding one of the shortest-serving incumbents in the autumn of "the year of three popes": Paul VI died on August 6 that year and was succeeded later the same month by John Paul I, who died on September 30, after just 33 days in office. Then, on October 16, the polish cardinal Karol Wojtyla was crowned Pope John Paul II—the first non-Italian Pontiff since Adrian VI of the Netherlands, who died in 1523.

John Paul II proved to be a popular, charismatic Pope, and made a large number of foreign visits early in his pontificate, each one prefaced with his trademark gesture of kissing the tarmac as he arrived at the airport. He drew huge, adoring audiences wherever he traveled, and he preached in the flesh to more people than any previous pope—but his stubborn conservatism over issues such as homosexuality, divorce and contraception led him to be dubbed "the pope they loved but could not obey."

John Paul II's reign was full of contradictions. He was hailed as a radical modernizer when he published his sermons on the Internet or pronounced on political issues such as Communist oppression and Third World debt, but he was dismissed as an antiquated reactionary over other issues, such as his negative attitude to the idea of women being ordained and his stated compassion for pedophile priests. He was praised for championing individual freedom but criticized for tightening church controls that had been relaxed by the Second Vatican Council during the 1960s—dichotomies that led one leading Catholic writer to describe the opposing sides of his personality as "the romantic freedom fighter [living] side by side with the terrifying autocrat."

THE FUNERAL

John Paul II's funeral was an unprecedented outdoor extravaganza that echoed his famous al fresco masses. It was attended by heads of church and state from around the world, as

Where were you when?

I made sure I went down to St. Peter's after work on the day Pope Benedict was elected. Of course, he had finished appearing on the balcony, but there were still huge numbers of people. Some were trying to get into St.Peter's, but most of them seemed to be milling about chatting to each other about the new pope—did anyone know his views on this or on that. What impressed me most was the fact that some enterprising chap was already selling T-shirts with the new pope's name on.

—Rupert Matthews, Surrey, England

What would the carpenter of Nazareth think about yesterday's events in Rome?

—Mabel Taylor, in a letter to *The Guardian*, April 9, 2005, on the pope's funeral well as by thousands of ordinary people who had made the pilgrimage to Rome, and it was watched on television by millions, if not billions more. In death as in life, the late pope managed to make a powerful visual gesture, in this case one that said more about him than all of the spoken eulogies. In the midst of all the pomp, circumstance and ceremony, the simple cypress-wood coffin he had requested in his will stood as a potent symbol of the humility he maintained despite the majesty of his position as head of the Catholic Church. Ten days later he was succeeded by a German cardinal, Joseph Ratzinger, who named himself Pope Benedict XVI.

Mourners reach out to touch a photograph of Pope John Paul II during a Mass at Our Lady of Angels Cathedral in Los Angeles, California (April 2, 2005).

2005

Hurricane Katrina

On August 29 2005, New Orleans bore the brunt of the most costly weather disaster and its deadliest hurricane since 1928.

Hurricane Katrina was headline news even before it hit New Orleans, so millions of people were already watching in awe as the storm swept across Florida and into the Gulf of Mexico, hoping against hope that it would deviate from its course before hitting the city. Katrina began life on August 23 as a tropical depression over the Bahamas, and the following day it intensified into Tropical Storm Katrina, continuing to gain strength until at 11:00 P.M. a hurricane warning was issued for Florida. A day later, on August 25, Katrina hit Miami as a Category 1 hurricane and swept across Florida, causing substantial damage, severe flooding, and killing 14 people.

Katrina then began to cross the Gulf of Mexico, where its warm waters helped to reintensify the storm until, on Sunday August 28, it was classified as a Category 5 ("catastrophic") hurricane, with sustained wind speeds peaking at nearly 175 mph. By now the world was expecting the worst as Katrina continued on course for New Orleans, making landfall in Lousiana at 6.10 A.M. on August 29 having diminished to a Category 3. Within hours it hit New Orleans with wind speeds of up to 100 mph, creating a storm surge that raised water levels by up to 25 ft./7.5 m, fulfilling the National Hurricane Center's earlier warning: "Some levees in the Greater New Orleans Area could be overtopped."

THE LEVEE BREAKS

The catastrophic damage wrought by Katrina was due less to high winds than to the unusually large storm surge, which caused the level of Lake Pontchartrain to rise, thus straining the levee system protecting New Orleans to breaking point. On August 30 the 17th Street Canal, Industrial Canal, and London Avenue Canal levees were breached, and water simply poured into the city until 80 percent of New Orleans was flooded to depths of up to 20 feet.

The city administration was evacuated, and some 25,000 inhabitants were forced to take shelter in the Superdome and Convention Center where they spent several days in squalid conditions with little or no sanitation and meager supplies of food, water, and medicine. Civil

TIME LINE

8.23.05 A tropical depression forms 175 miles southeast of Nassau.

8.24.05 The depression intensifies into Tropical Storm Katrina.

8.25.05 The storm continues to intensify and hits Miami as a Category 1 hurricane.

8.25–28.05 Hurricane Katrina gains yet more strength as it crosses Florida and the Gulf of Mexico.

8.29.05 Hurricane Katrina sweeps across Louisiana, destroying several small towns before hitting New Orleans.

8.30.05 The New Orleans levee system fails, flooding 80% of the city. The administration is evacuated and civil disorder breaks out.

8.31.05 A public health emergency is declared.

9.3.05 Troops are finally drafted in and an airlift of victims belatedly begins.

BILLION DOLLAR WEATHER DISASTERS

In the quarter of a century between 1980 and 2005 the United States suffered more than 60 "billion-dollar weather disasters" (adjusted to 2002 $ value). By far the worst in terms of lives lost was a severe drought and heatwave that afflicted the east and central United States in 1980, killing an estimated 10,000 people; the second worst was a repeat of the phenomenon in 1988, which killed an estimated 7,500. Hurricane Katrina was the third deadliest weather disaster in that period but the worst ever in financial terms, costing the nation more than $100 billion. It was also the deadliest hurricane since September 1928, when the Lake Okeechobee disaster in Florida killed an estimated 2,500 Americans, the same hurricane having already killed 1,000 people when it hit Puerto Rico days earlier.

Rights leader Jesse Jackson was not alone in claiming that racial injustice was to blame for the fact that the majority of those left stranded were poor, mainly black inhabitants, while many rich, white residents had the resources to escape the city before the hurricane hit.

The disaster was further exacerbated by looting and violent crime and by a slow and inadequate government response. More than 1,600 people were killed and some 250,000 rendered homeless.

Where were you when?

I told [Undersecretary Brown] that transportation into the city was nonexistent; that all of the roads, highways, bridges were either destroyed or flooded and impassable. And I told him that...the levee that I had witnessed myself...was just pouring water into the city and there was no sign that that was going to stop anytime soon.

—Marty Bahamonde, Federal Emergency Management Agency public affairs officer, speaking to a Senate committee investigating the handling of the disaster

We sat glued to the TV screen as we watched the unbelievable tragedy unfolding in New Orleans. Over and over, we kept asking ourselves: How can this be happening here in the United States?

—Susan Markson, Minneapolis, Minnesota

Above A satellite image of Hurricane Katrina crossing the Gulf of Mexico on its approach to New Orleans (August 27, 2005).

Opposite A Coast Guard helicopter rescues a victim of Hurricane Katrina in eastern New Orleans (September 3, 2005).

Other memorable events

1939 SEPTEMBER 12 The Lascaux cave paintings are discovered.

1939 DECEMBER 17 Canada signs the British Commonwealth Air Training Plan.

1940 JUNE 29 Swiss painter Paul Klee, one of the original masters of modern art, dies.

1940 AUGUST 5 Montreal mayor Camillien Houde is arrested on charges of sedition.

1940 AUGUST 21 Russian revolutionary Leon Trotsky is assassinated in Mexico City.

1940 DECEMBER 21 American author F. Scott Fitzgerald dies.

1941 Yankee center fielder Joe DiMaggio completes a 56-consecutive-game hitting streak.

1941 JANUARY 13 Irish writer and poet James Joyce dies.

1941 FEBRUARY 21 Charles Banting, Nobel–prizewinning co-discoverer of insulin, dies in plane crash.

1941 MARCH 30 English novelist Virginia Woolf commits suicide.

1941 MAY 5 Release of *Citizen Kane*.

1942 NOVEMBER 28 Coconut Grove fire in Boston kills 492.

1944 JANUARY 23 Norwegian symbolist/expressionist painter Edvard Munch dies.

1944 FEBRUARY 1 Dutch abstract painter Piet Mondrian dies.

1944 AUGUST 19 Paris is liberated.

1945 MARCH 18 Montreal Canadiens' hockey player Maurice "Rocket" Richard scores 50 goals in 50 games.

1945 APRIL 12 President Franklin Delano Roosevelt dies.

1945 SEPTEMBER 5 Soviet embassy clerk Igor Gouzenko defects in Ottawa, exposing Soviet espionage activity in the West.

1946 JANUARY 28 Racing schooner *Bluenose* founders on a reef in Haiti.

1946 MARCH 6 Winston Churchill makes his Iron Curtain speech at Westminster College in Fulton, Missouri.

1947 APRIL A Bedouin goat herder discovers the Dead Sea Scrolls 11 miles (18 km) east of Jerusalem.

1947 NOVEMBER 20 Princess Elizabeth (later Queen Elizabeth II) and Prince Philip marry.

1948 NOVEMBER 2 Harry S Truman is elected president of the United States.

1948 NOVEMBER 28 The Holden, the first all-Australian car, goes on sale in Melbourne.

1949 MARCH 31 Newfoundland becomes the 10th Canadian province.

1949 OCTOBER 1 Mao Tse-Tung, chairman of the Chinese Communist Party, proclaims the People's Republic of China.

1950 JANUARY 21 Alger Hiss, U.S. State Department official accused of being a Soviet spy, is convicted of perjury.

1950 OCTOBER 2 "Peanuts" comic strip debuts in seven newspapers.

1951 JULY 1 The New South Wales government introduces world-first legislation providing for paid sick and long-service leave.

1951 SEPTEMBER 1 Australia, New Zealand, and the United States sign the ANZUS mutual defense pact.

1952 FEBRUARY 6 King George VI of the United Kingdom dies.

1952 JULY 26 Eva Peron (Evita), First Lady of Argentina, dies.

1952 OCTOBER 3 The first nuclear explosion in Australia occurs when Britain tests an atomic bomb in Western Australia.

1952 NOVEMBER 4 Dwight D. Eisenhower is elected president of the United States.

1953 MARCH 5 Soviet leader Joseph Stalin dies.

1953 JUNE 19 American citizens Julius and Ethel Rosenberg are executed for spying for the Soviet Union.

1953 NOVEMBER 9 Welsh poet Dylan Thomas dies.

1954 FEBRUARY Dr. Jonas Salk's polio vaccine is field-tested.

1954 MARCH 30 Canada's first subway opens in Toronto.

1954 MAY 14 U.S. Supreme Court rules that segregation in public schools is unconstitutional.

1954 SEPTEMBER 9 Marilyn Bell becomes the first person to swim across Lake Ontario.

1954 NOVEMBER 3 Henri Matisse dies.

1955 The AFL and CIO merge under George Meany.

1955 MARCH 17 The Richard Riot erupts in Montreal.

1955 APRIL 18 Albert Einstein dies.

1955 JULY 11 U.S. Air Force Academy opens.

1956 MARCH France grants independence to Morocco and Tunisia.

1956 SEPTEMBER 16 Australia's first television broadcast is made from TCN Channel 9 in Sydney.

1956 OCTOBER 28 Maria Callas makes her Metropolitan Opera debut in *Norma* and gets 16 curtain calls.

1956 NOVEMBER 22—DECEMBER 6 Melbourne hosts the XVI Olympiad, the first Olympic Games held in the Southern Hemisphere.

1957 Jack Kerouac's *On the Road* is published.

1957 FEBRUARY 18 Walter James Bolton is the last person in New Zealand to be hanged.

1957 MARCH 25 The European Economic Committee (EEC) is founded by the Treaty of Rome.

1957 SEPTEMBER 12 The North American Air Defense Command (NORAD) is established.

1957 OCTOBER 4 U.S.S.R. launches *Sputnik I*, the first satellite to orbit Earth.

1958 Arthur L. Schawlow, a Bell Labs researcher, and Charles H. Townes, a consultant to Bell Labs, publish paper on laser technology.

1958 JANUARY 14 Australian airline Qantas introduces its first round-the-world service, flying to London via the United States and to London via India.

1959 JANUARY 1 Fidel Castro becomes premier of Cuba.

1959 JANUARY 3 Alaska becomes the forty-ninth state of the United States.

1959 JUNE 26 The St. Lawrence Seaway opens.

1959 AUGUST 21 Hawaii becomes the fiftieth state of the United States.

1959 SEPTEMBER 15 Georges Vanier becomes the first French Canadian governor general of Canada.

1959 OCTOBER 21 Frank Lloyd Wright's Guggenheim Museum opens in New York.

1960 Aborigines are recognized as Australian citizens for the first time, eligible for the same Social Security benefits.

1960 JANUARY 4 Albert Camus, French author and philosopher, dies in car crash.

1960 MAY 10 U.S. submarine *Triton* completes first submerged circumnavigation of the Earth.

1960 MAY 11 Nazi war criminal Adolph Eichmann is arrested in Argentina.

1960 JUNE 1 New Zealand's first official television transmission is broadcast to Auckland residents.

1960 JUNE 16 Release of *Psycho*.

1960 NOVEMBER 2 The "Lady Chatterley trial" ends with the publisher found not guilty of obscenity.

1960 NOVEMBER 16 Clark Gable dies.

1961 FEBRUARY The contraceptive pill goes on sale in Australia.

1961 JUNE 16 Rudolf Nureyev defects to the West after a performance in Paris.

1961 SEPTEMBER 18 U.N. Secretary Dag Hammarskjold dies in plane crash.

1962 Rachel Carson's *Silent Spring* is published.

1962 SEPTEMBER 3 The 7,821-kilometer-long Trans-Canada Highway opens.

1962 NOVEMBER 7 Eleanor Roosevelt dies.

1963 DECEMBER 27 Last episode of *That Was The Week That Was*.

1964 FEBRUARY 10 In Australia's worst peacetime naval disaster, HMAS *Voyager* collides with HMAS *Melbourne*, killing 82.

1964 FEBRUARY 25 Cassius Clay (later Muhammad Ali) beats Sonny Liston to become Heavyweight Champion of the World.

1964 OCTOBER 30 The Star of India is stolen from the American Museum of Natural History, New York.

1964 NOVEMBER 21 Verrazano Narrows Bridge, longest suspension bridge in the United States, opens in New York.

1965 FEBRUARY 15 Canada officially inaugurates its new flag at a ceremony on Parliament Hill, Ottawa.

1965 AUGUST 11 The Watts riots break out in the Watts district of Los Angeles.

1966 Launch of "Star Trek."

1966 JANUARY 20 Sir Robert Menzies retires as Australia's prime minister after a record 16 years in office.

1966 FEBRUARY 1 Buster Keaton dies.

1966 FEBRUARY 14 Australia adopts decimal currency.

1966 AUGUST 3 Comedian Lenny Bruce dies.

1966 OCTOBER Metropolitan Opera House moves to Lincoln Center, New York.

1966 NOVEMBER 4 Flash floods cause severe damage in Florence, Italy.

1967 President Lyndon B. Johnson appoints Thurgood Marshall to be the first African-American justice to head the U.S. Supreme Court.

1967 FEBRUARY 3 Ronald Ryan is the last person in Australia to be hanged.

1967 AUGUST 15 Belgian surrealist Rene Magritte dies.

1967 OCTOBER 3 Woody Guthrie dies.

1967 DECEMBER 17 Australian prime minister Harold Holt disappears, presumed drowned, while swimming near his holiday house.

1968 FEBRUARY 10 Figure skater Peggy Fleming wins only U.S. gold medal at winter Olympics.

1968 APRIL 20 Pierre Trudeau becomes Canada's fifteenth prime minister.

1968 JUNE 1 Helen Keller dies.

1968 JUNE 5 Senator Robert F. Kennedy is assassinated.

1969 Launch of *Monty Python's Flying Circus*.

1969 MARCH 7 Golda Meir becomes prime minister of Israel.

1969 APRIL 8 The Montreal Expos become the first non-American team to play major league baseball.

1969 JUNE 1 John Lennon and Yoko Ono record "Give Peace a Chance" in Montreal's Queen Elizabeth Hotel.

1969 JULY 3 Rolling Stones guitarist Brian Jones dies.

1969 JULY 18 Mary Jo Kopechne is killed when Senator Edward Kennedy drives his car off a bridge in Chappaquiddick, Massachusetts.

1969 AUGUST 9—11 Charles Manson and his "family" kill eight people in Beverly Hills.

1970 MAY 4 Four student protestors are killed by National Guard at Kent State University in Ohio.

1970 SEPTEMBER 18 Musician Jimi Hendrix dies.

1970 OCTOBER 4 Rock singer Janis Joplin dies.

1971 U.S. voting age is lowered to 18.

1971 JANUARY 10 Fashion designer Coco Chanel dies.

1971 FEBRUARY 7 Women get the vote in Switzerland.

1971 MARCH 4 Montreal snowstorm kills 17.

1971 JULY 3 The Doors lead singer, Jim Morrison, dies.

1971 NOVEMBER 15 Neville Bonner, elected senator for Queensland, becomes the first Aborigine to enter any Australian Parliament.

1972 U.S. military draft is phased out.

1972 JANUARY 22 The Treaty of Brussels brings Britain, Denmark, Ireland, and Norway into the European Economic Committee (EEC).

1972 MAY 2 FBI director J. Edgar Hoover dies.

1972 SEPTEMBER Seventeen-year-old Olga Korbut is the darling of the Munich Olympics.

1972 DECEMBER 2 The Australian Labor Party comes to office after 23 years of Liberal Party rule.

1973 FEBRUARY 27 Militant Native Americans occupy Wounded Knee, South Dakota, in a 71-day standoff.

1973 APRIL 8 Pablo Picasso dies.

1973 SEPTEMBER 11 General Augusto Pinochet carries out a violent coup and seizes power in Chile.

1973 SEPTEMBER 20 Billie Jean King defeats Bobby Riggs 6-4, 6-3, 6-3 in a "battle of the sexes" tennis match in Houston.

1973 OCTOBER 20 The Sydney Opera House is opened by Queen Elizabeth II.

1973 DECEMBER 10 Novelist Patrick White becomes the first Australian to be awarded the Nobel Prize for Literature.

1974 Frank Robinson is named manager of the Cleveland Indians, thereby becoming the first African-American major-league manager.

1974 President Ford offers partial amnesty to draft evaders and military deserters.

1974 After 25 years of construction, Australia's massive Snowy Mountains Hydroelectric Scheme is completed.

1974 FEBRUARY 4 Patty Hearst is kidnapped.

1974 JUNE 29 Mikhail Baryshnikov defects from the U.S.S.R. during a trip to Toronto.

1974 JULY 20 Turkey invades Cyprus.

1975 Serial killer David "Son of Sam" Berkowitz terrorizes New York.

1975 Sarah Caldwell is the first woman to conduct Metropolitan Opera orchestra in New York.

1975 APRIL 2 Construction of Toronto's CN Tower is completed.

1975 JUNE 20 Release of *Jaws*.

1975 NOVEMBER 11 Australian prime minister Gough Whitlam is dismissed by Governor General Sir John Kerr.

1976 Henry (Hank) Aaron retires, holding major-league record of 755 career home runs.

1976 JULY 4 The United States celebrates its bicentennial.

1976 JULY 17 Montreal Summer Olympics begin, during which Nadia Comaneci scores the first perfect 10 in Olympic gymnastics.

1976 OCTOBER 15 First vice-presidential debate, between senators Walter F. Mondale and Robert J. Dole.

1976 NOVEMBER 15 The Parti Quebecois wins the Quebec provincial election.

1977 Queen Elizabeth II celebrates her Silver Jubilee.

1977 Seattle Slew wins the Triple Crown of horse racing: the Kentucky Derby, the Preakness, and the Belmont Stakes.

1977 JANUARY 17 Career criminal Gary Gilmore is executed in Utah, becoming the first person legally executed in the United States after the death penalty was reinstated in 1976.

1977 JANUARY 18 83 people die in Sydney's Granville train disaster.

1977 MARCH 27 Two Jumbo jets collide on the ground on Tenerife.

1977 APRIL 2 Jacqueline Means becomes the first woman ordained a priest in the Episcopal Church in the United States.

1977 SEPTEMBER 12 Steve Biko, founder of the Black Consciousness movement in South Africa, is killed while in the custody of South African police.

1977 DECEMBER 25 British actor Charlie Chaplin dies.

1978 MARCH 16 Italian prime minister Aldo Moro is kidnapped (and later murdered) by the Red Brigades.

1978 AUGUST 11 Max Anderson, Ben Abruzzo, and Larry Newman complete first transatlantic crossing by balloon.

1978 SEPTEMBER 15 Bulgarian defector Georgi Markov is the victim of an "umbrella assassination" in London.

1978 NOVEMBER 17—18 The "Reverend" Jim Jones leads a mass suicide of cult members in Jonestown, Guyana.

1978 DECEMBER 25 Vietnam invades Cambodia.

1978–79 Britain's "Winter of Discontent," during which widespread strikes by trade unions demanded larger pay raises for their members.

1979 JUNE 4 Margaret Thatcher becomes Britain's first female prime minister.

1979 JUNE 1 American film actor John Wayne "the Duke" dies.

1980 Ted Turner establishes CNN.

1980 APRIL 12 In Newfoundland, amputee Terry Fox begins his Marathon of Hope, an epic cross-country journey to raise money for cancer research.

1980 APRIL 15 French novelist and philosopher Jean-Paul Sartre dies.

1980 APRIL 17 Britain grants independence to Rhodesia, its last African colony.

1980 APRIL 29 Film producer Alfred Hitchcock, master of the suspense thriller, dies.

1980 MAY 18 Mount St. Helens erupts in Washington State.

1980 JULY 1 "O Canada" becomes Canada's official national anthem.

1980 AUGUST 17 Nine-week-old Azaria Chamberlain goes missing at Uluru (Ayers Rock). Her mother, Lindy, claims a dingo took the baby.

1981 MAY 5 Sandra Day O'Conner is first woman appointed to U.S. Supreme Court.

1981 AUGUST 1 Launch of MTV (MTV Europe launched August 1, 1987).

1981 OCTOBER 6 Egyptian president Anwar Sadat is assassinated.

1982 FEBRUARY 15 The oil rig *Ocean Ranger* sinks off the coast of Newfoundland, killing 84.

1982 MARCH 5 Toronto downhill skier Steve Podborski becomes the first North American to win the World Cup title.

1982 MARCH 30 Bertha Wilson is the first woman appointed to the Supreme Court of Canada.

1982 APRIL 17 Queen Elizabeth II signs the Canada Act in Ottawa.

1982 MAY 9 Formula 1 driver Gilles Villeneuve is killed in an accident in Belgium.

1982 MAY 18 Reverend Sun Myung Moon marries 2,200 couples in Madison Square Garden, New York.

1982 OCTOBER 4 Pianist Glenn Gould dies.

1982 OCTOBER 31 Marguerite Bourgeoys is named Canada's first saint by the Pope.

1982 NOVEMBER Audio compact disc first released, in Asia.

1983 APRIL–MAY West German magazine *Stern* acquires what are purported to be Hitler's diaries but which later prove to be fakes.

1983 SEPTEMBER 26 *Australia II* wins the America's Cup.

1983 OCTOBER 25 United States invades Grenada.

1984 JANUARY 1 AT&T break-up is accomplished.

1984 FEBRUARY 1 The Australian federal government introduces Medicare, a universal health-care scheme.

1984 MAY 8 Denis Lortie sprays the Quebec National Assembly with sub-machine gun fire, killing 3 and wounding 13.

1984 AUGUST 5 Actor Richard Burton dies.

1984 SEPTEMBER 17 Brian Mulroney is elected prime minister of Canada.

1984 NOVEMBER 11 Vietnam War Memorial in Washington, D.C., opens.

1985 British scientists discover hole in ozone layer.

1985 Nintendo home-entertainment system introduced.

1985 MARCH 28 Surrealist painter Marc Chagall dies.

1985 JULY 10 *Rainbow Warrior* is sunk by French agents in Auckland Harbour, New Zealand.

1986 DNA first used to clear a criminal in British court.

1986 FEBRUARY Halley's Comet becomes visible from the Northern Hemisphere.

1986 FEBRUARY 28 Swedish prime minister Olof Palme is killed in Stockholm.

1986 MARCH 23 Queen Elizabeth II signs the Proclamation of Australia Act, severing the legal bond between Australia and Britain.

1986 AUGUST 31 Sculptor Henry Moore dies.

1986 NOVEMBER 8 Pope John Paul II arrives in Sydney, Australia, at the start of a six-and-a-half-day tour.

1986 NOVEMBER 26 Tower commission appointed to look into Iran-Contra affair.

1987 FEBRUARY 22 Pop artist Andy Warhol dies.

1987 JUNE 20 New Zealand's All Blacks win the inaugural rugby union World Cup.

1987 JUNE 30 Canada's one-dollar coin, the "loonie," is released into circulation.

1987 OCTOBER 19 Black Monday stock market crash.

1988 Antidepressive drug Prozac is introduced.

1988 JANUARY 26 Australia celebrates its 200th anniversary of white settlement.

1988 FEBRUARY 13 Canada's first Winter Olympics begin in Calgary.

1988 AUGUST 9 Wayne Gretzky is traded from the Edmonton Oilers to the Los Angeles Kings.

1988 SEPTEMBER 30 Ben Johnson is stripped of his 100-meter title after failing a drug test at the Seoul Olympics.

1988 DECEMBER 7 An earthquake in Armenia kills more than 50,000 people.

1989 JANUARY 23 Spanish surrealist painter Salvador Dali dies.

1989 JANUARY 24 Notorious serial killer Ted Bundy is executed for killing more than 35 women in the United States between 1974 and 1978.

1989 MARCH 29 Junk-bond trader Michael Milken is indicted on 89 fraud and racketeering charges.

1989 APRIL 26 Actress Lucille Ball dies.

1989 OCTOBER 19 San Francisco earthquake kills nine people and injures hundreds.

1989 DECEMBER 6 Marc Lepine kills 14 women and injures 13 at the Université de Montreal's Ecole Polytechnique.

1989 DECEMBER 22 Irish playwright Samuel Beckett dies.

1989 DECEMBER 28 An earthquake measuring 5.5 on the Richter scale hits the New South Wales city of Newcastle, killing 12 and causing substantial damage.

1990 APRIL Vast tracts of eastern Australia are devastated by the worst floods in the history of European settlement in Australia.

1990 JUNE 21 Earthquake in Iran kills more than 40,000 people.

1990 NOVEMBER 28 British prime minister Margaret Thatcher resigns.

1990 DECEMBER Helmut Kohl is reelected German chancellor after engineering German unification.

1991 FEBRUARY 7 The IRA fires a mortar bomb into the garden of 10 Downing Street, London.

1991 MAY 21 Former Indian prime minister Rajiv Ghandi is assassinated by Sri Lankan terrorists.

1991 JUNE Civil war breaks out in Yugoslavia.

1991 JUNE 12 Boris Yeltsin is elected Russian president.

1991 JUNE 15 Mount Pinatubo erupts on Luzon Island, Philippines.

1991 JUNE 15 Separatist political party Bloc Quebecois is founded.

1991 NOVEMBER 5 Robert Maxwell dies after falling off his yacht.

1991 NOVEMBER 24 Freddie Mercury, lead singer of Queen, dies.

1992 The Australian High Court's historic "Mabo Judgment" recognizes Aboriginal land rights under common law.

1992 MARCH Civil war breaks out in Bosnia.

1992 APRIL 9 John Major wins the British General Election.

1992 APRIL 29 Race riots break out in Los Angeles after the acquittal of police accused of beating motorist Rodney King.

1992 JUNE 15 Brett Whiteley, dubbed "the wild boy of Australian art," dies of an accidental heroin overdose, age 53.

1992 OCTOBER 8 Former German chancellor Willy Brandt dies.

1992 OCTOBER 26 Canadian voters the Charlottetown Accord.

1992 NOVEMBER 11 The Church of England votes for the ordination of women.

1992 NOVEMBER 20 Windsor Castle suffers severe damage in a fire.

1992 NOVEMBER 28 Renowned Australian artist Sir Sidney Nolan dies, age 75.

1993 FEBRUARY 28 FBI raids Branch Davidian complex in Waco, Texas, killing 4 agents and 5 Davidians. Subsequent 51-day siege ends when fire kills 76 members, including Davidian leader David Koresh.

1993 JUNE 11 Ali Akhbar Rafsanjani is reelected Iranian president.

1993 NOVEMBER 1 Treaty of Maastricht establishes European Union.

1994 JANUARY 1 The United States, Canada, and Mexico launch the North American Free Trade Agreement (NAFTA).

1994 APRIL 5 Kurt Cobain, lead singer of Nirvana, commits suicide.

1994 APRIL 22 Former U.S. president Richard Nixon dies.

1994 MAY 6 The Channel Tunnel opens, connecting England to France.

1994 MAY–JULY John Smith dies and Tony Blair becomes Labour leader.

1994 NOVEMBER GOP wins Congress. Newt Gingrich appointed Speaker of the House.

1994 DECEMBER 11 Russia invades Chechnya.

1995 JANUARY Devastating floods hit Europe.

1995 JANUARY 1 Austria, Finland, and Sweden join the EU.

1995 JANUARY 17 Kobe earthquake kills several thousand people.

1995 MARCH 20 Aum Shinrikyo cult releases sarin gas in the Tokyo subway.

1995 APRIL 19 Timothy McVeigh carries out the Oklahoma bombing.

1995 AUGUST 11 Three die in a Toronto subway crash.

1995 NOVEMBER 4 Israeli prime minister Yitzhak Rabin is assassinated.

1996 JANUARY 8 French president François Mitterand dies.

1996 APRIL 3 The United States's most wanted terrorist, the Unabomber, is arrested.

1996 APRIL 28 In the worst massacre in Australia's history, a lone gunman kills 36 people at Port Arthur in Tasmania.

1997 JANUARY 23 Madeline Albright is sworn in as first woman Secretary of State.

1997 FEBRUARY 17 Deng Xiaoping, China's maximum leader, dies.

1997 MAY 4 The catastrophic flooding of the Red River reaches its peak.

1997 JULY 1 Britain returns Hong Kong to China.

1997 JULY 2 Fall of the Thai Baath signals Asian financial crisis, spreads to Latin America.

1997 JULY 15 Fashion designer Gianni Versace is shot dead in Miami.

1997 JULY 30 A landslide at the New South Wales ski resort of Thredbo kills 18 people.

1997 AUGUST 2 Mohamed Khatami is elected president of Iran.

1997 NOVEMBER 22 Michael Hutchence, lead singer of internationally acclaimed Australian band INXS, commits suicide in his Sydney hotel room.

1997 DECEMBER 8 Jenny Shipley is sworn in as New Zealand's first female prime minister.

1997 DECEMBER 19 *Titanic*, highest-grossing film of all time at $1.8 billion, is released.

1998 JANUARY 4 Worst ice storm in Canadian history hits eastern Canada.

1998 MAY 11 India tests nuclear weapons.

1998 MAY 14 "Seinfeld" goes off the air after nine-year run.

1998 DECEMBER 6 Hugo Chavez is elected Venezuelan president.

1999 JANUARY The United States begins air strikes in Iraq.

1999 MARCH 24 NATO begins air strikes on Yugoslavia.

1999 APRIL 1 Nunavut becomes Canada's third territory.

1999 APRIL 18 Wayne Gretzky plays his last NHL game.

1999 APRIL 24 Legendary Australian artist Arthur Boyd (author of *The Magic Pudding*) dies, age 78.

1999 JUNE 28 The Goods and Services Tax (GST) is introduced in Australia.

1999 JULY 16-17 John F. Kennedy, Jr., wife Carolyn Bessette, and her sister Lauren are killed in a plane crash off Martha's Vineyard.

1999 JULY 28 14 Australians perish in a canyoning disaster in the Swiss town of Interlaken.

1999 NOVEMBER 6 In a historic referendum, Australians reject the republican model presented to them.

2000 JANUARY 10 AOL/Time-Warner merger is announced.

2000 MARCH 10 NASDAQ reaches all-time high of 5,048.62.

2000 MARCH 26 Vladimir Putin is elected president of Russia, succeeding Boris Yeltsin.

2000 MAY 12 Tate Modern opens in London.

2000 MAY 21 Actor Sir John Gielgud dies.

2000 MAY 27 Maurice "Rocket" Richard dies.

2000 JULY 2 Vincente Fox wins presidency in Mexico to become first non-PRI head of state after more than 70 years.

2000 DECEMBER 19 Colin Powell is appointed the first African-American U.S. Secretary of State.

2001 Australia celebrates its centenary of Federation.

2001 FEBRUARY 6 Ariel Sharon becomes Israel's prime minister.

2001 APRIL 26 Junichirio Koizumi becomes first modern Japanese prime minister.

2001 JUNE 11 Silvio Berlusconi is elected Italian prime minister for second time.

2001 JULY 11 Sir Peter Blake, New Zealand's most famous sailor, is murdered by pirates in the Brazilian Amazon.

2001 AUGUST In one of the most significant corporate collapses in Australian history, Ansett Airlines, founded in 1936, goes under.

2001 SEPTEMBER 28 Violinist Isaac Stern dies.

2002 JANUARY–FEBRUARY The euro replaces 12 European national currencies.

2002 MARCH 30 Queen Mother dies.

2002 SEPTEMBER 8 Pete Sampras wins his 14th grand slam at the U.S. Open and retires following year.

2002 OCTOBER The "Washington Sniper" terrorizes Washington, D.C.

2002 OCTOBER 27 Leftist Luiz Inacio Lula da Silva is elected president of Brazil.

2002 NOVEMBER 6 Republicans win control of the U.S. Senate.

2003 FEBRUARY 1 Vaclav Havel retires as Czech president.

2003 MAY 1 Jayson Blair resigns from *The New York Times*. Scandal rocks the paper, leading to resignation of editor Howell Raines.

2003 JULY 14 Robert Novak breaks Valerie Plame scandal.

2003 OCTOBER 14 The New Zealand parliament votes to establish a Supreme Court of New Zealand, severing the last judicial link with Britain.

2003 NOVEMBER 17 Arnold Schwarzenegger is elected governor of California.

2003 DECEMBER 1 New Zealand's capital, Wellington, hosts the world premiere of *Return of the King*, the final film in *The Lord of the Rings* trilogy.

2004 JANUARY 1 Forty-fifth anniversary of Fidel Castro coup.

2004 FEBRUARY 1 The *Ghan*, the first passenger train linking Australia's north and south, departs on its first, 1,800-mile journey from Adelaide to Darwin.

2004 APRIL 14 Australian Mary Donaldson marries Denmark's Crown Prince Frederik in Copenhagen.

2004 MAY 1 Ten new member states join the EU, which now comprises 25 nations.

2004 JUNE 5 Former U.S. presdient Ronald Reagan dies.

2004 JULY 3 Maria Sharapova wins the Wimbledon Ladies' Championship.

2005 JANUARY 26 Condoleeza Rice becomes U.S. Secretary of State, the second woman and second African-American to hold that post.

2005 FEBRUARY 6 Patriots win third Superbowl in four years.

2005 FEBRUARY 10 Pulitzer playwright Arthur Miller dies.

2005 MARCH 9 CBS anchor Dan Rather resigns, followed in April by ABC's Peter Jennings, then Ted Koppel in December.

2005 JULY 2 Live 8, a series of benefit concerts to pressure world leaders to drop the debt of the world's poorest nations, increase and improve aid, and negotiate fairer trade rules in the interest of poorer countries, was held in the G8 nations and South Africa.

2005 JULY 7&21 Islamic extremists perpetrate terrorist bombings on London's public transport system.

2005 AUGUST 2 An Air France Airbus A340 crashes at Toronto's Pearson International Airport.

2005 OCTOBER 26 Two-thousandth American dies in Iraq.

2005 NOVEMBER 22 Angela Merkel becomes German chancellor.

2006 JANUARY 30 Coretta Scott King dies.

2006 MARCH 11 Michelle Bachelet becomes Chile's president.

2006 MARCH 28 Caspar Weinberger, U.S. Secretary of Defense under Ronald Reagan, dies.

Index

See **Other Memoroable Events** on pages 276-279 for additional listings

Acknowledgments

Special thanks to Polly Powell for trusting me with another of her great ideas, and to Barbara Dixon and Thomas Keenes, my fellow triumvirs in what, after five titles in three years, has become the core of a finely tuned book-creating team. Thanks also to indexer Sue Bosanko for her perceptive queries on even the smallest of details, picture researcher Ali Khoja for his well-informed input, and to the following people for their help in researching *Where Were You When?*:

Victoria Alers-Hankey, Caroline Allen, John and Maureen Allen, Mitch Blank, Andrew Colquhoun of the Imperial War Museum, George Crosbie, John Handford, Phil Harrison, Roddy Langley, Margaret McAweaney, Susie Schofield, and Tim Tanner.

Picture credits

Chrysalis Books Group Plc is committed to respecting the intellectual property rights of others. We have therefore taken all reasonable efforts to ensure that the reproduction of all content on these pages is done with the full consent of copyright owners. If you are aware of any unintentional omissions please contact the company directly so that any necessary corrections may be made for future editions.

R=Right L=Left M=Middle T=Top B=Bottom

Getty Images: Front cover TL NASA, TR AFP, ML Getty Images, MR CBS Photo Archive, BL Time & Life Pictures BR Spencer Platt, 2TL Harold M. Roberts/US Army/National Archives/Time & Life Pictures, 2-3TM, 3TR, 2BL Dirck Halstead/Liaison, 2-3BM Anthony Suau, 3BR Andrea Nieto, 4-5 Getty Images, 10-11 Harold M. Roberts/US Army/National Archives/Time & Life Pictures, 12, 13, 14, 16, 17, 18 George Rodger/Time & Life Pictures, 19, 20 Richard Peter Snr ,21 J. A. Hampton, 22, 23, 24 Time & Life Pictures 25 Frank Scherschel/Time & Life Pictures, 26 David E. Scherman/Time & Life Pictures, 26T Robert F. Sargent, 27B AFP, 26 Preston Keres/AFP, 29 W. Eugene Smith/Time & Life Pictures, 30 AFP, 31 Margaret Bourke-White/Time & Life Pictures, 32 Jack Klemmer/Time & Life Pictures, 33 Harold M/ Roberts, 34, 35 Harold M. Roberts/US Army/National Archives 34-5B, 36, 37, 38BL, 38-9 Gordon Coster/Time & Life Pictures, 41 Harold M. Lambert, 42, 43 Margaret Bourke-White/Time & Life Pictures, 44BL Louise Ann Noeth/Time & Life Pictures, 44-5 AFP, 46, 47 Margaret Bourke-White/Time & Life Pictures, 48 Frank Scherschel/Time & Life Pictures, 49T, 49B, 50, 51T Walter Sanders/Time & Life Pictures, 51B, 52-3, 54 AFP, 55 Hank Walker/Time & Life Pictures, 56, 57T Time & Life Pictures, 57B Carl

Mydans/Time & Life Pictures 58 Indranil Mukhergee/AFP, 59 Bert Hardy, 60 Douglas Miller, 61T Reg Speller, 61B Nat Farbman/Time & Life Pictures, 62 George Silk/Time & Life Pictures, 63 Ralph Morse/Timepix/Time & Life Pictures, 64 Baron, 65, 66-7, 66B John Chillingworth, 67B, 68L, 68-9, 70, 71, 72L Allan Grant/Time & Life Pictures, 72-3 Alfred Eisenstaedt/Time & Life Pictures, 74, 75, 76, 78 Allan Grant/Time & Life Pictures, 79 Reg Birkett, 80TL CBS Photo Archive, 80-1 CBS Photo Archive, 83 Jack Esten, 84, 85T, 85B Haywood Magee, 86-7, 88 Peter Magubane/Time & Life Pictures, 89, 90 John Bryson/Time & Life Pictures, 91, 92, 93 Henry Grossman/Time & Life Pictures, 94 James Whitmore/Time & Life Pictures, 95 Time & Life Pictures, 96 Walter Sanders/Time & Life Pictures, 97, 98 E. Murray, 99 Lee Lockwood/Time & Life Pictures, 100, 102 Ralph Morse/Time & Life Pictures, 103T Carl Mydans/Time & Life Pictures, 103B Graf, 104 Robert W. Kelley/Time & Life Pictures, 105 AFP, 110, 111 Getty Images, 106 CBS Photo Archive, 107 Art Rickerby/Time & Life Pictures, 108TL Shel Hershorn/Time & Life Pictures, 108-9 Carl Mydans/Time & Life Pictures, 109BR, 113 Larry Burrows/Time & Life Pictures, 114TL, 114-15, 116 Matthew Peyton, 117 Ted Russell/Time & Life Pictures, 119 Time & Life Pictures, 120 Boris Spremo/Toronto Star 121 Mark Kauffman/Time & Life Pictures, 124T, 124B Joseph Louw/Time & Life Pictures, 125 Santi Visalli Inc., 126-7 AFP, 127, 128, 129 Libor Hajsky//AFP, 130 Michael Rougier/Time & Life Pictures, 131 Tony Duffy, 132TL NASA/AFP, 132-3 NASA/AFP, 134TL, 134-5 NASA/AFP, 135B NASA/AFP, 136TL Getty Images, 136-7 Bill Eppridge/Time & Life Pictures, 137TR Blank Archives, 138-9 Dirck Halstead/Liaison, 140 NASA/Time & Life Pictures, 141 NASA/AFP, 143 La Presse, 144TL AFP, 144-5 Co Rentmeester/Time & Life Pictures, 145B AFP, 146 Dmitri Kessel/Time & Life

Pictures 147, 150 Leonard Burt, 148 CP, 149 Toronto Star/Frank Lennon, 151 Tony McGrath/The Observer, 152-3 Bill Pierce/Time & Life Pictures 153 Michael Rougier/Time & Life Pictures, 155 Keystone/Hulton Archive, 156 Dirck Halstead/Time & Life Pictures, 158 NASA, 159 NASA/AFP, 160, 161, 162, 163 Graeme Robertson, 164, 165 National Photo Collection/The State of Israel/Sa'ar Ya'akov; 166 Paramount Pictures/Fotos International, 168 Pornchai Kittiwongsakul/AFP, 169T Mike Brown, 169B Fotos International, 174T George Freston, 174B AFP, 175 Michael Abramson/Time & Life Pictures, 176 S. Sobolev/AFP, 177 Hans Paul/AFP, 178-9 Anthony Suau, 180 Gabriel Duval/AFP, 181, 182 AFP,183, 184 CBS Photo Archive, 185T CBS Photo Archive, 185B Arthur Schatz/Time & Life Pictures, 186, 187 Luiz Alberto, 188 Stephen Thomas/The Observer, 189, 190TL, 190-1, 192 Rob Taggart, 193T, 193B Sven Nackstrand/AFP, 195 The Age/Fairfaxphotos.com, 196-7 Michael Abramson/Time & Life Pictures, 199 Diana Walker/Liaison, 200BL, 200-1 Sue Adler/The Observer, 202 Pablo Bartholomew, 203 BEDI/AFP, 204BL Lars Astrom/AFP, 204-5 Department of State/Time & Life Pictures, 205TR Dave Hogan, 206 NASA, 207T Dave Welcher, 207B Pete Souza/Time & Life Pictures, 208 AFP, 209 NASA/Time & Life Pictures, 210 Behrouz Mehri/AFP, 211 LETKEY/AFP, 212 Chris Wilkins/AFP, 214 Catherine Henriette/AFP, 215 Catherine Henriette/AFP, 216 Protzmann Eckart, 217 Chris Niedenthal/Time & Life Pictures, 218-19 Andrea Nieto, 220 Scott Peterson/Liaison, 221 Allan Tannenbaum/Time & Life Pictures, 222-3 Mike Nelson/AFP, 223BR Vincent Almavy/AFP, 224 Sergei Guneyev/Time & Life Pictures, 225 Anatoly Sapronenko/AFP, 226 Awad Awad/AFP, 227 Cynthia Johnson/Time & Life Pictures, 228BL Doug Wilson/Time & Life

Pictures, 228-9 Torsten Blackwood/AFP, 230 Jean-Marc Giboux/Liaison, 231T Myung Chun/AFP, 231B AFP, 232B, 233 Andre Pichette/AFP, 234 Mike Simmonds/AFP, 235 Stephen Ferry/Liaison, 236 Bruce Weaver/AFP, 237T NASA/Time & Life Pictures, 237B Mike Nelson/AFP, 238 Pierre Bousel/AFP, 239 Tim Graham, 241 Serge Attal/Time & Life Pictures, 242 Glenn Campbell, 243 Heimo Aga, 244 Getty Images, 245 Jamal A. Wilson, 246 Mark Wilson, 247 Robert King, 248 Porter Gifford, 249 Paul J. Richards/AFP, 250 Thomas Nilsson, 251T Spencer Platt, 251B Mario Tama, 251 Christophe Simon/AFP, 253 Choo Youn-Kong/AFP, 254 Patrick Barth, 255 Kurt Vinion, 257T Mirrorpix, 257B Al-Jazeera/Agence France Presse, 258 Hugo Philpott/AFP, 259 Martti Kainulainen/AFP, 260, 261 Chris Hondros, 262T Carlo Allegri, 262B, 263 Mark Mainz, 264 Yuri Tutov/AFP, 265 Alexander Korolkov/AFP, 266 Michel Porro, 265 Olaf Kraak/AFP 270T Dibyangshu Sarkar/ASP, 270B Dario Mitidieri, 271 Nils Petter Nilsson/AFP, 272 Vincenzo Pinto/AFP, 273 J. Emilio, Flores, 275 Handout/Getty Images News Back cover from top Getty Images; Luiz Alberto/Getty Images; Andy Newman/AFP/Getty Images; J. Emilio Flores/Getty Images

Alamy: 123 Popperfoto/Alamy
Corbis: 75 Bettmann, 157 Bettmann, 170 Bettmann, 122 Bettmann, 172-3 Bettmann, 215 Natalie Fobes
EMPICS/AP 142, 232T, 268-269, 274
Mirrorpix: 171
The Picture Desk: 13 Selznick/MGM/The Kobal Collection
The Ronald Grant Archive: 101 Courtesy EON, 167 Courtesy Lucasfilm
Science Photo Library: 196BL Chris Bjornberg
Taito Corporation: 172-3T TAITO CORP. 1978, 2005